INVESTMENT METHODS

INVESTMENT METHODS

A BIBLIOGRAPHIC GUIDE

JAMES B. WOY

Head, Mercantile Library
Free Library of Philadelphia

R.R. BOWKER COMPANY

New York & London, 1973
A Xerox Education Company

Published by R. R. Bowker Co. (a Xerox Education Company)
1180 Avenue of the Americas, New York, N.Y. 10036

Library of Congress Cataloging in Publication Data

Woy, James B
    Investment methods.

    1. Investments—Bibliography. 2. Investments—
Dictionaries. I. Title.
Z7164.F5W94   016.3326   73-9607
ISBN   0-8352-0631-9

CONTENTS

PREFACE

Investors who are mystified by the dozens of different investment methods
for stocks and bonds can use this volume to find out just what many of these
methods are and where practical information about them can be located. In
one convenient, alphabetical arrangement, 150 popular investment strategies or
factors are concisely defined, with relevant sources of information described im-
mediately after each definition.

Readers should note that broad, unspecific terms, such as "stock market" or
"stocks," and terms not related to specific *methods* of investment, are not included here. One seeming exception is "bonds," a term which is included because bond investment is often treated as a specific technique in popular investment books that have the stock market as their overall topic. Definitions are in
the author's own words, of course, and have been checked against such standard sources as *The Investor's Dictionary*, by Janet Low (Simon and Schuster,
1964), *The Wall Street Thesaurus*, by Paul Sarnoff (Ivan Obolensky, 1963), and
Dictionary of Stock Market Terms, by Peter Wyckoff (Prentice-Hall, 1964).
Unusual, colloquial, or relatively new terms relating to methods of investment
that are not included in available financial dictionaries were checked against
such sources as textbooks and periodical articles.

Investment methods vary from definitely speculative to quite conservative,
from an emphasis on the movements of prices themselves (so-called "technical"
analysis) to a stressing of the assets or values which a particular security rep-
resents (often called "fundamental" analysis). If there appears to be an emphasis
here on technical or chart techniques, it is because such methods show up so
often in the popular literature on investment and speculation.

As this combined dictionary–bibliography is intended primarily for use by the
individual, nonprofessional investor, the emphasis is on investment writing that
is easy to understand. Abstruse discourses have generally been avoided, although
a few academically written works have been included in cases where such
volumes provide unique coverage of a particular method of investment. Most
of the books included were written within the last few years, but a few stock
market classics that still have relevance for today's investor have been selected.

Entries from each investment book vary considerably in number, according to the extent that textual material in each volume was organized around what could be thought of as *methods* of investing or speculating. Most of the volumes scrutinized are well known and currently in print; a few may be available only in libraries. Complete bibliographic information, including latest-known price where available, will be found in the Bibliography section of this work.

To further assist the reader who is looking for sources of information about investment methods, a section lists periodical articles by subject. The articles selected were published from 1965 to early 1973. Articles are listed from a wide variety of periodicals (over 30 in all), such as *Barron's, Changing Times, Money, Financial Analysts Journal, Journal of Financial and Quantitative Analysis, Institutional Investor*, and *Medical Economics* (the last-named is a kind of *Changing Times* for medical entrepreneurs). Articles listed were deemed to have pertinence or interest for the individual investor seeking knowledge of particular methods of investing. In perusing investment articles in scholarly journals such as the *Journal of Finance*, the individual who does not happen to be a professional economist or mathematician may wish to read just the practical conclusions of certain articles and skip over the theory. A complete list of periodicals from which articles are cited, with addresses and subscription information, follows the section on periodical articles.

For convenience in locating all the works by a particular author cited in the text, an author index, covering both the books and periodical articles, is included. A title index, also covering both sections of the work, will enable the reader to refer by title to the books and articles noted herein.

James B. Woy

Head, Mercantile Library.
Free Library of Philadelphia

INVESTMENT METHODS

ADAGES (WALL STREET FOLKLORE)

Admonitions to investors or speculators are very common. Lists of rules, warnings, do's and don'ts, and nostrums in general are forever appearing in the popular literature of finance.

Bridwell, Rodger. "Advice from the Past." In his *Reality in the Stock Market*, pp. 15–20. 1965.
> A highly critical view of six ancient Wall Street maxims, such as "Cut your losses, let your profits run."

Engel, Louis. "The Folklore of the Market." In his *How to Buy Stocks*, 5th rev. ed., pp. 309–314. 1971.
> Analyzes the logic of eight hoary sayings, such as "Don't overstay the market." Engel finds each to have a certain amount of truth and a certain element of nontruth.

Laurence, Michael. "The Psychology of Successful Stock Speculation." In his *Playboy's Investment Guide*, pp. 66–73. 1971.
> Ten rules that the clear-thinking investor should keep in mind at all times. To follow them requires considerable self-discipline, even though most of the rules are based on ordinary common sense.

Leffler, George L. "Trading by Market Axioms." In his *The Stock Market*, 3rd ed., pp. 520–521. 1963.
> The author notes that "the list of market axioms is endless . . . . Some are of unquestioned merit; others are superficial as well as trite." Leffler quotes thirty-six trading maxims of all types.

Markstein, David L. "Points to Remember." In his *Investing in the 70s*, pp. 169–174. 1972.

These are "new era" adages—short paragraphs numbered from 1 to 23 which warn against growth stock fever and emphasize sensible, level-headed analysis.

Merritt, Robert D. "Old Adages." In his *Financial Independence through Common Stocks*, pp. 307–308. 1969.

Lists eleven traditional trading rules.

Mittra, Sid. "The Popular Myths." In his *Inside Wall Street*, pp. 206–208. 1971.

Nine Wall Street half-truths are analyzed and criticized.

Mittra, Sid. "The Ten Untouchables" and "The Ten Commandments." In his *Inside Wall Street*, pp. 261–262. 1971.

Ten things not to do in the stock market and ten rules that should be followed.

Owen, Lewis. "Twenty Rules to Help You Make It in the Market." In his *How Wall Street Doubles My Money Every Three Years*, pp. 114–116. 1969.

These are Owen's twenty commonsense rules for making money in common stocks. After listing the rules, he devotes one chapter of his book to each admonition.

Paris, Alexander P. "The Finishing Touches." In his *A Complete Guide to Trading Profits*, pp. 188–196. 1970.

Describes thirteen stock market trading pitfalls, with such headings as "Don't Trade with the Bread Money" and "Don't Trade against the Trend."

Rosenberg, Claude N. "Common Stock Commandments." In his *Stock Market Primer*, pp. 328–335. 1969.

Seventeen items of commonsense advice are discussed. The emphasis appears to be on buying and holding high quality growth stocks.

Weaver, Mark. "Don'ts for the Bull" and "Don'ts for the Bear." In his *The Technique of Short Selling*, rev. ed., pp. 67–69. 1963.

Twenty-nine rules for those who are buying stocks ("Don't be a hog") and twenty-five admonitions for those who are selling stocks short ("Don't short a strong 'dog' ").

Widicus, Wilbur W., and Stitzel, Thomas E. "Advice From Bernard Baruch." In their *Today's Investments for Tomorrow's Security*, p. 392. 1971.

> Nine rules for successful investing, based on Bernard M. Baruch's *My Own Story*.

ADVANCE-DECLINE LINE

(Also known as the "breadth index" or "breadth of the market.") Measures the difference between the number of stocks that go up during a particular period and the number that go down. Only direction of price, rather than amount of movement, is considered, and great significance is attached by some market analysts to the times that the advance-decline line diverges in direction from market price averages, such as the Dow-Jones Industrial Average. The advance-decline line is usually computed from stocks trading on the New York Stock Exchange or American Stock Exchange.

Arms, Richard W. "The Short Term Trading Index." In *Encyclopedia of Stock Market Techniques*, pp. 9–17. 1970 (cover date: 1971).

> "With the advent in recent years of electronic quotation devices . . . a set of new and very interesting figures has become available." These show the number of stocks advancing or declining and the *volume* of selling during advances or declines. Arms describes a timing device or index based on these data. The volume aspect makes this index different from the usual advance-decline line.

Cohen, Jerome B., and Zinbarg, Edward D. "Breadth of Market." In their *Investment Analysis and Portfolio Management*, pp. 504–507. 1967.

> Claims considerable validity for the advance-decline or breadth of market theory as a stock market forecaster. The advance-decline line (cumulative net advances and declines) is charted, with the Dow-Jones Industrial Average, from 1956 to 1966.

Dines, James. "Advances and Declines." In his *How the Average Investor Can Use Technical Analysis for Stock Profits*, pp. 502–518. 1972.

> Unusually complete discussion of stock market indicators based on the number of issues that go up and the number that go down. The ideas of Joseph Granville, C. V. Harlow, Harvey A. Krow, John W. Schulz, Edson Gould, and others are presented. Dines gives his own "6/3.5 A/D Rule," "Minus 6,000 A/D Rule," "Minus 21,000 A/D Rule," and "Fifty A/D Buy Signal." Includes charts of the various advance-decline forecasting methods.

Granville, Joseph E. "The Advance-Decline Line." In his *A Strategy of Daily Stock Market Timing for Maximum Profit*, pp. 125–131. 1960.

> Construction and use of the advance-decline line, with six observations regarding this indicator and nine rules to be followed.

Jacobs, William O. "Advance-Decline Line." In his *Stock Market Profile*, pp. 45–47. 1967.

> The advance-decline line is said to be an excellent indicator at the top of bull markets, but of no value whatever at bear market bottom reversals. Jacobs uses the line as one part of his stock market profile indicator.

Krow, Harvey A. "Evaluating Strength and Weakness by the Advance-Decline Line." In his *Stock Market Behavior*, pp. 61–79. 1969.

> Analyzes the standard advance-decline line, as well as the 200-day moving total, with charts and tables. Krow is more confident of the advance-decline line as an indicator at bull market tops than at bear market lows. He gives an example of a false signal generated by this indicator.

Krow, Harvey A. "Ten-Day Measurements of Market Movements." In his *Stock Market Behavior*, pp. 81–99. 1969.

> A consideration of buy and sell signals given by the ten-day advance-decline ratio. This ratio is an indicator of "overbought" or "oversold" conditions in the stock market. Eleven rules applicable to bull and bear markets are given.

Lerro, Anthony J. and Swayne, Charles B. "Advance-Decline Indices." In their *Selection of Securities*, pp. 109–111. 1970.

> Presents four specific principles to apply to any given set of facts in the use of the advance-decline line as a stock market indicator.

ADVISORY SERVICES. *See* Investment Advisory Services

AUTOMATIC INVESTMENT PLANS. *See* Formula Plans

AUTOMATIC TREND FOLLOWING. *See* Trend Following; Filter Technique; Moving Average; Formula Plans

AVERAGING UP

The technique of buying additional shares of a particular stock as the price of the stock rises.

Owen, Lewis. "Average Up—Never Down." In his *How Wall Street Doubles My Money Every Three Years*, pp. 181–183. 1969.

> An explanation of the advantage in buying more of a stock showing price strength and the danger of buying more of a stock that is weak. The weak stock may very well continue to drop in price, eventually causing the investor great loss.

AXIOMS OF THE MARKET. *See* Adages (Wall Street Folklore)

BANK-CREDIT INFLUENCES. *See* Money Supply and Stock Prices; Federal Reserve Board Actions

BARRON'S CONFIDENCE INDEX. *See* Confidence Index

BASE FORMATIONS. *See* Lines and Saucers

BEAR MARKET (*see also* Short Selling)

The stock market after it has become established in a downward trend. Typically, a bear market will not last as long as a bull market, but will display an unfortunate tendency to decline at a more rapid rate than a bull market ascends.

Fowler, Elizabeth M. "How the Bears Operate." In *The Anatomy of Wall Street*, ed. by Charles J. Rolo and George J. Nelson, pp. 36–47. 1968.

> Tells how to utilize various tactics in a down market including short selling, selling "against the box," buying bonds, and buying options or puts.

Markstein, David L. "Beware the Bear Years!" In his *How to Make Your Money Do More*, pp. 201–251. 1971.

> Includes such topics as "Bull or Bear Market? The Technical Tests" (turn signals) and "What to Do in a Bear Market" (sell).

Markstein, David L. "Can Investors Avoid Papa Bear?" In his *Investing in the 70s*, pp. 134–148. 1972.

> A discussion of technical methods by which the investor may detect bear markets before they proceed too far—early warning devices, so to speak. Outlines the analysis of secondary offerings, price action of the most active stocks, the "speculative fever index," price movements of New York Stock Exchange seats, changes in bank interest rates, stock group index movements, and analysis of put and call activity (option activity ratio).

Owen, Lewis, "How to Make Money in a Bear Market." In his *How Wall Street Doubles My Money Every Three Years*, pp. 260–261. 1969.

> "The best way to make money in a bear market is to sell out and then sit it out." The author recommends great patience in order to avoid buying stocks before a bear market is really over.

BEAR MARKET ENDING SIGNALS

Events that have come to be associated with the bottoming-out (ending) of a bear market, such as relatively high dividend yields on common stocks and a scarcity of new stock issues.

Granville, Joseph E. "The Classic Bear Market Ending—the Signs." In his *A Strategy of Daily Stock Market Timing for Maximum Profit*, pp. 157–159. 1960.

> Presents a list of thirty-six events that have been associated with the final stages of bear markets.

BEAR TRAP. *See* False Signal

BLUE CHIPS

The common stocks of the old-line, well-established, profitable, and enormous American corporations, such as General Electric, General Foods, and General Motors.

Bracker, Lewis A., and Wagner, Walter. "A Blue Chip Is a Stock That Goes Up." In their *The Trouble with Wall Street*, pp. 83–102. 1972.

> Bracker is a successful stockbroker who takes a somewhat cynical attitude toward blue chip stocks. He presents two tables, one showing the poor performance of the twenty-four most widely held stocks during 1969, and the other showing how a list of the top fifty stocks changed radically from 1946 to 1969. Seven other tables deal with various aspects of poor performance by blue chips. The author points out that profitable investing in the largest corporations is possible, of course, but good timing is vital.

Loeb, Gerald M. "The Big Blue Chips." In his *The Battle for Stock Market Profits*, pp. 241–244. 1971.

> Mainly a discussion of what to look for in selecting a blue chip stock for investment.

Owen, Lewis. "Beware the Blue Chips." In his *How Wall Street Doubles My Money Every Three Years*, pp. 199–201. 1969.

> The author regards blue chip stocks as generally lethargic in price movements, and therefore to be avoided.

BONDS. (*see also* Convertible Bonds; Government Bonds; Municipal Bonds)

Certificates of debt issued by corporations and governments (as opposed to corporate stock certificates, which represent ownership). Many corporate bonds are debentures, backed by the general credit of the company, while other bonds are backed by specific assets. The face amount of a bond is typically $1,000, even though prices are usually quoted relative to 100 (a bond quotation of 96 means $960). Many important corporate bonds are listed on the New York Stock Exchange.

American Research Council. "Profits in Taxable Corporate and Government Bonds." In *Your Investments*, 18th ed., pp. 124–130. 1970.

> Some of the types of bonds briefly considered are: term, sinking fund, serial, secured, guaranteed, unsecured, registered, coupon, federal government, federal agency, defaulted, and income. Six do's and don'ts for bond investors are listed, plus the five types of marketable government bonds, the five concepts of yield, and six pros and cons of taxable corporate and government bonds.

Ellis, Charles D. "Policy in Portfolio Management: Bonds." In his *Institutional Investing*, pp. 27–40. 1971.

> A negative view of bonds as long-term investments. Written for institutional investors, will also be useful to individual investors who have an interest in nonconvertible bonds. Ellis does not approve of plans which involve switching back and forth between stocks and bonds, according to market level. He mentions the Yale and Vassar formula plans, which took those institutions out of stocks and into bonds "in the late forties—just as the biggest bull stock market in history was gaining momentum."

Engel, Louis. "What You Should Know about Bonds. . . ." In his *How to Buy Stocks*, 5th rev. ed., pp. 29–41. 1971.

> A simplified explanation of corporate bonds, using the hypothetical Rod and Reel Company as an example.

Graham, Benjamin. "The Bond Component." In his *The Intelligent Investor*, 4th rev. ed., pp. 44–50, 147–151. 1973.

>   Graham takes a favorable view of the defensive investor's holding about half of his investment funds in bonds. Suitable bonds of a defensive nature are described. Under the heading "Bond Analysis," pp. 147–151, he tells specifically how to appraise corporate bonds.

Graham, Benjamin, and others. "The Selection of Fixed-Income Securities." In their *Security Analysis*, 4th ed., pp. 308–363. 1962.

>   Four principles for the conservative selection of bonds are thoroughly discussed. They are (1) the ability of a company generally to meet its obligations, (2) the ability of a company to meet its obligations, during a recession, (3) the fact that high yield alone cannot compensate for insufficient safety, and (4) the application of specific rules and tests.

Hayes, Douglas A. "Fixed-Income Securities: Bonds." In his *Investments: Analysis and Management*, 2nd ed., pp. 15–23, 51–59, 243–256. 1966.

>   General discussion of the advantages and disadvantages of investing in straight (nonconvertible) bonds. Contractual clauses and factors influencing prices are described. Hayes gives further details in "Investment Strategies: Fixed-Income Securities," pp. 51–59, and in "Selection of Fixed-Income Securities: Standards of Performance . . . Terms and Yields," pp. 243–265.

Karanfilian, James. "Investing in Bonds." In *The Anatomy of Wall Street*, ed. by Charles J. Rolo and George J. Nelson, pp. 63–84. 1968.

>   General discussion of investing in bonds, including U.S. government bonds, corporate bonds (including convertibles), and municipal bonds. Timing, risks, income, and capital gains in the bond market are all considered.

Knowlton, Winthrop, and Furth, John L. "The Revival of the Long-Term Bond Market." In their *Shaking the Money Tree*, pp. 176–181. 1972.

>   Five reasons are given for the renewed interest in long-term bonds that has come about in the early 1970s. The authors tell what to look for when investing in bonds, stressing safety. They point out that the overall return on bonds can be greater than the overall return on common stocks, depending upon timing.

Laurence, Michael. "The Bond Market." In his *Playboy's Investment Guide*, pp. 129–163. 1971.

>Sophisticated commentary on bonds of various types, including governments, municipals, corporates, and convertibles.

Loeb, Gerald M. "A Realistic Appraisal of Bonds." In his *The Battle for Investment Survival*, pp. 110–114. 1965.

>Loeb emphasizes that the prices of high grade bonds will decline and cause losses as interest rates advance. They are a desirable purchase only when a favorable yield can be obtained.

Markstein, David L. "When Bonds Are the Best Buys." In his *How to Make Your Money Do More*, pp. 195–199. 1971.

>A consideration of the speculative possibilities of straight, nonconvertible bonds. Opportunities sometimes arise because of changes in money conditions (interest rates).

Merritt, Robert D. "Bonds in the Bargain Basement." In his *Financial Independence through Common Stocks*, pp. 245–248. 1969.

>Bonds have not always been in the bargain basement, but they certainly have been there in recent years. Merritt discusses bond quality and interest rates and gives ABCs for bond investors.

Neal, Charles V. "Bonds, Bills, Notes, and Certificates." In his *How to Keep What You Have, or, What Your Broker Never Told You*, pp. 47–64. 1972.

>A general discussion of the art of investing in bonds of various kinds. Government obligations other than bonds are also discussed.

BONDS, CONVERTIBLE. *See* Convertible Bonds

BONDS, GOVERNMENT. *See* Government Bonds

BONDS, MUNICIPAL. *See* Municipal Bonds

BOOKS (LITERATURE) (*see also* Investment Advisory Services)

Commentary on the literature of investment will occasionally be found in books on the general subject of how to invest.

Hirsch, Yale. "Year's Best Investment Books." In his *The Stock Trader's Almanac*. Annual.

> Each year in his *Almanac*, Hirsch briefly describes new books on the stock market that he has noted.

Laurence, Michael. "Bibliography." In his *Playboy's Investment Guide*, pp. 263–268. 1971.

> Laurence states that the average investment book is "dreary, poorly written and uninformative." (Presumably, he does not place his own book in that category.) Laurence's bibliographic essay describes books about stocks, bonds, and mutual funds that he found to be somewhat better than average.

Loeb, Gerald M. "Books to Help the Investor." In his *The Battle for Stock Market Profits*, pp. 211–214. 1971.

> Loeb lists and tells about the books that have influenced him the most in his financial career.

Neal, Charles V. "Some Thoughts on Getting Rich." In his *How to Keep What You Have, or, What Your Broker Never Told You*, pp. 9–22. 1972.

> Rather strong criticism of some popular books on how to speculate, such as Morton Shulman's *Anyone Can Make a Million* and Nicolas Darvas's *How I Made $2,000,000 in the Stock Market*. Even the grand old man of Wall Street, Gerald Loeb, takes a few lumps for his *The Battle for Investment Survival*. On the other hand, Neal has a rather favorable opinion of *The Strategy of Investment*, by Richard Stillman.

Warren, Ted. "Advice from Books?" In his *How to Make the Stock Market Make Money For You*, pp. 222–228. 1966.

> The author is strongly critical of virtually all books on the stock market except his own. He discusses some examples without naming writers or titles.

Zerden, Sheldon. *Best Books on the Stock Market*. 1972. 195 pp.

> Consists of relatively long, critical essays on each of about 150 leading investment books. Author, title, and subject indexes are included.

BORROWING TO INVEST. *See* Leverage; Margin

BOTTOMS, DORMANT. *See* Dormant Bottoms

BOXES. *See* Rectangles

BREADTH-MOMENTUM INDEX (*see also* Advance-Decline Line)

A comparison of the amount of movement (momentum) up or down of the advance-decline line in comparison with the movement of the New York Stock Exchange Index of stock prices.

Markstein, David L. "Breadth-Momentum." In his *How to Make Your Money Do More*, pp. 235–237. 1971.

> Discusses construction and use of the breadth-momentum index, described as "a sophisticated refinement on a plain breadth index."

BREADTH OF MARKET. *See* Advance-Decline Line

BREAKOUTS

Sharp upward or downward stock price movements from a previously more or less horizontal pattern. Breakouts are presumed to signal a significant move in the price of a stock. If the price returns to its old level after having broken out of a pattern, a "false breakout" is said to have occurred. False breakouts are the bane of stock traders who rely heavily on charts.

Paris, Alexander P. "The Breakout." In his *A Complete Guide to Trading Profits*, pp. 165–187. 1970.

> The author carefully analyzes the usual reasons for breakouts, which are crucial factors for the short-term trader. Paris also tells how to determine the probability of a breakout's being false. He considers both technical and fundamental questions, and devotes a few pages to anticipating the breakout.

BROADENING FORMATIONS

Stock chart formations that resemble long triangles, more or less, with the triangle broadening gradually toward the right. Also known as "catapults."

Markstein, David L. "The Opportunity Patterns: Broadening Formations." In his *How to Chart Your Way to Stock Market Profits*, pp. 77–79. 1966.

> Markstein states that broadening formations on stock charts are just another kind of triangle, although likely to break out on the down side.

BULL MARKET

The stock market in an established, upward movement. Traditionally, bull markets are longer lasting than bear markets.

Loeb, Gerald M. "How a Bull Market Affects Your Investment Thoughts." In his *The Battle for Investment Survival*, pp. 196–197. 1965.

> Quotes some interesting ways in which investors become unglued during bull markets because of overconfidence. Three basic rules are given, the application of which should enable one to survive a bull market.

Sobel, Robert. *The Great Bull Market; Wall Street in The 1920s*. 1968. 175 pp.

> Investors who read this small volume will receive a useful course in the psychology of bull markets. The quotes from financial "experts" as the market expanded and collapsed are especially enlightening. Sobel points out the surprising sense of normality and optimism that existed in early 1930, as the stock market made a slight recovery before beginning its extended decline from 1930 to 1932. Incidentally, Sobel calls the 1920s an age of innovation and growth.

BULL MARKET ENDING SIGNALS

Events that through the years have come to be associated with the topping-out of a bull market, such as unusually low dividend yields on common stocks and the floating of many new stock issues.

Granville, Joseph E. "The Classic Bull Market Ending—The Signs." In his *A Strategy of Daily Stock Market Timing for Maximum Profit*, pp. 153–157. 1960.

> Granville lists thirty-six events that have been associated in the past with the final stages of a bull market.

Rosenberg, Claude N. "What's the Market Doing?" and "The Bulls vs. the Bears." In his *Stock Market Primer*, pp. 70–78. 1969.

> Both these chapters outline characteristics of a rising market that is about to run out of steam. Two lists of factors or considerations are included.

BULL TRAP. *See* False Signal

BUY-AND-HOLD

The strategy of buying a security, particularly a common stock, and holding it indefinitely. Market fluctuations are ignored after purchase, and the only justification for selling becomes a major change in the nature of the corporation or security.

Hayes, Douglas A. "Common-Stock Strategy: Buy and Hold." In his *Investments: Analysis and Management*, 2nd ed., pp. 70–73, 82–85. 1966.

> The author points out that the buy-and-hold strategy has been successful by definition during the past twenty years or so, because the stock market has stayed in a generally upward trend (this assumes wise selection of securities for initial purchase, of course). However, buy-and-hold is said to offer "a greater probability of at least adequate returns than do alternative strategies." There is further discussion in "The Buy-and-Hold Strategy and Market Fluctuations," pp. 82–85.

BUYING ON STRENGTH. *See* Relative strength; Trend Following

CASH

Cash is cash, except that short-term U.S. Treasury Bills are practically the equivalent, so far as investors are concerned.

Ellis, Charles D. "Policy in Portfolio Management: Cash." In his *Institutional Investing*, pp. 41–49. 1971.

> A discussion of "speculative cash balances," mainly aimed at managers of other people's money. Ellis warns against trying to predict the market by withholding large amounts of cash for investment at a more favorable time anticipated in the future. He believes that institutional investors should stay fully invested in common stocks.

Markstein, David L. "How a Cash Reserve Can Help You." In his *How to Make Your Money Do More*, pp. 248–251. 1971.

> Markstein recommends the holding of cash or Treasury Bills as an investment technique that can be very useful at times, such as during a bear market.

CASH FLOW

Net income of a corporation, plus expenses such as depreciation that are accounting entries not involving an actual outlay of cash. Some security analysts like to pay more attention to cash flow per share than to net income (earnings) per share.

Graham, Benjamin, and others. "The New Concept of 'Cash Flow.'" In their *Security Analysis*, 4th ed., pp. 172–178. 1962.

> In general, the authors are critical of the cash flow concept, especially if used to justify higher stock prices. They state that the transfer of emphasis in an annual report from traditional earnings to cash flow has a basically misleading effect.

Stillman, Richard N. "Cash Flow: The New Criterion." In his *The Strategy of Investment*, pp. 157–167. 1962.

> Stillman advises, ". . . we urge the investor to give attention to both the price-earnings ratio and the price-cash flow ratio, since both figures are relevant to the valuation of a security." He indicates that cash set aside for depreciation is sometimes used to underwrite corporate activities unrelated to the replacement of facilities.

CATAPULTS. *See* Broadening Formations

CATS AND DOGS. *See* Low-Priced Stocks

CENTRAL VALUE METHOD. *See* Normal Value Plans

CHARTS (*see also* Point-and-Figure Charts)
Graphic representations of stock prices and volume of trading, often used in attempts to predict the future course of prices.

Allen, Leon B. "What Is the Meaning of Technical Chart Reading as a Method of Stock Market Investment?" In his *A Method for Stock Profits without Price Forecasting*, pp. 203–209. 1962.

> A generally negative view of stock charting as a means of determining future price movements. The many ramifications of charting are viewed as needless complications of the fact that established price trends tend to persist for a while.

American Research Council. "Using Charts to Spotlight Stock Strength and Weakness." In *Your Investments*, 18th ed., pp. 106–108. 1970.

> Succinct comment on (1) simple-line charts, (2) relative-strength charts, (3) trend-line charts, (4) moving-average charts, and (5) point-and-figure charts.

Bridwell, Rodger. "Illusions Charted." In his *Reality in the Stock Market*, pp. 21–29. 1965.

> A highly critical view of charting as a means of forecasting stock prices.

Crane, Burton. "Using Charts for Profit." In his *The Sophisticated Investor*, pp. 117–143. 1964.

> General review of stock market charting, including both line (vertical) charts and the point-and-figure method. Moving average charts are also discussed.

Dines, James. "Criticisms of Technical Analysis' Validity." In his *How the Average Investor Can Use Technical Analysis for Stock Profits*, pp. 189–198. 1972.

> While Dines is concerned mainly with point-and-figure charting, he is also a staunch defender of technical analysis and stock market chart techniques in general. His particular *béte noire* is anyone who qualifies as an anti-chartist.

Edwards, Robert D., and Magee, John. *Technical Analysis of Stock Trends*, 5th ed. 1966. 486 pp.

> Since the first edition in 1948, this has been the stock market chart reader's bible (at least, so far as bar or line charts are concerned—point-and-figure technique is not discussed). Part 1 deals with the theory of charting and technical analysis, while the second part of the volume considers practical operations and tactics for the stock trader. Many different chart patterns or formations are analyzed in part 1, and over two hundred actual charts are used throughout the book to illustrate various points.

Foster, Orline D. "Charting with Summary Data." In his *Ticker Technique*, pp. 95–109. 1965.

> General summary of stock market charting, including a table of twenty-three chart formations. According to Foster, there are fourteen basic chart formations (seven indicating accumulation and seven indicating distribution), plus nine intermediate chart formations.

Graham, Benjamin, and others. "Two Kinds of Market Analysis." In their *Security Analysis*, 4th ed., pp. 712–716. 1962.

> A definitely negative view is taken of both chart reading and technical analysis in general. Four bad aspects of chart operations are listed and commented on. Stock market chart interpretation and chart readers' operating methods are likened to gambling, in particular roulette.

Hazard, John W. "Dangers of Charting." In his *Choosing Tommorrow's Growth Stocks Today*, p. 290. 1968.

> A brief reminder that charts are tricky tools that must be used with great care. Even professional market technicians are often wrong.

Krefetz, Gerald, and Marosi, Ruth. "The Technicians." In their *Money Makes Money* . . . , pp. 117–140. 1970.

> A popularly written view of technical analysis and charting of the stock market. Mainly descriptive, but includes some words of wisdom resulting from interviews with leading chartists.

Krow, Harvey A. "Vertical Chart Techniques" and "Other Aspects of Vertical Charting." In his *Stock Market Behavior*, pp. 159–196, 162–164. 1969.

> A good discussion of vertical line or bar charts as indicators of future price movements of individual stocks. Considers trend channels, reversal patterns, false breakouts, support and resistance, volume, and other aspects of charting. Under "The Theory" (p. 162–164), eleven basic principles of charting or technical analysis are stated.

Leffler, George L. "Charts and Chart Reading." In his *The Stock Market*, 3rd. ed., pp. 581–586. 1963.

> The author believes there is considerable truth in the saying that the stock market has no past. He states that charts as predictive devices must be used with caution and reservations. Of his list of 30 chart formations, he discusses only two, for purposes of illustration: the head-and-shoulders top and the triple top.

Lerro, Anthony J. and Swayne, Charles B. *Selection of Securities*. 1970. 131 pp.

> The entire book is devoted to the subject of charting stocks. The first half considers the analysis of bar charts and the second half the analysis of point-and-figure charts. Many illustrations are included.

Markstein, David L. "Can Stock Charts Really Help?" In his *How to Make Your Money Do More*, pp. 132–136. 1971.

> The author made a test of chart "upside signals," using the thirty stocks of the Dow-Jones Industrial Average, and found the results quite profitable. He includes table of results from a five-year test of chart signals in the Dow-Jones stocks.

Markstein, David L. *How to Chart Your Way to Stock Market Profits*. 1966. 259 pp.

> The six sections of this book include (1) "Introduction to Charting in General," (2) "Bar Charting," (3) "Point and Figure Charting," (4) "Volume-Price Trend Charting," (5) "Chart Analysis of the Overall Market," and (6) "A Strategy for Buying and Selling Profitably With Charts." Charts on a weekly basis are especially recommended, in that they "do not

suffer from either the over-sensitiveness of daily charts or the insensitive-
ness of monthly price pictures." Many illustrations are included.

Merritt, Robert D. "Charts Can Be Helpful." In his *Financial Independence
through Common Stocks*, pp. 184–200. 1969.

> Merritt states that charts serve a useful purpose, even though they "are
> frequently misunderstood and even downright misleading at times."
> Flags, triangles, pennants, etc., are designated as "mumbo jumbo."
> Relative strength (trend movement) is emphasized, and logarithmic rather
> than arithmetic charts are recommended.

Neal, Charles V. "Now Come the Technicians." In his *How to Keep What You
Have, or, What Your Broker Never Told You*, pp. 152–162. 1972.

> Neal puts stock market charting in the same category as astrology, Ouija
> boards, and haruspication (divination by inspecting the entrails of ani-
> mals). Dedicated chart readers will not appreciate Neal's remarks.

Paris, Alexander P. A *Complete Guide to Trading Profits*. 1970. 196 pp.

> An intelligent guide to stock-price charting by an institutional investment
> analyst. The first part of the book covers the theory of charting, the
> second part is on the practical use of various chart patterns and trend-
> lines, and the third part, "Trading Tactics," is concerned with speculative
> strategy and the emotions of the speculator.

Rosenberg, Claude N. "Charts." In his *Stock Market Primer*, pp. 275–278.
1969.

> The author takes a rather dim view of stock market charting. He states
> that interpretation of charts is often merely a personal matter, and that
> widespread charting contributes greatly to market instability, when a
> widely recognized signal causes all the chartists to try to get into or out
> of a stock at the same time, with chaos resulting.

Scheinman, William X. "Charting the Great Unknown." In his *Why Most Investors Are Mostly Wrong Most of the Time*, pp. 98–136. 1970.

> A philosophical view of stock market charting of various kinds. The
> author believes that charts are useful, but must be "integrated with funda-
> mental data and psychological measurements." He considers three kinds
> of charts: historic long-term; daily basis; and point-and-figure, along with
> other trend-determining techniques.

Smith, Adam (pseud.) "Can Footprints Predict the Future?" In his *The Money Game*, pp. 127–145. 1968.

> The author points out to his readers that stock market charting is as old as the hills, and quotes from a 1906 book on the subject. An amusing, irreverent view of charting and chart players.

Warren, Ted. "Where You Can Obtain Long Range Stock Charts." In his *How to Make the Stock Market Make Money for You*, pp. 145–149. 1966.

> Instead of daily or weekly stock market charts, the monthly charts published by M. C. Horsey are recommended. Warren specifically recommends looking through the charts to find stocks that are low in price and are forming bases.

Williamson, J. Peter. "Chart Reading: an Example." In his *Investments*, pp. 190–195. 1971.

> Williamson uses the classic "head and shoulders top reversal" to illustrate technical analysis of stocks by charting. The author appears to be very skeptical of chart reading as a technique.

CHARTS, POINT-AND-FIGURE. *See* Point-and-Figure Charts

CLIMAX FORMATIONS
Sudden, sharp price trend changes on stock charts, accompanied by great increases in volume of trading.

Markstein, David L. "Reversals: The Climax, or Spin-on-a Dime." In his *How to Chart Your Way to Stock Market Profits*, pp. 53–58. 1966.

> Eight signs of a climax are listed. The author points out that climax formations "are the trickiest of all technical signals to spot." Unfortunately, because a climax probably means that a stock is going to move very far vary fast (up or down), it is important that the technician be able to spot these tricky reversals.

CLOSED-END FUNDS. *See* Investment Companies

COILS. *See* Triangles (Coils)

COMMON TRUST FUNDS. *See* Trust Funds

COMPUTER ANALYSIS (*see also* Filter Technique)
The use of the computer as a screening device to obtain lists of stocks with particular characteristics or as an aid in statistical analysis.

Chase, Richard H., and others. *Computer Applications in Investment Analysis*. 1966. 54 pp.

> Short, technical articles on the use of the computer for analysis of stocks and portfolio management. Includes sample computer programs.

Cohen, Jerome B., and Zinbarg, Edward D. "The Role of the Computer." In their *Investment Analysis and Portfolio Management*, pp. 732–767. 1967.

> Emphasis is on the advantages of computer use in investment analysis. Four main areas are covered: screening, security evaluation, investment timing, and portfolio strategy. Examples of computer use are given.

Haas, Albert, and Jackson, Don D. "Computer: Student and Teacher." In their *Bulls, Bears and Dr. Freud*, pp. 110–120. 1967.

> A more or less philosophical discussion of the use of computers by investment analysts. The authors emphasize that there is always a man behind the machine who provides a well-designed or poorly designed computer program.

Krefetz, Gerald and Marose, Ruth. "The Mechanical Moneymen." In their *Money Makes Money*, pp. 91–116. 1970.

> General discussion of the use of computers in the investment world. Subjects include "Rate of Return," "The Random Walk," "First Financial Language," "Models of Value," "Leading Indicators," and "On-Line Real-Time." The book is written in layman's language.

Latané, Henry A., and Tuttle, Donald L. "Computer-Based Information." In their *Security Analysis and Portfolio Management*, pp. 119–130. 1970.

> Discusses some of the new sources of investment information stored in computers. Several charts illustrate computer graphics.

Loeb, Gerald M. "The Computer Is an Indispensable Investment Tool." In his *The Battle for Stock Market Profits*, pp. 244–246. 1971.

> A general discussion of the growing use of computerized information in making investment decisions.

Smith, Adam (pseud.). "Computers and Computeers." In his *The Money Game*, pp. 169–179. 1968.

> Tells why completely computerized approaches to the stock market are not as successful as might be expected: (1) "Perfect" schemes become self-defeating as more people catch on, and (2) computers depend on emotional human beings for input.

Throop, Enos T. "The Computerization of Technical Security Analysis." In *Current Issues on the Frontiers of Financial Analysis*, ed. by Leo Barnes, pp. 177–208. 1970.

> Considers two ways to use computers in stock market analysis. Throop's study includes results obtained in 1966–1967 by five organizations using the computer in purely technical analysis: Market Pacers, Shields & Co., Trendex, the UHV Report, and the Chestnutt Corporation (American Investors Service.) The second type of computer use is a combination of technical and fundamental analysis employed by Com-Stat, Electronic Stock Evaluator Corporation, Ernst Associates, and McDonnell and Co. Throop's tests of the two methods show results to be very good, with some qualifications in the case of purely technical analysis.

Williamson, J. Peter. "Computers, Quantitative Analysis, and Investments." In his *Investments*, pp. 3–11. 1971.

> General discussion of computerized investment analysis. Includes "a word on computer services and databanks that are currently available to investment men," such as the Compustat tapes, Crispe tapes, Analystics, and other commercial data bank services.

Williamson, J. Peter. "Leading Indicators: The Filter Approach." In his *Investments*, pp. 172–176. 1971.

> The phrase "leading indicators" in this case has nothing to do with economic forecasting, but simply refers to characteristics of common stocks that can be isolated by computer. An example used is acceleration of growth. Williamson describes the work of M. Kisor in screening out stocks with certain characteristics thought to be desirable (Compustat tapes were used). Results for investing were good, but was it luck? Williamson notes that "virtually any investment technique" will work sometime on some group of stocks.

CONCEPT STOCKS

Refers to stocks to which there is a "big idea" attached, such as a new scientific development or a new merchandising concept. Typically, the great expectations associated with such stocks cause sharp price fluctuations.

Ellis, John. "Rewards and Risks in Concept Stocks." In his *Self-Reliant Investing*, pp. 50–63. 1971.

> Ellis gives the four key factors that make the stock of a particular corporation a concept stock. He emphasizes that skepticism and agility are necessary for successful speculation in concept stocks.

CONFIDENCE INDEX (*see also* Speculation Indexes)

Established by *Barron's* magazine and often called *Barron's* Confidence Index, the confidence index is the ratio of the yield on Barron's High-Grade Bond Index to the yield on the Dow-Jones Composite Bond Average. It reflects the confidence of supposedly sophisticated investors in medium-grade corporate bonds, relative to high-grade bonds.

Cohen, Jerome B., and Zinbarg, Edward D. "Confidence Index." In their *Investment Analysis and Portfolio Management*, pp. 528–531. 1967.

> Asserts that, although quite accurate during 1960–1961, the confidence index was erratic as a stock price indicator at most stock market turning points.

Dell'Aria, Paul S. "The Confidence Index and Its Lead Time." In *Encyclopedia of Stock Market Techniques*, pp. 223–238. 1970 (cover date: 1971).

> "The confidence index has never lost its intrinsic value; instead experience has revealed additional characteristics that will enable wiser interpretation of its behavior." These additional characteristics are discussed and illustrated.

Dines, James. "Is Barron's Confidence Index an Early Warning Signal for You?" In his *How the Average Investor Can Use Technical Analysis for Stock Profits*, pp. 539–543. 1972.

> After an explanation and history of Barron's Confidence Index, Dines states that he is not overly confident about the confidence index. He describes William Gordon's work in setting up a ten-month moving average of the confidence index. The averaging seems to help the index as a forecaster.

Granville, Joseph E. "The True Theory of Confidence." In his *A Strategy of Daily Stock Market Timing for Maximum Profit*, pp. 101–125. 1960.

> A complete explanation of Barron's Confidence Index as a stock market indicator, by the analyst who first brought the predictive value of the index to the attention of the public. Tables show the behavior of the index at important turning points of the stock market (1936–1938, 1946, 1957, 1959–1960). In "Can the Confidence Index Finally Go Haywire?" (pp. 123–125), the future of the index is considered. Also, there are fifteen points to guide in interpreting the index movements (pp. 122–123).

Krow, Harvey A. "The Confidence Index." In his *Stock Market Behavior*, pp. 135–141. 1969.

>   Emphasizes the unreliability of this index as an indicator of future stock price movements and analyzes its defects.

CONSENSUS OF INDICATORS

An averaging together by various methods of many technical indicators of stock market price action, so as not to rely too heavily on any one indicator.

American Research Council. "Indicator Consensus Techniques." In *Your Investments*, 18th ed., pp. 183–184. 1970.

>   The consensus approach is said to have worked very well from 1929 to 1962, but not so well from 1962 to 1968.

Granville, Joseph E. *A Strategy of Daily Stock Market Timing for Maximum Profit*. 1960. 289 pp.

>   This entire volume is concerned with the development of a consensus of indicators method for predicting stock prices.

Jacobs, William O. *Stock Market Profile*. 1967. 184 pp.

>   Jacobs's "stock market profile" is a consensus indicator based on fourteen separate items, such as volume, short sales, and free credit balance. The Dow Theory is also utilized. The volume contains many charts of individual indicators for various years and of Jacobs's stock market profile for the period 1945–1966.

Milik, Robert W. "The Performance and Reliability of Selected Technical Stock Market Indicators, from January 1946 to December 1966." In *Current Issues on the Frontiers of Financial Analysis*, ed. by Leo Barnes, pp. 73–120. 1970.

>   Eleven selected technical indicators are mathematically analyzed as to reliability in stock price forecasting. Milik considers only two items to be reliable as leading indicators: the advance-decline line at market tops and total short interest at market bottoms. One item that is reliable as a coincident indicator, according to Milik, is the odd-lot short sales ratio at market tops.

CONSOLIDATION PATTERNS. *See* Charts or names of specific patterns, such as Flags and Pennants.

CONSTANT-DOLLAR PLAN

A plan wherein the investor keeps a fixed number of dollars in stocks, with a fluctuating amount in bonds or other defensive investments. If stocks go up, some shares are sold and the extra dollars (beyond the previously decided-upon fixed amount) are used to buy bonds. If stocks go down in price, bonds are sold and the money is used to buy enough shares to bring the dollars in stocks up to the correct amount.

Leffler, George L. "Constant Dollar Plan." In his *The Stock Market*, 3rd ed., pp. 556–557. 1963.

Basic features, performance, advantages, and limitations are briefly considered. Leffler is unimpressed with the performance.

Persons, Robert H. "The Constant-Dollar Plan." In his *Handbook of Formulas in the Stock Market*, pp. 54–57. 1967.

An unenthusiastic description of this plan of investing, including a discussion of pros and cons.

CONSTANT-RATIO FORMULA (*see also* Normal Value Plans)

A plan wherein the investor keeps a fixed ratio of money in stocks and bonds— 50 percent in stocks and 50 percent in bonds, for example. As the markets fluctuate, stocks are sold and bonds bought, or vice versa, to keep the ratio constant.

American Research Council. "Constant Ratio Plans." In *Your Investments*, 18th ed., p. 188. 1970.

Indicates that the constant-ratio investing formula will work well only in a complete market cycle that includes some comparatively wide swings.

Cohen, Jerome B., and Zinbarg, Edward D. "Constant Ratio Plans." In their *Investment Analysis and Portfolio Management*, pp. 545–548. 1967.

Two hypothetical constant ratio formula plans are illustrated by means of charts. One plan covers the years 1946–1955, the other is for 1956–1964. Both plans involve a 75 percent to 25 percent stock–cash ratio, with the stock portion assumed to have been invested in the combined 425 stocks of Standard and Poor's Industrial Stock Index.

Graham, Benjamin. "The Basic Problem of Bond-Stock Allocation." In his *The Intelligent Investor*, 4th rev. ed., pp. 41–43. 1973.

> A simple, conservative, constant-ratio formula is favored for the "defensive investor," in which half of available funds are kept in high quality bonds and half in common stocks.

Leffler, George L. "Constant Ratio Plan." In his *The Stock Market*, 3rd ed., pp. 557–559. 1963.

> Leffler outlines the plan and reviews its advantages and disadvantages. He finds performance is only fair.

Persons, Robert H. "The Constant-Ratio Formula." In his *Handbook of Formulas in the Stock Market*, pp. 58–63. 1967.

> Discusses how to begin this plan and keep it operating. Persons says it is suitable for conservative investing, as in the case of institutions. The Yale University and Kenyon College plans are briefly described.

Widicus, Wilbur W., and Stitzel, Thomas E. "Constant Ratio Plans." In their *Today's Investments for Tomorrow's Security*, pp. 360–361. 1971.

> The authors point out that constant-ratio formulas have not worked as well recently as in the past, because there have been disruptions in the traditional relationship between bond prices and stock prices.

CONTRARY OPINION (*see also* Psychology)

A course of action different from or contrary to what the general public happens to be doing at the moment. It is adopted in the hope of outsmarting the market, but contrary opinion is often wrong as a guide to the future course of stock prices. The contrary opinion approach to investing is usually associated with an investment advisor named Humphrey B. Neill.

Drew, Garfield A. "Theory of Contrary Opinion." In his *New Methods for Profit in the Stock Market*, pp. 167–193. 1966 (reprint of 1955 edition).

> General discussion of the profitability of doing the opposite of what the crowd is doing. The theory is based on the ideas that for a few to be right, many must be wrong; that what everyone knows is not worth knowing; and that the majority lose in the end.

Fraser, James L. "The Neill Theory of Contrary Opinion." In *Encyclopedia of Stock Market Techniques*, pp. 268–299. 1970 (cover date: 1971).

> Describes various historical situations in which majority opinion was wrong about the stock market. The author also states that most formulas

or systems for investing will eventually work out poorly, either because of the investor's emotional inability to follow his own system or because a particular system attracts too many followers and therefore becomes self-defeating.

Leffler, George L. "Theory of Contrary Opinion." In his *The Stock Market*, 3rd ed., p. 578. 1963.

States that there is little truth to the theory because of the difficulty in accurately assessing public psychology, even if one assumes that the prevailing opinion is generally wrong.

Loeb, Gerald M. "Contrary Opinion as a Tool in Stock Selection" and "Contrary Thinking." In his *The Battle for Stock Market Profits*, pp. 83–86, 239–241. 1971.

Two brief discussions of when to be contrary and when to go along with the crowd. Loeb believes that the increasing use of computers by portfolio managers with similar principles of operation is increasing the crowd effect.

Thurlow, Bradbury K. "Contrary Opinion Theory: The Psychological Approach." In *The Anatomy of Wall Street*, ed. by Charles J. Rolo and George J. Nelson, pp. 178–191. 1968.

States that there is much more to contrary opinion theory than the mere belief that the public is always wrong (such a belief in itself is described as sophomoric). Discusses contrary opinion in relation to "speculative aberrations," security analysis, technical analysis, economic forecasting, and institutional investing. Very well written.

CONVERTIBLE BONDS

Bonds that may be exchanged for (converted into) a specified amount of another security, usually common stock. In theory, but not necessarily in practice, a convertible bond offers the stability of a bond in down markets and the capital gains opportunity of common stock in up markets.

American Research Council. "Profits in Convertible Preferreds and Convertible Bonds." In *Your Investments*, 18th ed., pp. 117–124. 1970.

Considers many aspects of convertible securities, and includes a list of pros and cons. There is a good discussion of evaluating "downside protection," with four specific yardsticks. Margin buying of convertibles is briefly discussed. For those concerned with an industry approach, the book includes a classified list of convertible bonds, indicating main field of activity.

Dell'Aria, Paul S. "Convertible Bonds." In *Encyclopedia of Stock Market Techniques*, pp. 249–259. 1970.

> Five advantages and four disadvantages of convertibles are listed. A full-page graph shows bond prices versus stock prices with a path of the norm superimposed. Mathematical formulas for determining investment value are given. Proper timing for the purchase of convertible bonds is discussed at some length.

Cohen, Jerome B., and Zinbarg, Edward D. "Convertible Securities." In their *Investment Analysis and Portfolio Management*, pp. 414–430. 1967.

> Includes six tests that a convertible bond or convertible preferred stock should pass in order to be considered an attractive investment. ". . . The analysis of convertibles must be fairly precise if their theoretical advantages are to be realized."

Graham, Benjamin. "Convertible Issues . . ." In his *The Intelligent Investor*, 4th rev. ed., pp. 220–228. 1973.

> A somewhat skeptical look at convertible securities. While convertible bonds are supposed to provide a degree of safety, Graham states that "instances in which the convertible worked out well even though the common stock proved disappointing" are not easy to find. He discusses the old Wall Street maxim, "Never convert a convertible bond."

Hayes, Douglas A. "Hybrid Security Contracts." In his *Investments: Analysis and Management*, 2nd ed., pp. 39–47. 1966.

> Discusses theoretical advantages and disadvantages of investing in convertible securities. Six more or less technical measurements are listed which should be used to arrive at a decision regarding a convertible security, assuming that the related common stock is attractive.

Merritt, Robert D. "Convertible Bonds." In his *Financial Independence through Common Stocks*, pp. 259–269. 1969.

> Includes four important rules for selection in buying convertible bonds. Merritt says convertibles of good quality are "very close to the ideal investment."

Rosenberg, Claude N. "A Few Rules About Convertible Stocks and Bonds." In his *Stock Market Primer*, pp. 88–90. 1969.

> Eight fairly detailed rules for those who are considering the purchase of convertible securities.

Shulman, Morton. "Convertible Bonds." In his *Anyone Can Make a Million*, pp. 53–65. 1966

> The author is very fond of convertible bonds, rating this type of security as an ideal investment, if certain rules are followed. The five rules that are recommended are listed at the end of the chapter.

Widicus, Wilbur W., and Stitzel, Thomas E. "Convertible Bonds." In their *Today's Investments for Tomorrow's Security,* pp. 214–222. 1971.

> The advantages and pitfalls of investing in convertibles, stressing a careful search for value, as many convertible securities are overpriced most of the time.

CONVERTIBLE PREFERRED STOCKS

Preferred stocks that may be exchanged for specified amounts of other securities, generally the related common stock.

American Research Council. "Profits in Convertible Preferreds and Convertible Bonds." In *Your Investments*, 18th ed., pp. 117–124. 1970.

> Mainly a discussion of convertible bonds, but comments under the headings "Convertible Preferred Stocks Retain Some Advantages" and "Tax Advantages of Convertible Preferred Stocks as Corporate Investments" are included. There is a list of over one hundred selected convertible preferred stocks.

Loeb, Gerald M. "Things to Consider When Buying Convertible Preferred Stocks." In his *The Battle for Stock Market Profits,* pp. 261–263. 1971.

> Brief consideration of convertible preferreds as investment vehicles.

Shulman, Morton. "Convertible Preferred." In his *Anyone Can Make a Million*, pp. 85–99. 1966.

> Dr. Shulman states that "convertible bonds are ideal investments. Convertible preferreds are *almost* ideal . . ." He gives four specific rules for the intelligent selection of this kind of preferred stock.

CREDIT BALANCES IN BROKERAGE ACCOUNTS. *See* Margin Debit and Free Credit Indicators

CROWD PSYCHOLOGY. *See* Psychology

CUSTOMERS' BALANCES. *See* Margin Debit and Free Credit Indicators

CYCLES (SEASONS). *See* Seasonal (Cyclical) Variation

DINES MOMENTUM INDEX. *See* Momentum Index (Dines)

DISPARITY INDEX

A measurement of the difference or disparity between the movements of the Dow-Jones Industrial Stock Average and Standard and Poor's Composite 500 Stock Index.

Dines, James. "Is the Disparity Index Dividing the Inaccurate by the Indiscernible in an Intelligent Fashion?" In his *How the Average Investor Can Use Technical Analysis for Stock Profits*, pp. 569–575. 1972.

> Dines does not seem to be too fond of the "standard" Dow-Jones–Standard and Poor disparity measurement, but describes in favorable terms the Smilen and Safien Dual Market Principle. The Dual Market Principle involves disparity between a cyclical stock average and a growth stock average. Various charts illustrate the Dual Market Principle.

Granville, Joseph E. "The Index of Disparity." In his *A Strategy of Daily Stock Market Timing for Maximum Profit*, pp. 132–134. 1960.

> Suggests that the disparity index is a good measure of stock market "vulnerability." How to construct the index is shown, and its performance at various points of time (1958–1959) is indicated.

DIVERGENCE ANALYSIS

Analysis of the difference (divergence) between the actions of investors who are supposed to be sophisticated and investors who are supposed to be unsophisticated. For example, the sophisticated short selling of New York Stock Exchange specialists can be compared with unsophisticated odd-lot short selling. Many different ratios can be used for analysis of divergence, and odd-lot activity does not necessarily have to be involved.

Scheinman, William X. *Why Most Investors Are Mostly Wrong Most of the Time*. 268 pp. 1970.

> Scheinman's whole book is more or less concerned with divergence analysis, but the most specific chapter is "Divergence Analysis: Timing Stock Selections" (pp. 137–172). Several charts are used as examples.

DIVERSIFICATION

The holding of more than one stock or other security in order to reduce overall risk.

Cohen, Jerome B., and Zinbarg, Edward D. "Alternative Investment Strategies." In their *Investment Analysis and Portfolio Management*, pp. 757–766. 1967.

Analyzes the ideas of Harry M. Markowitz regarding diversification and portfolio construction and notes several criticisms of his approach.

Ellis, Charles D. *Institutional Investing*, pp. 55–57, 146–148. 1971.

Although this book is not intended for the individual investor, the author has some very interesting things to say about diversification, volatility, and risk. He states that the two purposes of diversification are to spread risk among various counterbalancing industries and to further spread risk among various corporations within each industry. Three real risks or problems that may be involved with diversification are considered.

Hayes, Douglas A. "Principles of Diversification." In his *Investments: Analysis and Management*, 2nd ed., pp. 446–459. 1966.

Suggests that individual investors generally might diversify their portfolios enough by owning from five to about fifteen securities. The purposes and methods of diversification are covered.

Kamm, Jacob O. "Scattering Your Risks." In his *Making Profits in the Stock Market*, pp. 27–32. 1966.

General discussion of diversification, with specific warnings against over-diversification.

Knowlton, Winthrop and Furth, John L. "Don't Buy Too Many Stocks." In their *Shaking the Money Tree*, pp. 155–159. 1972.

The authors believe that five or six different stocks will suffice for portfolios of less than $100 thousand in value. Between $100 thousand and $1 million, ten to twelve stocks will be appropriate. "The fewer companies on your list, the easier it will be to keep track of what you own." Knowlton and Furth also discuss time diversification (varying the length of time needed for investments to work out) and psychological diversification (attitudes of investors toward various stock groups).

Latané, Henry A., and Tuttle, Donald L. "Diversifiable vs. Non-Diversifiable Risk." In their *Security Analysis and Portfolio Management*, pp. 575–577. 1970.

Adequate diversification is obtained with fewer stocks than most investors imagine. A table is presented showing that "the added benefit from additional diversification drops off quite sharply after sixteen stocks from various industries are placed in the portfolio." Industry diversification is emphasized.

Loeb, Gerald M. "Diversification of Investments." In his *The Battle for Investment Survival*, pp. 119–121. 1965

Loeb believes that most portfolios are characterized by overdiversification. He favors concentration in only a few issues that the investor expects will do much better than average.

Markowitz, Harry M. *Portfolio Selection: Efficient Diversification of Investments.* 344 pp. 1959.

This volume has earned a reputation among professional, institutional investors as a classic on the subject of diversification. Unfortunately, the nonprofessional investor who does not happen to have a good mathematical background will find the Markowitz book to be very difficult reading. The emphasis here is entirely institutional, stressing investment in large numbers of securities. Markowitz is generally concerned with mathematical methods of arriving at efficient portfolios that yield an expected return, with as little deviation as possible.

Merritt, Robert D. "Investment Diversification—Why and How Much?" In his *Financial Independence through Common Stocks*, pp. 273–280. 1969.

In answer to the question "How many stocks should you own?" the author states that there is no final answer for everyone. Broad ownership, as with most mutual funds, reduces both risk and the possibility of beating the averages, while owning just a few stocks normally increases both risk and the chances of making an unusually good gain. However, Merritt does make specific suggestions as to suitable numbers of stocks for small investors to hold.

Owen, Lewis. "Diversify." In his *How Wall Street Doubles My Money Every Three Years*, pp. 195–198. 1969.

A general discussion of why diversification is necessary to reduce risk. While no specific formula is given, the author states that he has always held between eight and fifteen stocks.

DIVIDEND INCOME. *See* Income Stocks

DIVIDEND VALUE APPROACH
A method of judging stocks based on the theory that the present worth of any stock should be determined by the expected dividend payout over future years.

Graham, Benjamin, and others. "The Dividend Factor in Common-Stock Valuation." In their *Security Analysis*, 4th ed., pp. 480–493. 1962.

The authors assert that contradictory forces have affected the historical primacy of dividends in recent years. While the traditional dividend value approach may still be suitable for nongrowth companies, an acceptable approach for some growth corporations may be to ignore dividends entirely when evaluating them. There are also companies for which a compromise method should be used.

Whitmore, Fred. "An Approach to Value Through Yield-Dividends." In *Encyclopedia of Stock Market Techniques*, pp. 693–706. 1970 (cover date, 1971).

A nontechnical view of dividends as the key to stock evaluation.

DIVIDEND YIELD SPREAD. *See* Stock-Bond Yield Spread

DIVIDENDS *See* Income Stocks

DOLLAR AVERAGING (*see also* Dollar Averaging, Modified)
The investing of equal amounts of money at stated intervals (such as monthly over a period of years) in a particular security or group of securities. The emphasis is on investing the same amount of money at each interval, so that the advantage of buying at low price levels will balance the disadvantage of buying at high prices.

American Research Council. "How to Build Up Your Capital Through Dollar Averaging." In *Your Investments*, 18th ed., pp. 191–196. 1970.

Tells how dollar averaging works and discusses how to select stocks for averaging. A table, "Results of Dollar Averaging," shows what would happen to $600 per period invested in both a volatile cyclical stock and a moderate growth stock through a complete market cycle. Several methods of improving dollar averaging are given and nine pros and cons are listed.

Cohen, Jerome B., and Zinbarg, Edward D. "Strict Dollar Averaging." In their *Investment Analysis and Portfolio Management*, pp. 536–542. 1967.

Three tables show the results obtained from three hypothetical dollar-averaging situations: (1) low volatility, no growth; (2) high volatiligy, no growth: (3) low "downside volatility," strong growth. Results are also given for dollar-averaging the combined 425 stocks of Standard and Poor's

Industrial Stock Index for various lengths of time. Finally, five requirements are listed for having a successful dollar-averaging plan.

Engel, Louis. "Can you 'Beat the Market'?" In his *How to Buy Stocks*, 5th
rev. ed., pp. 239–244. 1971

Two tables are presented "to demonstrate the validity of the dollar
cost averaging principle." In one table, the price of a stock falls by half,
then triples, then returns to its original price; in the other table, the
theoretical stock rises by 50 percent, then drops by two thirds, and finally
returns to its starting price. Through all these vicissitudes, the faithful
dollar averager would, in both cases, have come out with a hypothetical
profit of 10 percent. Another table shows what would have happened to
$500 per year invested in various large corporations from 1929 to 1969.

Graham, Benjamin, and others. "Dollar Averaging." In their *Security Analysis*,
4th ed., pp. 73–76. 1962.

Dollar averaging with proper selection of stocks, and over a long enough
period of time, is said to have real advantages for the investor, although
institutions may find averaging more practical over long periods than individuals.

Graham, Benjamin. "Dollar-Cost Averaging." In his *The Intelligent Investor*,
4th rev. ed., pp. 56–57. 1973.

Graham is generally in favor of dollar averaging for the conservative individual investor.

Hayes, Douglas A. "Dollar-Cost Averaging." In his *Investments: Analysis and
Management*, 2nd ed., pp. 453–455. 1966.

A somewhat critical survey of dollar averaging, concentrating upon the
fact that this technique must be used with securities with pronounced
price fluctuations to really be advantageous. Also, the use of dollar averaging by institutions tends to make favored stocks become overvalued, since
there is constant buying pressure.

Hazard, John W. "Dollar Cost Averaging." In his *Choosing Tomorrow's
Growth Stocks Today*, pp. 181–193. 1968.

Dollar averaging is described as "one of the most foolproof ways of investing in the stock market." Four rules for successful dollar averaging are
given.

Kamm, Jacob O. "Dollar Averaging." In his *Making Profits in the Stock Market*, pp. 105–109. 1966.

> Dollar averaging is discussed in a general manner. One table shows the results of dollar-averaging the Dow-Jones Industrial Average on a basis of $1000 invested at the beginning of each year from 1926 to 1964. Another table shows the results of the same procedure, same years, but using IBM, American Telephone, or General Electric.

Leffler, George L. "Dollar Cost Averaging." In his *The Stock Market*, 3rd ed., pp. 552–556. 1963.

> Leffler considers dollar averaging to be one of the best formula plans. However, in addition to six advantages to the plan, he presents five limitations or dangers.

Loeb, Gerald M. "Miracle Plan Investing." In his *Battle for Investment Survival*, pp. 216–220. 1965.

> Loeb takes a dim view of dollar averaging, especially of those plans which involve regular purchase of the shares of one particular stock. No one knows what will happen to a particular corporation over the years. Loeb believes that, if dollar averaging must be engaged in, the shares of a good investment company should be bought.

Merritt, Robert D. "A Way to Make Your Extra Dollars Grow." In his *Financial Independence through Common Stocks*, pp. 281–288. 1969.

> Generally favorable view of dollar averaging, stressing the importance of good stock selection and persistence.

Person, Carl E. "Dollar-Cost Averaging." In his *The Save-by-Borrowing Technique*, pp. 114–119. 1966.

> The author recommends dollar averaging on an annual basis, for use with his borrowing-to-invest program.

Persons, Robert H. "Dollar Averaging: Investment 'Magic'." In his *Handbook of Formula Plans in the Stock Market*, pp. 19–52. 1967.

> Full coverage of the dollar-averaging method of investing, including general principles, and how you can lose, for those wishing to know the negative aspects. The author tells how to select common stocks or mutual funds for dollar averaging.

Sherwin, Lowell A. "The Performance of Growth vs. Cyclical Stocks in Dollar-Cost Averaging and Formula Plans, 1961–1965." In *Current Issues on the Frontiers of Financial Analysis*, ed. by Leo Barnes, pp. 230–254. 1970.

> An analysis of common stocks to discover which types are best suited for use in dollar-cost averaging and formula plans. Sherwin found that volatile rapid-growth stocks did much better than stocks in four other categories. He adds that it cannot be determined from his study which factor is more important—growth or volatility. In any event, he found that buy-and-hold is better than dollar averaging in a generally rising stock market (1961–65).

Widicus, Wilbur W., and Stitzel, Thomas E. "Dollar Cost Averaging." In their *Today's Investments for Tomorrow's Security*, pp. 355–360. 1971.

> Good explanation of dollar averaging. This method of investing is generally recommended, but the investor must be careful, according to the authors, not to tinker with the regular timing of the plan.

DOLLAR AVERAGING, MODIFIED

Dollar averaging tied to a formula of some kind, so that the amount of periodic investment is increased when overall stock prices are low and decreased when prices are high.

American Research Council. "How to Improve Dollar Averaging Results." In *Your Investments*, 18th ed., pp. 195–196. 1970.

> Discusses "Dollar Averaging Plus Technical Timing Techniques," "Dollar Averaging on Credit" (use of margin or bank loans), and "Dollar Averaging Plus a Formula Plan."

Cohen, Jerome B., and Zinbarg, Edward D. "Modified Dollar Averaging." In their *Investment Analysis and Portfolio Management*, pp. 542–543. 1967.

> Four deviations from straight dollar averaging are briefly described.

Persons, Robert H. "Modified Dollar Averaging: a Flexible Formula." In his *Handbook of Formula Plans in the Stock Market*, pp. 71–74. 1967.

> Included is a table which illustrates dollar averaging geared to a formula.

DOMED HOUSE FORMATION. *See* Three Peaks and Domed House Formation

DORMANT BOTTOMS

Stock market chart formations made by inactive stocks trading at low prices.

Edwards, Robert D., and Magee, John. "The Dormant Bottom Variation." In their *Technical Analysis of Stock Trends*, 5th ed., pp. 81–82. 1966.

> After illustrating an extreme case of "Dormant Bottom," the authors point out that this particular chart pattern is sometimes a prelude to an important rise in the price of a stock.

DOUBLE TOPS AND BOTTOMS (*see also* Triple Top)

Stock price chart patterns in the form of an "M" at market tops and in the form of a "W" at market bottoms. These are thought to be important price-trend reversal patterns.

Edwards, Robert D., and Magee, John. "Double and Triple Tops and Bottoms." In their *Technical Analysis of Stock Trends*, 5th ed., pp. 128–139. 1966.

> The authors do not consider double tops and bottoms as vital to stock chart analysis as certain other formations, such as the head-and-shoulders. The difficulty is in recognizing a true double top or bottom.

Jiler, William L. "Double Tops and Bottoms." In his *How Charts Can Help You in the Stock Market*, pp. 73–83. 1962.

> Descriptions of double top and bottom formations, including variations, such as double tops and bottoms with platforms and triple tops and bottoms. Four questions are given that investors should ask themselves before taking a position based on these chart patterns. Six pages of charted examples appear in this chapter.

Markstein, David L. "Reversals: The Double Top." In his *How to Chart Your Way to Stock Market Profits*, pp. 43–47.

> Markstein says the double top formation on stock price charts is always freakish but is often significant after a definite upward movement has taken place. The double top signals a downward reversal, of course. Double bottoms signify a change upward. Either formation is "of considerable (although not infallible) reliability."

DOW THEORY

The idea that if the Dow-Jones Industrial Average breaks through old price boundaries, the average, and the stock market, will continue on to significant new territory. The basic thought is that prices established in one direction will continue for a while in that direction. This is an oversimplification, because the theory takes into consideration various kinds of price fluctuations and confirmations by other averages. Most so-called technical or chart analysis of the stock market reflects the Dow Theory promulgated around the turn of the century.

American Research Council. "The Dow Theory: Useful—But Far From Infallible." In *Your Investments*, 18th ed., pp. 178–179. 1970.

>Discusses the Dow Theory in relation to a possible bull market, a confirmed bull market, a bull market in progress, a possible bear market, a confirmed bear market, and a bear market in progress. Comments on various difficulties associated with the Dow Theory, and includes a table showing Dow Theory timing results from February 1960 to the top of the bull market in August 1968.

Bridwell, Rodger. "Can the Stock Market Forecast?" In his *Reality in the Stock Market*, pp. 63–68. 1965.

>The author answers his own question with a resounding "NO," asserting that technical analysis of stock trends in general and the Dow Theory in particular are unsound.

Dines, James. "Can You Make Money with the Dow Theory?" In his *How the Average Investor Can Use Technical Analysis for Stock Profits*, pp. 528–538. 1972.

>While Dines is not wildly enthusiastic about the Dow Theory, he does state that the theory "has been fairly profitable to its followers for most of this century." History of the Dow Theory is given, and the ideas of E. George Schaefer, Edson Gould, and others are discussed.

Drew, Garfield A. "Dow Theory and Various Offshoots." In his *New Methods for Profit in the Stock Market*, pp. 25–31. 1966 (reprint of 1955 edition).

>Speaking of the Dow Theory, Drew states "it could almost be said that its prominence represents a triumph of publicity rather than of merit." The theory is explained, with the comment that the original concept of Charles Dow in which he merely defined the trend has become, in some cases, confused and complicated.

Edwards, Robert D., and Magee, John. "The Dow Theory," "Dow Theory in Practice," and "The Dow Theory's Defects." In their *Technical Analysis of Stock Trends*, 5th ed., pp. 11–45. 1966.

>A comprehensive discourse on the "granddaddy of all technical market studies." The authors outline the twelve "basic tenets" of the theory, show how the theory actually operates, and present some objections to this type of stock market analysis. In general, Edwards and Magee are apologists for the Dow Theory, but even they admit that the time-lag

criticism has some validity. For those interested in results, a table shows what happened to $100 invested according to the Dow Theory from July 1897 to October 1956.

Graham, Benjamin. "Market Fluctuations as a Guide to Investment Decisions." In his *The Intelligent Investor*, 4th rev. ed., pp. 95–98. 1973.

A generally negative view of the Dow Theory. Graham says that the theory worked very well from 1897 to 1938. After 1938, as the theory became more popular, its usefulness diminished. With regard to trend-following formulas in general, Graham states ". . . as their acceptance increases, their reliability tends to diminish."

Greiner, Perry P. "The Dow Theory—an Anthology." In *Encyclopedia of Stock Market Techniques*, pp. 304–372. 1970 (cover date: 1971).

A carefully written history and description of the Dow Theory as an indicator of stock price movements. Criticisms, advantages, and limitations of the Dow Theory are discussed. Seven full-page charts show the Dow-Jones Industrial Stock Average and the Dow-Jones Railroad Average on a daily basis from 1962 to 1968. Daily stock sales are also charted, and rallies and declines are given in tabular form. Two tables give a statistical summary of eighteen bear markets and of eighteen bull markets from 1896 to 1966.

Hamilton, William P. *The Stock Market Barometer; a Study of Its Forecast Value Based on Charles H. Dow's Theory of the Price Movement, with an Analysis of the Market and Its History Since 1897*. 1960 (reprint of 1922 edition). 278 pp.

Richard Russell, in an introduction to this reprint (originally published by Harper & Brothers), states that "Hamilton was probably the greatest exponent of Dow's theory . . ." Hamilton describes primary and secondary movements of the stock averages in some detail, aided by quotes from Dow's original editorials in the *Wall Street Journal*, 1900 to 1902, which are the basis of the Dow Theory.

Jacobs, William O. "How to Identify Bull and Bear Markets." In his *Stock Market Profile*, pp. 30–42. 1967.

The ten principles of the Dow Theory are given. Criticisms are stated, but "the fact is that Dow Theory works, and works as well today as it ever did." Jacobs therefore uses the Dow Theory as one part of his "Stock Market Profile" indicator.

Krow, Harvey A. "Identifying the Trend by the Dow Theory." In his *Stock Market Behavior*, pp. 21–47. 1969.

> A thorough analysis of the famous technical indicator. Examines seven different precepts or principles connected with the Dow Theory, illustrating them with charts and tables. Both the positive and negative aspects of the theory are given, and actual results from 1897 to early 1967 are presented in detail, a total of thirty-nine major movements.

Latané, Henry A., and Tuttle, Donald L. "The Origins of Technical Analysis: the Dow Theory." In their *Security Analysis and Portfolio Management*, pp. 354–357. 1970.

> The Dow Theory is summarized and important criticisms of the theory are outlined.

Leffler, George L. "The Dow Theory." In his *The Stock Market*, 3rd ed., pp. 533–550. 1963.

> After outlining the history of the Dow Theory, Leffler describes its basic features at some length and summarizes the eight essential features . . . as first presented by Dow, Nelson, and Hamilton. Next, the action of the theory in 1929, 1946, 1948, 1949, 1953, 1957, and 1960 (all "signal" years) is described. Finally, the theory is strongly criticized and nine specific indictments are presented. Leffler observes that the Dow Theory appears to have declined greatly in popularity in recent years.

Lerro, Anthony J., and Swayne, Charles B. "Philosophy of Market Trends." In their *Selection of Securities*, pp. 6–9. 1970.

> Reviews principles relating to the Dow Theory. The authors believe that the Dow-Jones Transportation (Railroad) Average is still important to the functioning of the Dow Theory.

Markstein, David L. "Dow Theory—an Old Forecaster that Still Works." In his *How to Make Your Money Do More*, pp. 239–242. 1971.

> The "false signal" of 1965 and other Dow Theory matters are considered. Markstein believes the theory is still useful.

Markstein, David L. "The Famous Dow Theory." In his *How to Chart Your Way to Stock Market Profits*, pp. 165–171. 1966.

> Lists the twelve major tenets of the Dow Theory. According to Markstein, the theory is useful in determining major market trends.

Merrill, Arthur A. "What is the Dow Theory? Is It Profitable?" In his *Behavior of Prices on Wall Street*, pp. 46–53. 1966.

> Gives a seven-point summary of the Dow Theory and states that, while the theory does not always forecast correctly, it has been reasonably accurate over the years. The work of Robert Rhea in analyzing the theory is discussed. Dow Theory dates and data covering the years 1896–1939 are given in an appendix on pages 139–141.

Rosenberg, Claude N. "The Dow Theory." In his *Stock Market Primer*, pp. 273–274. 1969.

> A critical view of the Dow Theory, with the inference that the theory produces results no better than those obtained by pure chance.

Sauvain, Harry. "The Dow Theory." In his *Investment Management*, 3rd ed., pp. 496–497. 1967.

> Some people regard the Dow Theory as a mechanistic device for prediction of stock prices. "When the Dow Theory is construed in this manner, there is not much to be said for it." Sauvain takes a generally negative view of trying to predict stock prices by chart patterns or movements.

Warren, Ted. "The Dow Jones Trends." In his *How to Make the Stock Market Make Money for You*, pp. 133–144. 1966.

> A skeptical view of the classic Dow Theory, which Warren says gives many false signals. The theory may have worked well years ago, but Warren thinks it is now obsolete. He gives his own interpretation of moves in the Dow-Jones Industrial Average since 1929.

DUAL FUNDS

Closed-end investment companies with two classes of stock: capital and income. All dividends go to the income shareholders, while owners of the capital stock hope to benefit from capital gains. Most dual funds are listed on the New York Stock Exchange.

Laurence, Michael. "Discount Merchandise: Closed-End Funds." In his *Playboy's Investment Guide*, pp. 121–127. 1971.

> Interesting and perceptive discussion of dual-purpose investment companies and why they might be attractive to sophisticated investors. Much of the comment is devoted to the discounts that commonly prevail on the capital shares of dual funds.

Loeb, Gerald M. "Dual Funds Offer Investors Maximum Income or Capital Gains." In his *The Battle for Stock Market Profits*, pp. 254–257. 1971.

> A general discussion of how the investor can use dual funds to good advantage.

Markstein, David L. "These Funds Bring Built-In Leverage." In his *How to Make Your Money Do More*, pp. 184–189. 1971.

> Methods of investment or speculation using dual funds, including the use of a fund's capital shares for short-term trading "in tune with market signals."

Mead, Stuart B. "The Dual Funds." In his *Mutual Funds: A Guide for the Lay Investor*, pp. 22–25. 1971.

> Income shares and capital shares of dual funds are explained. The author mentions that dual funds are "open to the possibility of changes in investment policy that can harm one group while assisting the other" (holders of income shares versus holders of capital shares).

Stevenson, Richard A. "The Dual Fund Indicator." In *Encyclopedia of Stock Market Techniques*, pp. 666–671. 1970 (cover date: 1971).

> Discusses (1) nature and history of dual funds, (2) the dual fund indicator, (3) the indicator and market movements, (4) advantages of the dual fund indicator, and (5) disadvantages. Stevenson describes a stock market price indicator based on the discounts associated with capital shares of dual funds.

DU PONT INSTITUTIONAL PLAN

Developed by Francis I. Du Pont and Co., a brokerage firm, for institutional customers. According to R. H. Persons, this plan is based on a 120-month moving average of the Dow-Jones Industrial Average, with special delaying rules. Somewhat unique rules are involved for determining the relative amounts of stocks and bonds held.

Leffler, George L. "F. I. Du Pont Plan." In his *The Stock Market*, 3rd ed., p. 567. 1963.

> Brief description of the Du Pont Plan. Results of the plan have apparently been unimpressive.

Persons, Robert H. "Moving Average Formulas." In his *Handbook of Formula Plans in the Stock Market*, pp. 81–82. 1967.

> Persons asserts that retrospective studies show that this plan, developed in 1947, would have been successful "at least to the early fifties." The plan is described in some detail.

ELLIOTT WAVE PRINCIPLE

A theory formulated by the late R. N. Elliott, which states that stock prices exhibit periodicity and, therefore, move in regular patterns or waves. Some of the waves are tidal, while others are quite small.

Dines, James. "The Dow Theory, Elliott Waves and Mysticism." In his *How the Average Investor Can Use Technical Analysis for Stock Profits*, p. 535. 1972.

> Like others, Dines has little use for the Elliott wave theory. He regards the various waves as virtually impossible to define.

Drew, Garfield A. "Elliott's Wave Principle." In his *New Methods for Profit in the Stock Market*, pp. 159–161. 1966 (reprint of 1955 edition).

> "The practical difficulty lies in the confusion which is likely to attend identification of the correct waves as they develop."

Krow, Harvey A. "The Elliott Wave Principle." In his *Stock Market Behavior*, pp. 45–47. 1969.

> A critical view of this principle as a practical indicator of future stock prices. Krow hints it is akin to metaphysics or mysticism.

Merrill, Arthur A. "What is the Elliott Wave Theory?" In his *Behavior of Prices on Wall Street*, pp. 55–58, 99–117. 1966.

> States that the ideas of Ralph Nelson Elliott are very interesting, but so open to interpretation as to make practical use difficult. Further information about the Elliott Wave Principle (variations and applications) is given in two appendixes on pages 99–117.

EMOTIONS OF INVESTORS. *See* Psychology

FALSE SIGNAL

A stock market chart formation that does not lead to correct market predictions; a chief cause of stomach ulcers among stock market technicians.

Dines, James. "False Breakouts." In his *How the Average Investor Can Use Technical Analysis for Stock Profits*, pp. 368–377. 1972.

> "Sometimes, for reasons only dimly understood, things do not work out right. . . ." Many people don't use charts because they have had one or two bad experiences with them." The author goes on to say that the chart user can make money in spite of false signals, if he is careful to restrict losses to small amounts by use of stop-loss orders. One topic covered is "The Dropout Bottom and Successive Breakouts."

Jiler, William L. "The Trap." In his *How Charts Can Help You in the Stock Market*, pp. 149–155. 1962.

> "Bull traps" and "bear traps," otherwise known as false breakouts, are illustrated and analyzed. Four pages of charted examples appear in this chapter.

Krow, Harvey A. "False Breakouts." In his *Stock Market Behavior*, pp. 188–190. 1969.

> With reference to predicting stock-price movements by chart formations, the author says, "It may well come to pass one day that this whole technique will be self-defeating." Some reasons for false signals are given.

Warren, Ted. "False Support Levels: Encouraging Action that Hides Trouble Ahead." In his *How to Make the Stock Market Make Money for You*, pp. 82–87. 1966.

> Warren declares ". . . perfect support levels are usually phony," by which he means that the investor should be wary of a stock whose price always rebounds from exactly the same point over a period of months or even years. Insiders may be supporting the price artificially.

FEDERAL RESERVE BOARD ACTIONS (*see also* Three-Steps-and-a-Stumble Theory; Money Supply and Stock Prices)

The Board of Governors of the Federal Reserve System is able to exert a tremendous influence on business in general and the stock market in particular because it controls discount (interest) rates, margin requirements, and member banks' reserves (money supply).

American Research Council. "Changes in Money Supply as Determined by Federal Reserve Policies Influence Stock Prices." In *Your Investments*, 18th ed., p. 177. 1970.

> Brief discussion of the effect that changes in credit policy can have on the stock market. The Council finds that indicators based on actions of

the Federal Reserve Board have worked well when stock market activity was based on strictly monetary considerations.

Merrill, Arthur A. "How Does the Market Behave after a Move by the Federal Reserve System?" In his *Behavior of Prices on Wall Street*, pp. 36–88, 159–160. 1966.

> Considers market patterns in the days following a policy change by the Federal Reserve Board in the rediscount rate, margin requirements, or member bank reserve requirements. Major actions by the Federal Reserve are listed in an appendix on pp. 159–160, covering the years 1914–1965.

FILTER TECHNIQUE (*see also* Computer Analysis)

Use of a specified percentage of rise or fall in the price of a stock or stock index to determine buy or sell points. For example, use of a 5 percent filter for a particular stock would mean simply that the stock is purchased each time its price rises by 5 percent and sold or sold short each time its price falls by 5 percent. This price filter technique is simplistic; most results of profitability investigations have been unfavorable, especially after commissions, regardless of size of filter. Some "automatic trend-following" investment plans use simple price filters.

Latané, Henry A., and Tuttle, Donald L. "Filter Technique." In their *Security Analysis and Portfolio Management*, pp. 358–360. 1970.

> The filter technique is described, and its weaknesses are discussed.

FINANCIAL SERVICES. *See* Investment Advisory Services

FLAGS AND PENNANTS

Stock chart formations of particular shapes. A flag is more or less a parallelogram, tilting up or down, while a pennant is triangular.

Edwards, Robert D., and Magee, John. "Flags and Pennants." In their *Technical Analysis of Stock Trends*, 5th ed., pp. 168–181. 1966.

> Complete discussion of flags and pennants, with many illustrations. "These pretty little patterns of consolidation are justly regarded as among the most dependable of chart formations . . ." Three specific tests are given to help the stock trader determine the authenticity of these formations.

Lerro, Anthony J., and Swayne, Charles B. "Wedges, Flags, Rectangles, Pennants." In their *Selection of Securities*, pp. 39–44. 1970.

> Describes various consolidation or congestion configurations and their market characteristics.

Markstein, David L. "The Flag Flies at Half-Mast." In his *How to Chart Your Way to Stock Market Profits*, pp. 81–85. 1966.

> Outlines the four characteristics of the true flag or pennant on a stock price chart. The value of the flag is discussed.

FOREIGN INVESTMENTS

Securities originating in countries other than the United States and Canada.

Lewin, Kurt I. "Investing Abroad." In *The Anatomy of Wall Street*, ed. by Charles J. Rolo and George J. Nelson, pp. 124–142. 1968.

> This general discussion of investing in the securities of companies located in foreign countries includes a list of considerations that require special attention. Lewin tells briefly how to analyze foreign securities and mentions some of the technical problems that the investor may encounter.

Markstein, David L. "Opportunity Outside the U.S.A." In his *Investing in the 70s*, pp. 100–107. 1972.

> The high industrial growth rates of some foreign countries can produce superior opportunities for investment or speculation. The methods of overseas investing for U.S. citizens are discussed.

FORMULA PLANS (*see also* names of individual plans)

Investment procedures in which decisions are made automatically according to external signals, events or trends, and not according to individual analysis, judgment or intuition, except in the initial selection of the plan. See under Constant-Dollar Plan, Constant-Ratio Formula, Dollar Averaging, Du Pont Institutional Plan, Genstein Formula, Graham Formula, Keystone Plan, Leffler Formula, Normal-Value Plans, Oberlin Plan, Scale Trading, Ten-Percent Plan, Vassar Plan, and Yale Plan.

American Research Council. "How to Beat Market Swings by Formula Plans." In *Your Investments*, 18th ed., pp. 188–191. 1970.

> Covers various formula or ratio plans, with a listing of eight pros and cons.

Cohen, Jerome B., and Zinbarg, Edward D. "Formula Plans." In their
Investment Analysis and Portfolio Management, pp. 536–555. 1967.
>   Explains strict dollar averaging, modified dollar averaging, constant ratio
>   plans, and variable ratio plans.

Drew, Garfield A. "Formula Plans." In his *New Methods for Profit in the
Stock Market*, pp. 98–141. 1966. (reprint of 1955 edition).
>   Drew discusses about a dozen different investment formulas, and states
>   that it will always be arguable which plan is best. He says that formula
>   plans will show somewhat poor results during the course of a bull mar-
>   ket and somewhat favorable results during a bear market.

Leffler, George L. "Formula Plans." In his *The Stock Market*, 3rd ed., pp.
551–572. 1963.
>   Formula plans that are discussed are dollar-cost averaging, constant-dollar
>   plan, constant-ratio plan, ten-percent plan, and normal-value plans.
>   Leffler's final word of advice is: *Caveat emptor*.

Persons, Robert H. *Handbook of Formula Plans in the Stock Market*. 92 pp.
1967.
>   Persons is concerned mainly with dollar averaging and plans which at-
>   tempt to determine by formula what portion of investment funds should
>   be in bonds and what portion in stocks (variable stock-bond ratio formu-
>   las).

FREE CREDIT BALANCE. *See* Margin Debit and Free Credit Indicators

FUNDAMENTAL ANALYSIS. *See* specific subjects, such as Growth Stocks;
Price-Earnings Ratio; Undervalued Securities.

GAPS AND ISLANDS

In stock-price charting, a gap is a blank space representing prices at which a
stock did not trade, as when a stock opens at a price higher than the previous
day's high (the price must stay higher for at least a day, if the gap is to be ap-
parent on a daily chart). The pattern formed by a gap, followed by a few days
of trading within a reasonably limited price range, followed by another gap,
makes a kind of "island" appear on a chart.

Edwards, Robert D., and Magee, John. "Gaps" and "The Island Reversal." In their *Technical Analysis of Stock Trends*, 5th ed., pp. 190–210. 1966.

> Examines several kinds of gaps. The common superstition that a gap must be closed is considered at some length. The authors point out that prices may move very far away from a gap before it is closed, an event that may take years. Many gaps formed in 1929 were never closed.

Lerro, Anthony J., and Swayne, Charles B. "Gaps and Islands." In their *Selection of Securities*, pp. 56–59. 1970.

> Briefly discusses common gaps, breakaway gaps, runaway gaps, and exhaustion gaps. It is noted that runaway gaps are sometimes called "measuring gaps."

Paris, Alexander P. "Gaps." In his *A Complete Guide to Trading Profits*, pp. 104–108. 1970.

> The breakaway gap, the measuring or runaway gap, and the exhaustion gap are each discussed.

GENERAL MOTORS INDICATOR

A stock market price forecaster based on the movements of the common stock of the General Motors Corporation. The underlying principle is the importance of General Motors to the overall U.S. economy.

American Research Council. "GM—A Very Imperfect 'Bell-wether.' " In *Your Investments*, 18th ed., pp. 179–180. 1970.

> A generally negative view of the GM indicator, which worked quite well from 1928 to 1956, less well from 1956 to 1962, and not well at all from 1962 to 1968.

Dines, James. "General Motors and DuPont are Technical Indicators Unto Themselves." In his *How the Average Investor Can Use Technical Analysis for Stock Profits*, pp. 576–579. 1972.

> A generally favorable view of General Motors common stock as a stock market prognosticator. Dines adds his own personal touch by bringing in the "Dines Du Pont Indicator," based on movements of Du Pont common. If Du Pont flattens out and breaks its upward trendline, the stock market in general is supposed to be in trouble.

Latané, Henry A., and Tuttle, Donald L. "The General Motors Theory." In their *Security Analysis and Portfolio Management*, p. 271. 1970.

> Indicates that, while it is simplistic to use price movements of General Motors common stock to predict the market as a whole, the GM theory has worked reasonably well in the past. Certain difficulties in applying the theory are mentioned.

Stovall, Robert H. "General Motors as a Stock Market Bellwether." In *Encyclopedia of Stock Market Techniques*, pp. 672–676. 1970 (cover date: 1971).

> Stovall states that the record of GM as a stock market indicator has been "as good or better than any subjective theory or econometric model with which the writer is familiar." The GM indicator, which the author describes fully, also has the advantage of simplicity. Tables show signals given by General Motors stock from March 1929 to July 1969.

GENSTEIN FORMULA

An intrinsic- or normal-value formula (see definition under "Normal-Value Plans") devised by Edgar S. Genstein. Genstein's computation of central or normal value involves a ten-year average of the Dow-Jones Industrial Average, a ten-year average of dividends on the Dow-Jones Industrials, and current dividends from the Dow-Jones Industrials.

Leffler, George L. "Genstein Price-Dividend Formula." In his *The Stock Market*, 3rd ed., p. 571. 1963.

> Brief description of Genstein's intrinsic-value plan for investment timing. Leffler notes that strict adherence to the formula would have kept the investor out of the market from early 1956 to the middle of 1962 (which may or may not be a good thing).

Persons, Robert H. "The Genstein Formula." In his *Handbook of Formula Plans in the Stock Market*, pp. 85–88. 1967.

> Detailed description, with list of data required, plus the five steps that must be followed to arrive at the median or "normal value" of the Dow-Jones Industrial Average. Tables show the results of Genstein Formula computations from 1948 to 1966 and alternate plans for the Genstein Formula. Results to 1966 were reasonably good.

GLAMOUR STOCKS. *See* Growth Stocks; High Velocity Stocks

GOLD STOCK PRICE INDICATOR

A stock market indicator based on the fact that the prices of gold-mining common stocks often move in a direction opposite to that of the popular stock averages. If gold mine stocks are moving down, other stocks should move up, and vice versa, varying more with relative strength of movement than with actual price direction.

Dines, James. "Contracyclical Golds Tip Off General Market Direction." In his *How the Average Investor Can Use Technical Analysis for Stock Profits*, pp. 543–546. 1972.

> *"The Dines Letter* pioneered the concept: when golds go up, stocks go down. But this is not a strictly mathematical relationship. . . ." The Dines Gold Rule is described, use of relative strength of gold-mine stocks is shown in a chart, and an example is given of Dines' "Gold-Bug Corner" (charts of a wide variety of gold statistics).

GOVERNMENT BONDS

United States Treasury Bonds and other bonds issued by agencies of the Federal government. Generally speaking, the term "government bonds" refers to issues that fluctuate in price on the open market, and not to fixed-price savings bonds.

Crane, Burton. "The Almost-Sure-to-Win Speculation." In his *The Sophisticated Investor*, pp. 35–43. 1964.

> A discussion of buying government bonds on margin when a business recession is on the way. Presumably, as the government leans in the direction of easier money, interest rates will drop and bond prices rise.

Engel, Louis. "What You Should Know about Government and Municipal Bonds." In his *How to Buy Stocks*, 5th rev. ed., pp. 47–50. 1971.

> Treasury bonds, Treasury bills, and savings bonds are briefly described.

Laurence, Michael. "Speculating in Bonds." In his *Playboy's Investment Guide*, pp. 160–163. 1971.

> Tells about the opportunities for high gain and great loss in buying government bonds on 5 to 10 percent margin (one borrows 90 to 95 percent of the value of the bonds).

Sauvain, Harry. "United States Government Securities." In his *Investment Management*, 3rd ed., pp. 55–62. 1967.

> Clear discussion of the various kinds of federal securities, including marketable issues (bills, certificates, notes, and bonds) and nonmarketable issues and special issues (Series E and H Savings Bonds and Series B Treasury Bonds).

GRAHAM FORMULA

This formula, devised by Benjamin Graham, is probably the best known of the normal- or intrinsic-value investment timing plans (see definition under "Normal-Value Plans"). Graham's computation of normal or central value involves earnings on the Dow-Jones Industrial Average and the yield on Moody's Corporate Aaa Bond Average.

Graham, Benjamin, and others. "Our Suggested Multipliers for Common Stocks as a Whole." In their *Security Analysis*, 4th ed., pp. 511–513. 1962.

> Describes Graham's newer, more liberal central-value formula—the original formula would have evaluated the Dow-Jones Industrial Average at only 356 at the beginning of 1962. But the authors are careful to point out that they are not presenting a scientific calculation of exact central value: "We are not qualified to do this, and we doubt if anyone else is so qualified."

Leffler, George L. "Graham Earnings-Yield Formula." In his *The Stock Market*, 3rd ed., pp. 570–571. 1963.

> Brief description of Benjamin Graham's plan. The plan has not worked very well in recent years.

GROUPS, STOCK. *See* Stock Groups

GROWTH STOCKS

These are stocks of companies with earnings increasing at a faster-than-average annual rate. Hopefully, the prices of such stocks will increase at a rate much faster than average. These stocks tend to become "overvalued" and to move about in a volatile manner.

American Research Council. "Growth Approaches to Common Stock Selection." In *Your Investments*, 18th ed., pp. 43–62. 1970.

> General discussion of investing in growth stocks, including seven pros and cons of investing for long-term growth and ten do's and dont's for growth investors. Includes lists of growth stocks and two tables, "A Growth

Stock Price Evaluator" and "Prudent Price-Earnings Multiples for Growth Stocks," for determining whether or not the price of a growth stock is reasonable.

Cohen, Jerome B., and Zinbarg, Edward D. "Analysis of Growth." In their *Investment Analysis and Portfolio Management*, pp. 249–353. 1967.

This full discussion of how to analyze growth industries and stocks is divided into four parts: (1) "Some Basic Concepts," (2) "Sales Growth," (3) "Earnings Growth," and (4) "Management as an Independent Factor." An appendix to the first part describes statistical techniques for analysis of growth, explaining the uses of semilogarithmic charts, relative-growth ratios, scatter diagrams, simple regression analysis, and seasonal adjustment.

Crane, Burton. "If They Say 'Growth', Make 'Em Prove It!" In his *The Sophisticated Investor*, pp. 103–117. 1964.

A somewhat skeptical version of how to invest in growth stocks.

Dines, James. "Can Growth Stocks Make You Rich?" In his *How the Average Investor Can Use Technical Analysis for Stock Profits*, pp. 609–615. 1972.

Most of Dines' discussion is devoted to a consideration of the level at which a growth stock may be considered reasonably priced. Two tables show examples of Dines' listing of America's smartest managements and his listing of unusual earnings upswings.

Ellis, John. "Growth: Where the Big Gains Are." In his *Self-Reliant Investing*, pp. 36–49. 1971.

Includes six rules for finding a growth situation. Some of the dangers associated with investing in growth stocks are also outlined.

Graham, Benjamin. "Growth-Stock Approach." In his *The Intelligent Investor*, 4th rev. ed., pp. 75–78. 1973.

Graham's view of growth stocks is quite different from that of most writers on the subject. He points out that most mutual funds specializing in growth stocks have not done particularly well over the years, and most individual investors should not expect to do any better. Recognized growth stocks are, in general, not recommended.

Graham, Benjamin, and others. "Our Approach to Growth-Stock Valuation."
In their *Security Analysis*, 4th ed., pp. 536–538. 1962.

> Describes two highly simplified methods which give, according to the
> authors, approximately the same results as those produced by complicated,
> mathematically difficult formulas for evaluating growth stocks.

Hayes, Douglas A. "Buy and Hold: Growth-Stock Strategy." In his *Investment:
Analysis and Management*, 2nd ed., pp. 73–77. 1966.

> A general discussion of the difficulties involved in long-term investing in
> growth stocks. The main question: Can earnings growth be sustained over
> a long period of years?

Hazard, John W. *Choosing Tomorrow's Growth Stocks Today*. 1968. 305 pp.

> Much of this volume is devoted to discussion of how to select industries
> and corporations that will grow the fastest in future years. Specific in-
> dustries and companies are discussed and compared. See especially "A
> Stake in an Expanding America," pp. 68–84, and "Selecting Industries
> and Companies," pp. 85–114.

Herold, John S. "Profitable Common Stocks." In *Encyclopedia of Stock
Market Techniques*, pp. 387–411. 1970. (cover date: 1971).

> Comprehensive discussion of the advantages of investing in growth stocks,
> with emphasis on the determining of reasonable price-earnings ratios. A
> table shows the compound growth rate of one dollar over one to seven
> years at percentages from 10 to 200. A chart shows "Prudent Capitaliza-
> tion Rates (P/E Ratio) Corresponding to Various Growth Rates."
> Finally, various guide-rules are outlined.

Kamm, Jacob O. "Growth Stocks." In his *Making Profits in the Stock Market*,
pp. 56–69. 1966.

> Lists four fundamental growth factors, nine growth factors influencing
> industries, three factors influencing company growth, and ten growth com-
> pany characteristics. Three advantages and three disadvantages of owning
> growth stocks are discussed.

Knowlton, Winthrop, and Furth, John L. *Shaking the Money Tree; How to Find
New Growth Opportunities in Common Stocks*. 1972. 190 pp.

> A modern exposition of growth stock investment, featuring sections on
> rate of return, kinds of companies that should be bought, the factors that
> make a corporation successful, and the selection of advisers and portfolios.

Leffler, George L. "Growth Stocks." In his *The Stock Market*, 3rd ed., pp. 524–527. 1963.

> Notes three advantages to buying growth stocks, as well as seven specific criticisms of the purchase of growth issues.

Lufkin, Dan W. "Investing for Growth." In *The Anatomy of Wall Street*, ed. by Charles J. Rolo and George J. Nelson pp. 97–103. 1968.

> A brief introduction to the philosophy of investing in growth stocks, including when to buy and when to sell.

Markstein, David L. "The Collapse of the Growth-Stock Balloon." In his *Investing in the 70s*, pp. 1–22. 1972.

> Included in this general treatment of investment in growing companies is a list of seven tests to apply in identifying a true growth stock.

Peisner, Robert N. *How to Select Rapid Growth Stocks: Six Practical Investment Tools for Finding Stocks with a Potential for Rapid Growth*. 1966. 160 pp.

> Peisner devotes a chapter to each of his six growth-stock factors: (1) strong increase in quarterly earnings, (2) upward trend in annual earnings, (3) upward trend in quarterly earnings, (4) stock in "strong hands," (5) stock price in uptrend, (6) review of quarterly earnings. Other chapters consider the strategy and techniques of investing in stocks with rapidly growing earnings.

Rosenberg, Claude N. "Spotting Growth Companies." In his *Stock Market Primer*, pp. 206–210. 1969.

> Rosenberg tells how to identify the stock of a growth company. He includes a five-point checklist to use as an aid to locating growth stocks.

Shade, Philip A. "Determining PE Ratio Levels of Growth Companies." In his *Common Stocks: A Plan for Intelligent Investing*, pp. 236–257. 1971.

> Discussion includes identifying growth companies, distinguishing between fast-and slow-growth companies, factors affecting the future earnings growth of fast-growth companies, and estimating the current price-earnings ratio level of fast growth companies.

Stillman, Richard N. "What Price Growth?" In his *The Strategy of Investment*, pp. 71–102. 1962.

> Describes the discounted cash-flow method as a way of evaluating growth stocks. As an example, a complete evaluation of IBM is given, as of 1961.

In contrast to the actual price increase of roughly 400 percent from 1960 to 1970, the author's estimate of price increase in IBM stock, based on this method, was 110 percent. Stillman suggests that the investor search for overlooked growth stocks that have not become overpriced, although he admits that such issues are few and far between.

HEAD-AND-SHOULDERS FORMATION

A stock price pattern which makes a formation on a chart similar in appearance to a head and shoulders. This best-known of the many stock-price chart patterns is thought by chart analysts to be a reasonably reliable indicator of a price-trend reversal. A regular head-and-shoulders is supposed to signal a change from an uptrend to a downtrend, while an upside-down head-and-shoulders is supposed to signal a reversal from down to up.

Edwards, Robert D., and Magee, John. "The Head-and-Shoulders." In their *Technical Analysis of Stock Trends*, 5th ed., pp. 50–74. 1966.

This is one of the more common and, by all odds, the most reliable of the major reversal patterns, according to the authors. Includes comments upon volume during these formations, relation to the Dow Theory, multiple patterns, and symmetry; illustrated by various charts.

Jiler, William L. "Head and Shoulders." In his *How Charts Can Help You in the Stock Market*, pp. 55–72. 1962.

Complete discussion of head-and-shoulders tops and bottoms, with analysis of the left shoulder, the head, the right shoulder, and the neckline. Jiler points out that some of these formations are complex and not neatly delineated. Under "Tactics," four rules are given to help the investor decide when to take action. Six pages of charted examples appear in this chapter.

Lerro, Anthony J., and Swayne, Charles B. "Head and Shoulders Formation." In their *Selection of Securities*, pp. 30–38, 84–85. 1970.

Includes analyses of the right shoulder and the inverted head-and-shoulders. The authors discuss the head-and-shoulders pattern on point-and-figure charts on pages 84–85.

Markstein, David L. "Reversals: Head and Shoulders." In his *How to Chart Your Way to Stock Market Profits*, pp. 37–42. 1966.

Tells how to identify a head-and-shoulders formation. Markstein points out that a reversal pattern such as a head-and-shoulders chart pattern must occur at the end of some definite trend to be significant. One can hardly have a trend reversal without a trend to reverse.

Warren Ted. "Head and Shoulders Bottoms: Stocks Building Technical Strength." In his *How to Make the Stock Market Make Money for You*, pp. 63–68. 1966.

> Eight charts of individual stocks are illustrated and are interpreted relative to head-and-shoulders formations.

Williamson, J. Peter. "Chart Reading: An Example." In his *Investments*, pp. 190–195. 1971.

> Williamson uses the classic head-and-shoulders "top reversal" to illustrate technical analysis of stocks by means of chart formations. One gets the impression that the author is quite skeptical of charting as a technique of analysis.

HEDGE FUNDS

Investment companies which actively engage in short selling to counterbalance or "hedge" their long positions. Most hedge funds have not been available for public investment. These funds are notorious for their poor performance during the market break of 1970.

Loeb, Gerald M. "'Hedged Funds' Are for Experts, Not Average Investors." In his *The Battle for Stock Market Profits,* pp. 181–183. 1971.

> A brief description of how hedge funds operate, with some discussion of the risks involved.

Markstein, David L. "Sometimes Hedge Funds Multiply Investment Leverage." In his *How to Make Your Money Do More*, pp. 190–194. 1971.

> Considers the hedge fund idea for individual investors, with either actual stock positions being used or puts and calls being purchased. The investor forms his own little hedge fund in effect.

HEDGING

Hedging may be done in various ways in the stock market, for example by using options, but, in general, to hedge means to have long positions in stocks viewed favorably along with short positions in stocks viewed unfavorably. One may be "fully hedged" (50 percent long, 50 percent short) or "net long" (mostly long) or "net short" (mostly short).

Graham, Benjamin, and others. "Hedging." In their *Security Analysis*, 4th ed., pp. 625–626. 1962.

> Describes a form of hedging in which the investor buys the convertible bond and sells short the common stock of the same corporation. Assuming a relatively stable convertible bond and a common stock that fluctuates with the market, this form of hedging constitutes a conservative way to make money in a bear market. If the stock market moves up instead of falling, the convertible issue is converted into common stock to cover the short position, thus limiting loss.

Kamm, Jacob O. "The Art of Hedging." In his *Making Profits in the Stock Market*, pp. 121–134. 1966.

> How to use convertibles, industry selection, formula plans, and warrants for conservative hedging.

Scheinman, William X. "Selling Strategies." In his *Why Most Investors Are Mostly Wrong Most of the Time*, pp. 193–218. 1970.

> While this chapter is concerned with selling stocks in general, pages 205–218 are specifically about the art of hedging. Examples are given comparing an ordinary account with a margin account utilizing hedging.

HIGH FLIERS. *See* High Velocity Stocks

HIGH-LOW INDEX

A measurement of the difference between the number of stocks making new highs in price for the year and those making new lows.

Dines, James. "Using the New High-New Low Index to Detect Trouble Ahead." In his *How the Average Investor Can Use Technical Analysis for Stock Profits*, pp. 563–568. 1972.

> General discussion of the high-low index, with four pages of charts, including American Stock Exchange new highs and new lows from the beginning of 1963 to the end of 1970.

Jacobs, William O. "New High Index." In his *Stock Market Profile*, pp. 48–52. 1967.

> Jacobs asserts that an index of new highs is a good indicator of bull market tops, if interpreted in special ways. He uses a new-high index as one part of his stock market profile indicator.

Krow, Harvey A. "New Highs and New Lows." In his *Stock Market Behavior*, pp. 101–104. 1969.

> Explains the value of watching for changes in the new-high–new-low numerical relationship as a kind of early warning signal for the stock market.

Markstein, David L. "The Hi-Lo Index." In his *How to Make Your Money Do More*, pp. 230–232. 1971.

> An explanation of the cumulative differential method of constructing a high-low index, which results in a one-line chart, in contrast with the two-line chart representing moving averages of new highs and new lows used by some indexes.

HIGH VELOCITY STOCKS

Stocks that are showing high volatility on the up side—shooting upward in price.

Paris, Alexander P. "High-Velocity Stocks." In his *A Complete Guide to Trading Profits*, pp. 99–114. 1970.

> Tells how to use charts as an aid in speculating in stocks that are moving upward unusually rapidly. Paris says that these stocks offer unusual opportunities for gain, but with correspondingly high risk. The three phases of a high-velocity stock price move are outlined and illustrated.

HIGHS AND LOWS. *See* New Highs and New Lows

HOURLY VARIATIONS. *See* Seasonal (Cyclical) Variations

INCOME STOCKS

Stocks of corporations noted for paying dividends that are both liberal and reliable. Public utility stocks, for example, are often held for income. In addition to conservative income stocks, such as utilities, there is usually available a number of very high-yield, high-risk income stocks.

American Research Council. "Income Approaches to Common Stock Selection." In *Your Investments*, 18th ed., pp. 36–43. 1970.

> Covers many aspects of dividend income, as well as the two main ways of using capital gains as income. Characteristics of high-yielding stocks are discussed, and six do's and don'ts for income investors are given.

Bridwell, Rodger, "The Income Illusion." In his *Reality in the Stock Market*, pp. 47–51. 1965.

> The author does not recommend buying stocks mainly for income, for, as he points out, "the higher the yield, the higher the risk."

Merritt, Robert D. "Buying Stocks for Income." In his *Financial Independence through Common Stocks*, pp. 71–83. 1969.

> The author advises against buying common stocks with currently high dividend yields. Instead, stocks should be selected on the basis of growth prospects and the probability of paying dividends that increase over the years.

Owen, Lewis. "Duck Dividends." In his *How Wall Street Doubles My Money Every Three Years*, pp. 207–209. 1969.

> Stocks which pay high dividends should generally be avoided, according to Owen, as the fast-moving stocks are generally those of corporations which put profits back into the business. Stocks which are good for dividend income are generally stodgy.

INCOME TAX. *See* Tax Transactions

INDICATOR CONSENSUS. *See* Consensus of Indicators.

INDUSTRY GROUPS. *See* Stock Groups

INSIDER TRANSACTIONS

The buying and selling activities of officers, directors, and large stockholders in individual corporations, reported monthly in the *Official Summary of Security Transactions and Holdings*, often called the "Insiders Report," compiled by the Securities and Exchange Commission. Unusual insider activity in the stock of a particular corporation may give an important clue to the future of its price.

Ellis, John. "Companies with Bullish Insiders." In his *Self-Reliant Investing*, pp. 85–88. 1971.

> Describes the work of Perry Wysong and others, in the study of buying and selling by insiders. Ellis considers insider buying of a particular stock to be much more significant than insider selling.

Wysong, Perry. *How You Can Use the Wall Street Insiders*. 1971. 188 pp.

> Wysong is the leading authority on judging stocks by what the insiders are up to. His book is a conglomeration of material, mainly from the Wysong

investment advisory service, "Consensus of Insiders," but also including articles from newspapers and magazines, as well as reprints of scholarly studies of the stock transactions of corporate insiders. The three main parts of the book are (1) "When to Buy and When to Sell," (2) "What Stocks to Buy," and (3) "Wysong's Library of Insider Lore."

INSTITUTIONAL INVESTING

The investment activities of endowment funds, pension funds, mutual funds, and other large accumulations of capital. This kind of investing dominates today's stock market.

Ellis, Charles D. *Institutional Investing*. 1971. 253 pp.

An examination of "the theory and practice of managing large portfolios of other people's money . . ." This is not a volume intended for the individual investor. Nevertheless, Ellis writes much better than might be expected, so this book is a relatively painless way for individuals to find out what strategies the institutions are employing or, according to Ellis, should be employing. He gives worthwhile information about trying to beat the market, staying fully invested, the volatility of stocks, diversification, and risk.

INTEREST RATES AND STOCKS. *See* Money Supply and Stock Prices

INTRINSIC VALUE. *See* Dividend Value Approach; Normal-Value Plans

INVESTMENT ADVISORY SERVICES

Printed advice or information about the stock and bond markets, generally published in loose-leaf or newsletter form. Weekly publication is typical.

Cheney, Harlan L. "Subscription Investment Advisory Services: How Good Are They?" In *Encyclopedia of Stock Market Techniques*, pp. 83–97. 1970 (cover date: 1971).

The author has a kind word to say for published advisory services, based on his study of four services that have a "relatively prominent position in the industry." The four services are not named, and the results of the four are averaged together, according to recommendations for growth stocks. On average, the four services combined gave recommendations for stocks that performed moderately better than Standard and Poor's Composite 500 Stock Average, during the period from 1957 to 1968.

Dines, James. "Market Letters, Advisory Services, and Tout Sheets." In his *How the Average Investor Can Use Technical Analysis for Stock Profits*, pp. 653–656. 1972.

> General discussion of what to look for in investment letters or services. Dines recommends that an investor set aside a few hundred dollars to try a large number of market letters for at least a six-month period.

Ellis, John. "A Guide to Advisory Services." In his *Self-Reliant Investing*, pp. 127–140. 1971.

> A generally skeptical look at advisory services.

Engel, Louis. "Financial Advice—At a Price." In his *How to Buy Stocks*, 5th rev. ed., pp. 213–226. 1971.

> In discussing the limited amount of control that the Securities and Exchange Commission has over printed advisory services, Engel says that "many publishers of market letters can continue to ply their dubious trade without too much interference from regulatory authorities." He then describes the services of thirteen of the "most reputable companies" in the field of published investment information and advice.

Graham, Benjamin. "Financial Services." In his *The Intelligent Investor*, 4th rev. ed., pp. 133–135. 1973.

> Graham regards the fundamental investment services as being generally useful for information and suggestions, but superficial in predictions of the near future of stock prices. He dismisses charting and technical forecasting stock market services as not being of concern to "investors" as he uses the term.

Hirsch, Yale. "Interesting New Services." In his *The Stock Trader's Almanac*. Annual.

> Each year, Hirsch lists new investment services that he found interesting or worthwhile. A short description is given of each service.

Kamm, Jacob O. "The Experts Are Wrong." In his *Making Profits in the Stock Market*, pp. 143–149. 1966.

> Five major criticisms of stock market advisory services are listed and discussed.

Krefetz, Gerald, and Marosi, Ruth. "The Advisory Services." In their *Money Makes Money* . . ., pp. 46–53. 1970.

> Emphasizes the fact that just about any person can start a printed, stock market advisory service, regardless of education or background.

Loeb, Gerald M. "Money From Market Letters." In his *The Battle for Investment Survival*, pp. 259–262. 1965.

> A reasonably favorable discussion of stock market letters. Loeb says these advisory publications are worth reading, but only if one thinks independently. Taking advice blindly on Wall Street generally leads to trouble.

Neal, Charles V. "Investment Advisory Services—Whom Do They Serve?" In his *How to Keep What you Have, or, What Your Broker Never Told You*, pp. 236–252. 1972.

> Asserts that "it pays to be just a little cynical" when looking at the publications of investment advisory services, because in the past some of the services have not been above making a few deals on the side with companies whose stocks are being recommended.

Springer, John L. *If They're So Smart, How Come You're Not Rich?* pp. 198–211. 1971.

> Although Springer knocks investment services in general, the Value Line Investment Survey ("How Much Value in Value Line?") receives special attention. The author regards Value Line's practice of projecting the prices of individual stocks into the relatively distant future (three to five years) as "sheer guesswork." In "The Art of Self-Defense", pp. 198–211, Springer discusses eight principles that should be scrupulously followed by the individual investor wishing to avoid bad advice. Springer's overall conclusion is that the advisory-service industry is pitiful in its lack of standards.

Warren, Ted. "Advisory Services: A Spider's Web of Conflicting Claims and Confusion." In his *How to Make the Stock Market Make Money for You*, pp. 184–199, 200–211. 1966.

> As indicated by the chapter title above, this is a severe criticism of printed, stock market advisory services. Warren says the advertising of these services is especially blameworthy. The chapter, "Two Big Advisory Services: My Predictions and Theirs," pp. 200–211, shows how superior Warren's predictions were to those of two very popular services.

INVESTMENT CLUBS

Groups of people who have agreed to pool investment funds and have meetings to decide jointly which securities will be invested in. Typically, small amounts are invested monthly by a club made up of individuals who are at least reasonably compatible. Organizational structure is generally informal.

Hazard, John W. "Investment Clubs." In his *Choosing Tomorrow's Growth Stocks Today*, pp. 187–193. 1968.

> Tells why investment clubs are popular and how to form one. Three guiding principles are given that a club should follow if it is to be successful.

Sederberg, Arelo. *The Stock Market Investment Club Handbook. How to Organize, Maintain and Profit from an Investment Club*. 1971. 277 pp.

> This book espouses the National Association of Investment Clubs' method of forming and operating an investment club. Organization, portfolio management, record keeping, and legal aspects are covered.

INVESTMENT COMPANIES (*see also* Mutual Funds)

Corporations which pool investment money from a number of individuals or others and then see to it that the money is professionally (although not necessarily profitably) invested. One of the chief advantages of buying shares in an investment company is that broad diversification can be achieved with a small amount of capital. Some investment companies issue a fixed number of shares that trade on the open market, perhaps on the New York Stock Exchange; these companies are called closed-end. Other investment companies are open-end (mutual funds) and stand ready to issue or redeem their shares continously at net asset value plus fees, if any. Closed-end funds may sell above or below asset value, according to investor supply and demand.

American Research Council. "How to Select Investment Companies and Operate Personal Retirement Plans." In *Your Investments*, 18th ed., pp. 153–167. 1970.

> Discusses eleven tests of eligibility for investors to consider when selecting investment companies, under the heading, "Which Eligible Investment Companies are Suitable for You?".

Cohen, Jerome B., and Zinbarg, Edward D. "Investment Companies." In their *Investment Analysis and Portfolio Management*, pp. 613–645. 1967.

> Compares open-end investment companies (mutual funds) with closed-end investment companies. A good deal of space is devoted to a description

of how best to measure the performance of investment funds. Formulas are included. Cohen and Zinbarg point out ". . . while investment companies on the whole turn in average performances, a great many do quite poorly."

Graham, Benjamin. "Investing in Investment Funds." In his *The Intelligent Investor*, 4th rev. ed., pp. 116–130. 1973.

Three major questions about investment companies are asked and answered: how to (1) choose a fund that will give better than average results, (2) at the very least, avoid a fund that will do worse than average, and (3) choose a suitable type of fund. The author states: "We do not think the mutual-fund industry can be criticized for doing no better than the market as a whole." Nevertheless, Graham recommends buying closed-end investment companies at a discount, rather than mutual funds.

Laurence, Michael. "Discount Merchandise: Closed-End Funds." In his *Playboy's Investment Guide*, pp. 117–127. 1971.

General discussion of closed-end investment companies, including dual funds.

Loeb, Gerald M. "Investment Trust Investing Is Average Investing." In his *The Battle for Investment Survival*, pp. 168–169. 1965.

States that the investor who wants to do substantially better than the crowd must invest for himself, not through a mutual fund or other investment company.

Mead, Stuart B. 'The Closed-End Investment Companies. . . ." In his *Mutual Funds: a Guide for the Lay Investor*, pp. 18–22. 1971.

The author recommends that investors consider closed-end investment companies as well as mutual funds (open-end). "Some of them are good investments." Discount and leverage features of closed-end funds are discussed.

Sauvain, Harry. "Investment Company Securities for the Small Investor." In his *Investment Management*, 3rd ed., pp. 608–613. 1967.

Asserts that investment companies provide a valuable service for the small investor just by providing "average returns and the probability of above average returns in the future . . ." because they can provide the broad diversification that an individual investor can not normally afford by himself.

Widicus, Wilbur W., and Stitzel, Thomas E. "Investing in Investment Companies." In his *Today's Investments for Tomorrow's Security*, pp. 250–281. 1971.

> Discusses closed-end investment companies, open-end investment companies (mutual funds), no-load funds, accumulation plans, automatic dividend reinvestment, withdrawal accounts, balanced funds, income funds, tax-free exchange funds, growth funds, hedge funds, dual-purpose funds, and funding companies.

ISLANDS. *See* Gaps and Islands

"KERAN MODEL." *See* Money Supply and Stock Prices

KEYSTONE PLAN

A seven-step investment plan or formula based on stock market zones or levels. The zones are established by superimposing a set of trend-lines on a chart of the Dow-Jones Industrial Average. When stock prices are within zone four (the middle one of the seven zones), the plan calls for holding 50 percent stocks and 50 percent defensive bonds. The proportion of stocks to bonds is lowered gradually to 10 percent as stock prices go up to zone seven and raised gradually to 90 percent as stock prices fall to zone one.

Leffler, George L. "Keystone Plan." In his *The Stock Market*, 3rd ed., p. 565. 1963.

> Brief description of Keystone Plan. States that the plan worked well from 1940 to 1953, but poorly thereafter.

Persons, Robert H. "Trend Line Formulas." In his *Handbook of Formula Plans in the Stock Market*, pp. 75–80. 1967.

> Emphasizes the "Keystone Seven-Step Plan" introduced in 1941 and publicized by Keystone Custodian Funds. While the channel or zone lines used produced a very good "fit" from 1897 to 1941, things went haywire after about 1955 because of acceleration in the rate that stock prices increased. Revised channels were adopted in later years, but Persons says that any long-term trend-line plan is subject to unforeseen obsolescence. This chapter of his book has charts of three Keystone zone plans, based on rates of ascendancy of 3.0 percent, 4.4 percent, and 8.23 percent. A logarithmic chart of the Dow-Jones Industrials is included to 1966, while the zone lines continue to 1972.

LEFFLER FORMULA

An intrinsic- or normal-value investment timing plan (see definition under "Normal-Value Plans") devised by George L. Leffler for small investors. Normal or central value is determined by two factors: dividend yield on the Dow-Jones Industrial Average and the price-earnings ratio for the same average.

Leffler, George L. "The Two-Signal Intrinsic Value Formula." In his *The Stock Market*, 3rd ed., pp. 569–570. 1963.

> Brief description of Leffler's formula for the average investor. Stock prices are regarded as being very high, normal, or very low according to the yield and price-earnings ratio of the Dow-Jones Industrials. The plan would have worked very well from 1942 to the early 1960s.

LEVERAGE (*see also* Margin)

Generally, the investment power gained by adding borrowed money to original capital, as in the use of margin to buy securities. Corporations gain leverage by using borrowed money to expand operations. Of course, losses as well as gains are magnified by leverage.

American Research Council. "How to Use Corporate and Investor Leverage for Maximum Gain." In *Your Investments*, 18th ed., pp. 111–112. 1970.

> The kinds of leverage briefly discussed are capitalization leverage (trading on the equity), operating leverage (the condition in which a corporation has high fixed costs and low variable costs), ordinary margin for speculators, and special instruments (warrants, puts and calls, and so forth).

Markstein, David L. "Make Your Investment Capital Do More." In his *How to Make Your Money Do More*, pp. 177–183. 1971.

> Various ways of obtaining leverage in the stock market are briefly considered, such as use of margin, warrants, margined warrants, puts and calls, and convertibles.

Person, Carl E. *The Save-By-Borrowing Technique*. 1966. 289 pp.

> A book about borrowing money through ordinary monthly installment loans and then investing the money in the stock market. The psychology of the plan is that money that is borrowed must be paid back, while voluntary savings programs often get side-tracked.

LINES AND SAUCERS

These are stock-price chart pattern formations in the shape of long, relatively straight lines, although in the case of "saucers," the lines are rounded. Sometimes these patterns are referred to as bases or base formations.

Jiler, William L. "Line and Saucer Formations." In his *How Charts Can Help You in the Stock Market*, pp. 85–95. 1962.

> Jiler describes lines and saucers as "dream patterns" because they (1) are easy to recognize, (2) usually indicate an extensive price move, and (3) give adequate time to "take a position." Six pages of charted examples appear in this chapter.

Lerro, Anthony J., and Swayne, Charles B. "Saucers, Sauce Plans, Bowls, M- and W-Triple Tops and Bottoms." In their *Selection of Securities*, pp. 45–55. 1970.

> Describes some fairly exotic chart formations such as horizontal bowls, inverted bowls, downward-tilting bowls and upward-tilting bowls.

LIQUIDITY OF MUTUAL FUNDS. *See* Mutual Fund Liquidity

LITERATURE OF INVESTING. *See* Books (Literature)

LOANS FOR INVESTING. *See* Leverage; Margin

LOSSES (*see also* Profits)
The opposite of profits; the chief cause of mental distress among investors.

"Anonymous Investor." *Wiped Out; How I Lost a Fortune in the Stock Market while the Averages Were Making New Highs.* Simon and Schuster, 1966. 125 pp.

> A horror story about an "average investor" who managed to run 62 thousand dollars down to 298 dollars between October 1957 and May 1964, while the Dow-Jones Industrial Average advanced from 485 to 820. The anonymous author dedicates his book to his brokers, "whose capacity for self-delusion was commensurate with my own." Most of the losses were brought about by buying stocks of low quality, with the expectation of making a lot of money in a short period of time.

Loeb, Gerald M. "Gaining Profits by Taking Losses" and "What to Do About Losses." In his *The Battle for Investment Survival*, pp. 91–95, 190–191. 1965.

> In his book, Loeb returns again and again to the theme of cutting losses before they become great. He advises, "Accepting losses is the most important single investment device to insure safety of capital."

Loeb, Gerald M. "Losses" and "Three Ways to Lose in the Stock Market." In his *The Battle for Stock Market Profits*, pp. 139–142, 204–207. 1971.

> The first of these chapters outlines when, why, and how to take losses. Stressing the general theme, "don't delay." The second chapter analyzes three principle ways to lose money in the stock market, all involving over-evaluation (paying too much) and underanalysis (failing to recognize a company's poor financial position).

Rosenberg, Claude N. "On Losing Cold, Hard Dollars." In his *Psycho-Cybernetics and the Stock Market*, pp. 75–97. 1971.

> Rosenberg takes a dim view of mechanical methods of limiting losses, such as the use of stop-loss orders, and he also warns against overdiversification. He discusses the psychological side of the problem, the debilitating fear of losing money in the stock market and the six symptoms of fear of poverty or losses. A loss questionnaire is presented to help the individual investor analyze his or her own attitude toward losing.

Rosenberg, Claude N. "Ugh!" In his *Stock Market Primer*, pp. 260–266. 1969.

> Most of this chapter is concerned with the tax aspects of stock market losses.

LOW-PRICED STOCKS (*see also* Speculation Indexes)

Stocks selling below twenty dollars per share, although twenty dollars is an entirely arbitrary figure. Low-priced stocks are noted for their price volatility.

Graham, Benjamin, and others. "Low-Priced Stocks." In their *Security Analysis*, 4th ed., pp. 649–656. 1962.

> Emphasizes the arithmetical advantage of low-priced stocks, noting, "It is a commonplace of the securities market that an issue will rise more readily from 10 to 40 than from 100 to 400."

Krow, Harvey A. "Low-Priced Stocks." In his *Stock Market Behavior*, pp. 105–110. 1969.

> Indicates that the movement of an index of low-priced stocks may be of more value as a leading indicator at stock market tops than at bottoms. A two-page chart shows Standard and Poor's Twenty Low-Priced Common Stocks Index plotted on the same scale as Standard and Poor's 425 Industrial Stocks Index, from 1940 to 1967.

Silverman, Richard. "How to Make Big Money with Canadian Penny Stocks while Other Investors Are Losing Their Shirts." In his *$100 Gets You Started*, pp. 34–47. 1965.

> Description of a method of making money in very low-priced stocks (under one dollar per share) which have had "consistently wide fluctuations over the years." The idea is to buy toward the bottom of a typical yearly price range and sell toward the top of this range.

MARGIN (*see also* Leverage)

Wall Street's word for credit. Margin involves the use of securities as collateral for a loan from a broker or bank, the money received from the loan being used to buy additional securities. Margin loans are regulated by the Federal Reserve Board. Margin requirement is the percentage of a stock's price that must be furnished from the buyer's own funds. This figure has varied from 40 percent to 100 percent.

American Research Council. "How to Buy Securities on Margin or Credit." In *Your Investments*, 18th ed., pp. 208–213. 1970.

> Many aspects of margin are considered, including key formulas to figure current equity, excess margin, cash-withdrawal power, and security-buying power. The Council also considers borrowing on life insurance or on a real estate mortgage (to obtain money to buy stocks). Three ways are listed to save money on the interest paid on a margin acocunt.

Bridwell, Rodger. "Invest Only Your Own Money." In his *Reality in the Stock Market*, pp. 52–58. 1965.

> The disadvantages of buying stock on margin are outlined.

Engel, Louis. "How You Buy Stocks on Margin." In his *How to Buy Stocks*, 5th rev. ed., pp. 173–180. 1971.

> Engel points out that the small investor or speculator should not buy stocks on margin unless he is prepared to "accept his losses with reasonable equanimity." The operation of margin accounts is explained in an easy-to-understand manner.

Granville, Joseph E. "Margin Requirements." In his *A Strategy of Daily Stock Market Timing for Maximum Profit*, pp. 147–148. 1960.

> Brief discussion of changes in margin requirements as an indicator of stock price movement.

Hazard, John W. "Buying Stocks on Margin." In his *Choosing Tomorrow's Growth Stocks Today*, pp. 277–283. 1968.

> Good discussion of what is involved in buying stock on margin. Various formulas are given for determining equity, margin call levels, and so forth. A table shows the effect of staying fully invested on 70 percent margin, assuming three successive 20 percent rises in the price of the stock purchased. Finally, the dangers of margin trading are emphasized.

Leffler, George L. "Margin Trading." In his *The Stock Market*, 3rd ed., pp. 364–381. 1963.

> Topics include the advantage and disadvantages of margin trading, how to compute margins, and the history of margin requirements.

Owen, Lewis. "Buy on Margin." In his *How Wall Street Doubles My Money Every Three Years*, pp. 174–180. 1969.

> A recommendation of margin as a "quick, painless" way to extend one's buying power in the stock market. The details of opening and maintaining a margin account are discussed.

Silverman, Richard. "What You Should Know about Margin—and How to Use It." In his *$100 Gets You Started*, pp. 173–184. 1965.

> A reasonably complete discussion of buying stocks on margin and selling short, written for the small investor. Advantages and disadvantages of using margin are included.

Warren, Ted. "Why You Should Consider Buying on Margin." In his *How to Make the Stock Market Make Money For You*, pp. 109–118.

> Interesting presentation of some of the advantages of using margin accounts, although the author believes that nervous or even forced selling from these accounts can make market breaks more severe than they would have been otherwise.

Zerden, Sheldon. *Margin: Key to a Stock Market Fortune*. 1969. 53 pp.

> This small volume tells the average investor about all he will ever need to know about margin, subject, of course, to changes in current regulations. The mechanics of a margin account are well explained.

MARGIN DEBIT AND FREE CREDIT INDICATORS

Stock price predictors based on the activity of those who buy stock on margin (New York Stock Exchange customers' margin debit balances) and those who buy on a cash basis (customers' free credit balances). Free credit balances decrease as cash customers buy and margin debit balances increase as margin customers buy. Various interpretations of these figures are made by market technicians.

American Research Council. "Cash and Credit Ratio Techniques." In *Your Invesments*, 18th ed., p. 183. 1970.
> Discusses customers' free credit balances and customers' net debit balances as stock market indicators. States that these are slow-moving indicators that can be ambivalent.

Cohen, Jerome B. and Zinbarg, Edward D. "Credit Balances in Brokerage Accounts." In their *Investment Analysis and Portfolio Management*, pp. 514–516. 1967.
> A chart shows the relationship between free credit balances in brokerage accounts and Standard and Poor's 425 Industrials Index of stock prices. Customers' credit balances are shown to peak in advance of the stock market.

Dines, James. "Credits and Debits Suggest No Two People Were Ever Created Equal." In his *How the Average Investor Can Use Technical Analysis for Stock Profits*, pp. 551–558. 1972.
> Explains credits and debits, describing Indicator Digest's credit-debit ratio, broker's borrowings, margin requirements, net (free) credit balances, and net debit balances. A chart shows the free credit index and the net debit balances from 1931 to 1967 and compares them with the Dow-Jones Industrial Average. Edson Gould's chart, "Stock Prices and Customers' Balances" (total) is shown for 1936–1964.

Jacobs, William O. "Debit Balance." In his *Stock Market Profile*, pp. 85–87. 1967.
> Jacobs says "a turn-down or even a leveling out of [an index of margin debt] in a bull market has always meant trouble ahead . . . ." On the other hand, an increase of margin debt in a bear market is said to predict higher stock prices. Jacobs makes use of an index of margin debt in customers' brokerage accounts in his stock market profile indicator.

Jacobs, William O. "Free Credit Balance." In his *Stock Market Profile*, pp. 81–84. 1967.

> States that the free credit (cash) balances of stock market customers tend to go up as a bull market proceeds, indicating skepticism on the part of the customers. As might be expected, skepticism disappears during late stages of a bull market, free credit balances drop sharply, and customers have their final fling before the bear appears on the scene. Jacobs uses the free credit balance indicator as part of his stock market profile system.

Wilson, Sloan J. "The Customers' Free Credit and Margin Debit Balances." In *Encyclopedia of Stock Market Techniques*, pp. 707–722. 1970 (cover date: 1971).

> Wilson tells what typically happens to free credit and margin debit balances during bottom formations, top formations, and post-peak and post-crash eras. The psychology of the credit and debit balance groups is discussed. Various charts are shown, including free credit and debit balances during the 1963–1968 period.

MARKET AXIOMS. *See* Adages (Wall Street Folklore)

MARKET FUEL INDICATOR

A money market indicator based on the movements of the Dow-Jones Utility Stock Average and the Dow-Jones Composite Bond Average. Bond prices and utility stock prices are favorably affected by increases in money supply.

Markstein, David L. "The Market Fuel Indicator." In his *How to Make Your Money Do More*, pp. 232–235. 1971.

> This long-term indicator is described as well as charted for the period from April 1966 to November 1967.

MARKET LETTERS. *See* Investment Advisory Services

MARKET-NORM PLANS. *See* Normal Value Plans

MARKET PHILOSOPHY. *See* Adages (Wall Street Folklore); Psychology

MARKET SCARES

News events which cause the stock market to decline sharply within a short period of time. In the case of a market scare, such declines are not based on economic happenings. The market generally recovers rapidly, and many investors regard these drops as buying opportunities.

American Research Council. "Market Scares, Surprises, Jitters, and Reactions."
In *Your Investments*, 18th ed., p. 187. 1970.

> Discusses scares briefly and includes a table showing response to market
> scares since 1897, beginning with the sinking of the battleship *Maine* in
> 1898 and ending with the Arab-Israeli War in 1967. Twenty-two events
> are listed, with percent of loss, days of decline, percent of loss recovered,
> and number of days lapsed before recovery.

Dines, James. "Is the Stock Market Cause or Effect?" In his *How the Average
Investor Can Use Technical Analysis for Stock Profits*, pp. 608–609. 1972.

> Dines summarizes: ". . . We do not believe news is terribly important to
> the stock market, unelss it actually affects future corporate earnings and
> therefore dividends." He elaborates on this theme.

MAXIMS. *See* Adages (Wall Street Folklore)

"MECHANICAL" INVESTMENT FORMULAS. *See* Filter Technique; Formula
Plans; Moving Average; Trend Following

MEMBER SHORT SELLING. *See* Short Selling Activity of New York Stock
Exchange Members

MODIFIED DOLLAR AVERAGING. *See* Dollar Averaging, Modified

MOMENTUM INDEX (DINES) *(See also* Breadth-Momentum Index; Relative
Strength
An index, devised by James Dines, which is the ratio of the current price of a
stock or stock average to the price of the same stock or average one year ago.

Dines, James. "The Momentum Index as a Near-Infallible Indicator." In his
How the Average Investor Can Use Technical Analysis for Stock Profits, pp.
447–450. 1972.

> Dines examines a monthly momentum index of Standard and Poor's
> Industrial Stock Index and asserts "This is an extremely valuable indicator
> which has proved almost infallible in calling past market turns." In
> addition to momentum indexes of stock averages, the author tells about
> weekly momentum indexes of stock industry groups. A table shows an
> example of the Robot Group Selector, which is a weekly listing of 111
> industry groups according to momentum.

MONEY SUPPLY AND STOCK PRICES (*see also* Federal Reserve Board Actions; Three-Steps-and-a-Stumble Theory)

Money is the fuel of the stock market. Therefore, considerable interest exists among investment analysts about whether the supply of money is expanding or contracting. The relationship between stock prices, interest rates, and money supply is complex, to say the least.

Dines, James. "The Impact of Interest Rates on the Stock Market Is Profound." In his *How the Average Investor Can Use Technical Analysis for Stock Profits*, pp. 559–562. 1972.

> Comments on five monetary indicators: (1) net free reserves, (2) member banks' borrowings, (3) the three-month Treasury bill rates, (4) the federal funds rate, and (5) money supply.

Jacobs, William O. "Indicators of Money and Credit." In his *Stock Market Profile*, pp. 88–96. 1967.

> The discount rate, member bank reserves, and margin requirements are discussed as stock market indicators. Jacobs uses all three of these as part of his stock market profile system.

Markstein, David L. "The Keran Model." In his *Investing in the 70s*, pp. 143–144. 1972.

> Description of Michael W. Keran's model of stock price movements combining the current stock price, the expected stock price, expected dividends, and interest rate. The predictive value of the Keran Model was very good from 1960 to 1970.

Mittra, Sid. "Dough Makes a Difference." In his *Inside Wall Street*, pp. 73–83. 1971.

> The author says that finding a reliable system for predicting stock prices is about as difficult as finding a flying saucer. Nevertheless, he seems to feel that the relationship between money supply or interest rates and stock prices is worth looking into, despite the uncertainties. Various money measures are discussed.

Poole, D. B. "Bank-Credit—a 'Forecast' ". In *Encyclopedia of Stock Market Techniques*, pp. 535–553. 1970 (cover date: 1971.)

> Poole offers a relatively non-technical presentation of the various relationships existing in the economy between bank-credit, or money, and prices, particularly stock prices.

Ritter, Lawrence S., and Silber, William L. "Does Monetary Policy Affect the Stock Market?" In their *Money*, pp. 128–139. 1970.

> Notes that stock market reaction to changes in monetary policy has been more prompt and predictable recently than from 1930 to 1960. The two reasons given for the change are that the Federal Reserve is acting more authoritatively, and that more and more people, including investors, are starting to sit up and pay attention when the Federal Reserve takes action.

Sprinkel, Beryl W. "Money and the Stock Market." In his *Money and Markets; a Monetarist View*, pp. 217–241. 1971.

> Sprinkel is a leading authority on the subject of money supply and the stock market. While his entires book deals with the way that money flow affects business, the above chapter is specifically on the stock market. How money affects stock prices is explained and a special chart shows turning points in money and stock prices from 1918 to 1970.

MONTHLY INVESTMENT PLAN

An arrangement devised by the New York Stock Exchange in 1954 to enable small investors to buy individual stocks in amoutns as small as forty dollars on a periodic basis.

Engel, Louis. "How the Monthly Investment Plan Works." In his *How to Buy Stocks*, 5th rev. ed., pp. 108–111. 1971.

> Fully explains the Monthly Investment Plan, which, Engel notes, ". . . does have the advantage of helping investors establish regular habits of thrift."

Person, Carl E. "Comes the Monthly Investment Plan." In his *The Save-by-Borrowing Technique*, pp. 128–148. 1966.

> A complete explanation of the Monthly Investment Plan (MIP) is given. Person does not generally recommend monthly investment of small amounts under this plan, because of the relatively high commission rate.

MONTHLY PRICE VARIATIONS. *See* Seasonal (Cyclical) Variations

MOST ACTIVE STOCKS

The individual stocks showing the greatest volume of trading during a certain period—daily or weekly, for example. Newspapers often list the ten or fifteen most active stocks on the New York and American Stock Exchanges.

Dines, James. "The 'Most Actives' Tell Where the Action Is! West's Most Actives Rule." In his *How the Average Investor Can Use Technical Analysis for Stock Profits*, pp. 596–597. 1972.

> Refers to the work of F. R. West, in which the number of most active stocks advancing is compared on a weekly basis with the number declining. Despite the fact that an index based on this data has sometimes been unreliable as a stock market indicator, Dines believes that it has value and should be watched closely in coming years.

Markstein, David L. " 'Most Active' Stocks." In his *Investing in the 70s*, pp. 137–138. 1972.

> Describes a study made by F. R. West, which showed that an increasing number of negative price movements in lists of most active stocks is often a prelude to a bear market.

MOVING AVERAGE

An arithmetic mean that changes (moves) according to a specified period of time. Two-hundred-day moving averages, for example, are commonly used to measure stock price trends. The figure plotted each day, in this case, would be the average or mean of closing prices for the most recent two hundred days.

Allen, Leon B. *A Method for Stock Profits without Price Forecasting*. 1962. 216 pp.

> Allen's method combines several moving averages to determine the general trend of the stock market. Individual stocks are selected by charting their relative strengths. Allen achieved very good results with his method over a period of about thirty years (1932–1961).

Bridwell, Rodger. "The Golden Egg." In his *Reality in the Stock Market*, pp. 69–73. 1965.

> Discusses the advantages and disadvantages of dollar-averaging, with emphasis on the latter.

Cohen, Jerome B., and Zinbarg, Edward D. "Rate-of-Change Analysis." In their *Investment Analysis and Portfolio Management*, pp. 517–520. 1967.

> Cohen and Zinbarg believe that moving averages reveal the underlying direction and rate of change of stock prices. But they assert that the commonly used 200-day moving average does not necessarily produce results superior to other averages using different time periods. A full-page chart is used to show a twelve-month moving average of Standard and Poor's 425 Industrials Index from 1945 to 1966.

Dahl, Curtiss. "Moving Averages and the Dahl Approach to Profits in the Stock Market." In *Encyclopedia of Stock Market Techniques*, pp. 175–209. 1970 (cover date: 1971).

> More than thirty charts are used to illustrate the use of moving averages to generate signals to buy and sell individual stocks.

Dines, James. "How to Use the 200-Day Moving Average to Spot a Bear Market." In his *How the Average Investor Can Use Technical Analysis for Stock Profits*, pp. 452–460. 1972.

> Very good explanation of moving averages, including such details as the exact difference between a 200-day and thirty-week average. "Present technical literature uses the terms interchangeably—we do not." The work of Joseph E. Granville and of Indicator Digest on moving averages is discussed in some detail. Ten-day and twenty-day averages as short-term indicators are commented upon.

Drew, Garfield A. "Moving Average Methods." In his *New Methods for Profit in the Stock Market*, pp. 42–50. 1966. (reprint of 1955 edition).

> An interesting, realistic consideration of moving-average and other mechanical methods of trend-following in the stock market. "The net result is ordinarily many small losses and a few large profits." Drew emphasizes that mechanical methods must be followed religiously if they are to work at all, and that relative success or failure depends entirely on the character of the stock market, because a method that works beautifully at one time may flop at another. However, Drew is generally in favor of using a market system of one kind or another.

Granville, Joseph E. "The 200-Day Moving Average Price Line Analysis." In his *A Strategy of Daily Stock Market Timing for Maximum Profit*, pp. 237–261. 1960.

> Provides eight "basic ways of reading" 200-day moving-average charts of individual stocks. The author considers 200-day charts to be more reliable than ten-day, fifty-day, eighty-day, or one hundred-day charts. Twelve full-page charts are included, with commentary.

Jacobs, William O. "Moving Average of the DJI." In his *Stock Market Profile*, pp. 56–59. 1967.

> Jacobs says a thirty-week moving average of the Dow-Jones Industrial Average is a good indicator of both bull and bear markets; he uses such an average as part of his stock market profile system.

Jiler, William L. "The '200 Day Moving Average.' " In his *How Charts Can Help You in the Stock Market*, pp. 179–186. 1962.

> Eight basic rules are listed for the interpretation of 200-day moving average lines. Five pages of charted examples appear in this chapter.

Krow, Harvey A. "The Moving Average Theory of Market Trends." In his *Stock Market Behavior*, pp. 49–60. 1969.

> Six rules are given for the use of a thirty-week moving average of stock prices as a trend indicator. Various charts illustrate the use of a thirty-week moving average line with Standard and Poor's 500 Stock Index.

Latané, Henry A., and Tuttle, Donald L. "Two-Hundred-Day Moving Average Price Line Analysis." In their *Security Analysis and Portfolio Management*, pp. 366–367. 1970.

> Clear explanation of how to use a 200-day moving average as a stock price indicator.

Lerro, Anthony J., and Swayne Charles B. "Moving Average Index." In their *Selection of Securities*, pp. 116–118. 1970.

> Lists Joseph E. Granville's eight rules for interpreting the 200-day moving average of stock prices.

Persons, Robert H. "Moving Average Formulas." In his *Handbook of Formula Plans in the Stock Market*, pp. 81–82. 1967.

> Long-term moving-average formulas are discussed, such as a ten-year moving average using yearly means. Persons says these long-term formulas are much too sluggish to be of any use. He describes in detail a more successful formula, the DuPont Institutional Plan using a 120-month moving average.

Williamson, J. Peter. "Relative Strength in Stock Prices." In his *Investments*, p. 195. 1971.

> Describes the results obtained by two professors, J. C. Van Horne and G. G. C. Parker, in testing the 200-day moving average as a stock price forecaster. They theoretically bought individual stocks at prices above their 200-day moving average and sold them below the average price. Results of a thirty-stock sample from 1960 to 1965 were uniformly bad.

MUNICIPAL BONDS

Debt certificates issued by cities, states, or other local governments. Interest income from municipal bonds is usually free of federal income tax.

Allen, Leon B. "How Attractive an Investment Are Municipal Bonds;" In his *A Method for Stock Profits without Price Forecasting*, pp. 155–157. 1962.

Allen says that "It is usually foolish for a man in a low tax bracket to buy municipal bonds." He regards bonds in general as poor investments in an inflationary economy.

American Research Council. "Profits in Tax-Exempt Bonds." In *Your Investments*, 18th ed., pp. 136–140. 1970.

Lists the six basic types of tax-free bonds, and indicates five factors that should be pondered by investors before buying tax-exempts. A table shows tax-free versus taxable income.

Engel, Louis. "What You Should Know About Government and Municipal Bonds." In his *How to Buy Stocks*, 5th rev. ed., pp. 50–54. 1971.

Various kinds of municipal bonds are briefly considered. Engel says that "in the main they offer the investor a good degree of safety. . . ." A table compares after-tax yields from taxable versus tax-exempt securities based on Federal tax rates as of January 1971. Tabulations are included of joint tax returns of 24 thousand dollars to 200 thousand dollars for non-taxable yields of 2 percent to 7 percent.

Hayes, Douglas A. "Municipal Bonds: General Obligations." In his *Investments: Analysis and Management*, 2nd ed., pp. 365–389. 1966.

Various aspects of municipal bonds are discussed, including classification, technical aspects, and analysis of debt record, political stability, social and economic factors, and other factors. On pp. 388–389, a concise outline summarizes the major analytical factors to consider in an investigation of municipal credit.

Sauvain, Harry. "Securities of Political Subdivisions." In his *Investment Management*, 3rd ed., pp. 62–70. 1967.

Easy-to-understand consideration of bonds issued by states, counties, cities, towns, villages, parishes, boroughs, and townships. General obligation, revenue, and rental revenue bonds are explained.

MUTUAL FUND LIQUIDITY

The total cash position of mutual funds. High liquidity or buying power is generally regarded as a favorable sign for stock prices, while low liquidity is not, because mutual funds will not be able to support the market.

Dines, James. "Use Mutual Funds' Knowledge for Your Profit—SMFLI." In his *How the Average Investor Can Use Technical Analysis for Stock Profits*, pp. 500–501. 1972.

> Generally favorable comment on the theory of John Slatter, originator of Slatter's Mutual Fund Liquidity Index (SMFLI), that the cash position of mutual funds rises significantly when stock prices are at important low points and about to turn higher. Therefore, SMFLI is one of the many contrary-opinion or cynical indicators, because mutual funds are shown to be accumulating the most cash at the time when they should be buying stocks.

Latané, Henry A., and Tuttle, Donald L. "Mutual Fund Liquidity Theory." In their *Security Analysis and Portfolio Management*, p. 376. 1970.

> Asserts that analysis of mutual fund liquidity is good for forecasting stock market bottoms, but not so good for predicting tops.

MUTUAL FUNDS (*see also* Investment Companies)

Open-end investment companies; their shares are "open" in number because they are issued and redeemed on a continuous basis. Some mutual funds charge commissions to the buyer, while others (no-load funds) do not.

American Research Council. "How to Select Investment Companies and Operate Personal Retirement Plans." In *Your Investments*, 18th ed., pp. 153–167. 1970.

> Discusses eleven tests of eligibility for investors to consider when selecting mutual funds or other investment companies.

Bracker, Lewis A., and Wager, Walter. "What! You Still Don't Own Any Mutual Funds?'" In their *The Trouble with Wall Street*, pp. 203–219. 1972.

> Bracker and Wager summarize their attitude by saying, "The truth is that mutual funds are bad news from whatever angle they are viewed." Nevertheless, they have a few good words to say about no-load funds and give three important factors that should be considered by any prospective mutual-fund investor.

Dacey, Norman F. *Dacey on Mutual Funds*. 1970. 272 pp.

> The controversial author of *How to Avoid Probate* presents his views on investing in mutual funds. Dacey is generally in favor of the funds and states that "Investment is not a do-it-yourself job." Pages 139–238 are devoted to elaborate tables and charts of forty-nine individual mutual funds from 1944 to 1968. A unique feature is the computation of

"living estate" and "death estate" for each fund, wherein results are shown for a combination of term insurance and the fund.

Ellis, Charles D. "The Individual as Client." In his *Institutional Investing*, pp. 219–226. 1971.

"The individual investor is obsolete," according to Ellis. The author believes that the individual is out of his depth in a stock market that is dominated by professional, institutional investors. Therefore, mutual funds are recommended for personal investment.

Engel, Louis. "Should You Buy a Mutual Fund?" In his *How to Buy Stocks*, 5th rev. ed., pp. 249–266. 1971.

Engel notes, ". . . Mutual funds are likely to turn in surprisingly inconsistent results." Great care must therefore be taken in selecting a mutual fund to invest in. The author gives a very good summary of the mild reforms brought about by the Investment Companies Amendments Act of 1970 (". . . a far cry from what the S.E.C. had originally asked for"). The dangers of heavy, forced selling by mutual funds in a rapidly declining stock market are described (the redemption factor.)

Hazard, John W. "Mutual Funds and Other Investment Companies." In his *Choosing Tomorrow's Growth Stocks Today*, pp. 163–180. 1968.

Emphasizes that the large number of mutual funds available makes careful selection a necessity. About a dozen different types of mutual funds are described. Important factors to consider are size, acquisition costs, the quality of management, and performance.

Laurence, Michael. "Mutual Funds." In his *Playboy's Investment Guide*, pp. 75–127. 1971.

Points out that over 800 mutual funds are now available, making selection of a fund almost as difficult as picking an individual common stock. Different types of funds and some of their problems are discussed. The chapter, "Load Versus No-Load" (pp. 108–116), generally favors the mutual funds that make no sales charge. Laurence lists and briefly describes seven no-load mutual funds that are characterized as "well-established" and having "performed creditably. . . in recent years."

Lawrence, John F., and Steiger, Paul E. "How to Pick a Mutual Fund—If You Must." In their *The 70s Crash and How to Survive It*, pp. 200-207. 1970.

The authors are highly critical of mutual funds, so their advice on how to pick one takes on added significance. The vast differences in various types of funds are emphasized, as is the matter of timing.

Loeb, Gerald M. "Yardsticks for Selecting Mutual Funds." In his *The Battle for Stock Market Profits*, pp. 225-232. 1971.

An interesting discussion of various factors that should be considered in the selection of a mutual fund, including management, type, size, cost, and performance. Various published sources of information about funds are mentioned.

Markstein, David L. "The Real Place of Mutual Funds." In his *Investing in the 70s*, pp. 49-62. 1972.

Tells how to select a suitable mutual fund. Markstein recommends that the investor who sees a bear market coming should get out of mutual funds and into cash.

Mead, Stuart B. *Mutual Funds; a Guide for the Lay Investor*. 1971. 161 pp.

This is a general volume on mutual funds by a professor emeritus of the Graduate School of Business of Michigan State University. The various kinds of funds, including no-loads, are described. Mead also devotes considerable space to the market decline of 1969 and 1970 and its effect on mutual funds. Pages 103-160 carry tables of results obtained by individual funds.

Merritt, Robert D. "How Good Are Mutual Funds?" In his *Financial Independence through Common Stocks*, pp. 221-244. 1969.

The author does not really give an answer to the question posed by his chapter heading, except to say that some mutual funds are very good, while others have had unfavorable results. The intelligent investor must therefore select a mutual fund as carefully as he would an individual common stock. Merritt asks and answers seven important questions about the selection of a fund, and discusses the pros and cons of mutual funds.

Neal, Charles V. "How Mutual Is Your Fund?" In his *How to Keep What You Have, or, What Your Broker Never Told You*, pp. 185-220. 1972.

Neal has many negative things to say about the more speculative mutual funds, and winds up with this bit of sage advice: "Stick with the older, proven investment companies, especially those which have managed to ride out sharp market declines without losing much of their assets. . . ."

Owen, Lewis. "Kick the Mutual Crutch." In his *How Wall Street Doubles My Money Every Three Years*, pp. 210–217. 1969.

> The author believes that the intelligent investor or speculator can get better results by doing his own trading in individual stocks than by buying a mutual fund.

Person, Carl E. "What to Tell a Mutual Fund Salesman." In his *The Save-by-Borrowing Technique*, pp. 159–179. 1966.

> This is mainly a plea to the small investor to avoid mutual fund contractual plans or front-end load plans. No-load funds are especially recommended for the average person.

Smith, Ralph L. *The Grim Truth About Mutual Funds*. 1963. 122 pp.

> This little book brought to light some of the questionable practices of mutual funds, long before the furor of the early 1970s. Smith tells about poor performance by the majority of funds, withholding of information by salesmen, wasteful compensation of fund management groups, overtrading, and other matters. He asks what he refers to as the 64 billion dollar question: "What happens if mutual funds have to dump large blocks of stock on a falling market in order to meet a heavy position of net redemption?"

Springer, John L. "Mutual Funds: Everyman's Investment Expert." In his *If They're So Smart, How Come You're Not Rich?*, pp. 106–130. 1971.

> Under "Why some Funds Fail to Deliver," Springer discusses ten specific criticisms of mutual funds. Various studies are cited, and all arrive at the same conclusion: The performance of the average mutual fund leaves much to be desired.

Sullivan, George. "Mutual Funds." In his *The Dollar Squeeze and How to Beat It*, pp. 93–98. 1970.

> Simplified discussion of how to select a suitable mutual fund.

Warren, Ted. "Why You Can Distrust Trust Funds." In his *How to Make the Stock Market Make Money for You*, pp. 217–221. 1966.

> By "trust funds" the author means mutual funds, of which he is very critical. While investment companies in general are criticized, closed-end funds are regarded as superior to mutual funds (open-end).

Williamson, J. Peter. "Evaluating Mutual Fund Performance." In his *Investments*, pp. 69–78. 1971.

> Indicates that the prevalent, popular ways of ranking mutual funds measure rate of return only, with no consideration of other important factors such as risk or level of diversification. Sophisticated ways of evaluating mutual funds are briefly discussed.

NEILL THEORY OF CONTRARY OPINION. *See* Contrary Opinion

NEW HIGHS AND NEW LOWS. *See* High-Low Index

NEW ISSUES

Common stock of corporations that are going public and are therefore selling stock to the public for the first time. At least, this is the popular concept of new issues, even though the term has broader meaning and may refer, for example, to new issues of corporate or municipal bonds.

Bridwell, Rodger. "The New Issue Illusion." In his *Reality in the Stock Market*, pp. 159–165. 1965.

> A warning against new stock issues. Bridwell says the odds against these issues working out well are overwhelming.

Cobleigh, Ira U. "New Issues." In his *All About Stocks*, pp. 54–65. 1970.

> A good explanation of new common stock issues for the average investor. The new issues market is described as quite risky, but for those who want to take the plunge, such matters as when to sell, and what to look for are discussed.

Fisher, Milton. *How to Make Big Money in the Over-the-Counter Market*. 1970. 237pp.

> Being a securities underwriter, Fisher emphasizes new issues throughout his book. Typical chapter titles are "New Issues—Good!," "New Issues—Bad," "How to Get New Issues," and "How to Read a Prospectus."

Graham, Benjamin. "New Common-Stock Offerings." In his *The Intelligent Investor*, 4th rev. ed., pp. 69–72. 1973.

> New common stock issues of companies going public for the first time are poison for the individual investor, according to Graham.

Hazard, John W. "New Issues—Should You Buy Them?" pp. 194–211.
Choosing Tomorrow's Growth Stocks Today. 1968.

> Hazard stresses that new issues offer many opportunities for above-
> average capital gains, but only to the careful investor who is willing to
> read prospectuses and use common sense. He warns of gimmicks to be-
> ware of, particularly the "bail-out" and the "lock-up".

Widicus, Wilbur W., and Stitzel, Thomas E. "New Issues." In their *Today's
Investments for Tomorrow's Security*, pp. 294–297. 1971.

> Cogent treatment of the tremendous opportunities and risks involved in
> purchasing corporate common stock that is being offered to the public for
> the first time. The author emphasizes that new issues must be carefully
> investigated and selected.

NEW YORK STOCK EXCHANGE SEAT PRICES

The cost of membership on the New York Stock Exchange is generally referred
to as the price of a seat. These seat prices fluctuate considerably.

Markstein, David L. "NYSE Seats." In his *Investing in the 70s*, pp. 139–140.
1972.

> A description of the New York Stock Exchange seat price trend as a
> stock market indicator.

NEW YORK STOCK EXCHANGE TURN SIGNAL

A short-term market price indicator based on weekly moves of the New York
Stock Exchange Index. Only direction (up or down) is considered, not the
amount of movement.

Markstein, David L. "The NYSE Turn Signal." In his *How to Make Your
Money Do More*, pp. 226–230. 1971.

> Markstein gives a full description of this short-term market indicator, and
> includes a chart showing signals given from December 1967 to July 1969.
> The author thinks that the NYSE turn signal is one of the more reliable
> short-term indicators.

NEWS EVENTS. *See* Market Scares

NO-LOAD FUNDS. *See* Mutual Funds

NORMAL-VALUE PLANS (*see also* Graham Formula)

Formula investment plans based on a determination of the "normal" or "proper" stock market level that should prevail at a particular time. This level is calculated from the relationship of a stock average (such as the Dow-Jones Industrials) to selected fundamental values, such as industrial earnings, dividends, or interest rates. Normal-value plans may also be based on the level of stock prices themselves. In a typical normal-value plan, the ratio of holdings of stocks to cash or bonds is varied as stock prices move above or below the calculated central or normal value.

American Research Council. "Variable-Ratio Plans." In *Your Investments*, 18th ed., pp. 188–191. 1970.

> Briefly discusses the four main problems associated with variable-ratio or normal-value investment plans and explains how to determine central or normal value by examining history, growth or trend, and ratio. Finally, four methods of improving formula-plan results are listed and eight pros and cons of formula plans are given. All these plans have the investor buy stock as prices fall and sell stock as prices rise.

Buck, Frank H. "Portfolio Control by Value Median." In *Encyclopedia of Stock Market Techniques*, pp. 69–82. 1970 (cover date: 1971).

> Offers a fairly complicated formula for determining a reasonable value for the Dow-Jones Industrial Stock Average at any particular time. Results must be computed from the most recent 10-year moving average of earnings for the Dow-Jones Industrials and a specially computed multiplier. The multiplier takes into consideration both interest rates on savings and the current rate of inflation. A table shows recommendations of the percentage of investment funds that should be placed in defensive or conservative risks, and in aggressive securities, according to the variance of the Dow-Jones Industrial Average from its value median.

Cohen, Jerome B., and Zinbarg, Edward D. "Variable Ratio Plans." In their *Investment Analysis and Portfolio Management*, pp. 548–551. 1967.

> The authors assert that "Variable ratio plans obviously involve far more long-term forecasting than constant-ratio plans." The pitfalls in trying to determine what level of stock prices is historically reasonable are emphasized.

Hayes, Douglas A. "Common-Stock Strategy: Cyclical Timing." In his *Investments: Analysis and Management*, 2nd ed., pp. 66–70. 1966.

> Hayes discusses the market-norm approach to a cyclical timing strategy and comes to the conclusion that it is very difficult to arrive at normal in-

trinsic values for the stock market. He advances the idea that there has been a structural change in the market in the last twenty years and historical precedents no longer apply.

Leffler, George L. "Normal Value Plans with Variable Ratios." In his *The Stock Market*, 3rd ed., pp. 559–572. 1963.

Two basic types of plans are described: normal-value plans based on price and normal-value plans based on intrinsic values. Advantages and limitations of various plans are given.

Persons, Robert H. "Intrinsic Value Techniques." In his *Handbook of Formula Plans in the Stock Market*, pp. 83–88. 1967.

Persons describes Benjamin Graham's central-value formula, the Birmingham Plan of the First National Bank of Birmingham, Alabama, Edgar S. Genstein's formula, and the Tomlinson compromise plan.

Persons, Robert H. "Variable Ratio Formulas." In his *Handbook of Formula Plans in the Stock Market*, pp. 66–92. 1967.

Considers modified dollar averaging, trend-line formulas, moving-average formulas, and intrinsic-value techniques.

Widicus, Wilbur W., and Stitzel, Thomas E. "Variable Ratio Plans." In their *Today's Investments for Tomorrow's Security*, pp. 361–365. 1971.

The authors emphasize the problem of determining what a normal level of stock prices is. Rules are given for evaluating a simple variable-ratio formula, and a table shows how a hypothetical variable-ratio plan operates.

OBERLIN PLAN

A normal-value variable-ratio plan started at Oberlin College in 1944. The normal value is based on an arithmetic projection of the trend of the Dow-Jones Industrial Average.

Leffler, George L. "Oberlin Plan." In his *The Stock Market*, 3rd ed., pp. 566–567. 1963.

A brief description of the Oberlin Plan, which points out that the plan worked very well up to the late 1940s, but was revised in 1949.

ODD-LOT SHORT SALES

Short sales in quantities of less than one hundred shares are odd-lot short sales. As small-time short sellers are born losers, their activities are widely followed. A significant rise in the volume of odd-lot short selling nearly always means that the stock market will soon go up in price to provide the little short sellers with their usual losses. The odd-lot short sales ratio is the ratio of odd-lot short sales to regular odd-lot sales.

American Research Council. "Odd-Lot Short Sales Ratio." In *Your Investments*, 18th ed., p. 183. 1970.

> A brief description of the odd-lot short sales ratio as a stock market indicator, with the comment: ". . . that very rare bird, the odd-lot short seller, is the wrongest of all."

Dines, James. "Odd-Lot Short Selling." In his *How the Average Investor Can Use Technical Analysis for Stock Profits*, pp. 491–497. 1972.

> After reviewing Garfield A. Drew's interpretations of odd-lot short selling, Dines devotes several pages to his own innovative thinking on the subject. He comments on ". . . the short sellers' astonishing ability to become most pessimistic precisely when the market has already over-discounted the worst, and is about ready to start a recovery."

Jacobs, William O. "Odd-Lot Short Sales Ratio." In his *Stock Market Profile*, pp. 78–81. 1967.

> The odd-lot short sales ratio is mainly useful as an indicator of a reversal from bear market to bull market, according to Jacobs. He uses this ratio (computed on a weekly basis) as part of his stock market profile system.

Krow, Harvey A. "Odd-Lot Short Sales." In his *Stock Market Behavior*, pp. 131–134. 1969.

> Notes that odd-lot short interest, like short interest in general, usually peaks when stock prices are at historically low points. The odd-lot short sales ratio is explained.

ODD-LOT THEORY

The somewhat cynical idea that it is wise to do the opposite of what is being done by the small- or odd-lot investor, who buys stock in lots of less than one hundred shares. If small investors are buying more odd-lots than usual, the stock market is due for a fall. On the other hand, if odd-lotters have been selling more than they usually do, the market should rise. Odd-lot short selling is regarded as especially significant.

American Research Council. "Odd-Lot Clues to Unsophisticated Investor Attitudes." In *Your Investments*, 18th ed. p. 183. 1970.

> Describes (1) the odd-lot selling ratio, (2) the odd-lot trading ratio, and (3) the odd-lot short selling ratio.

Cohen, Jerome B., and Zinbarg, Edward D. "Odd-Lot Trading." In their *Investment Analysis and Portfolio Management*, pp. 511–513. 1967.

> Notes that while the actions of odd-lotters or small investors can be useful as a clue to future stock prices, caution is necessary when interpreting odd-lot statistics. The small investor is usually wrong, but not always.

Dines, James. "How to Profit Symbiotically from the Odd-Lotter's Losses." In his *How the Average Investor Can Use Technical Analysis for Stock Profits*, pp. 460–501. 1972.

> An extensive, favorable, and unusually complete exposition of the odd-lot theory, although Dines occasionally finds himself at odds, so to speak, with Garfield A. Drew, the original promoter of the odd-lot indicator. Under "What Does Dines Say?", the author examines how to use these indicators for detecting market turns, with the aid of various, more or less esoteric rules, such as the Dines 300–550 Rule, the Dines Odd-Lot Four-Week Rule, and the Dines Odd-Lot One Thousand Rule.

Drew, Garfield A. "Odd Lot Indexes." In his *New Methods for Profit in the Stock Market*, pp. 193–234. 1966 (reprint of 1955 edition).

> A major discussion of the odd-lot theory by the analyst whose name is most often associated with the theory. Even Drew admits that the odd-lot indexes are far from perfect stock market forecasters, and he says: "As a rule the indexes have been more decisive in their indications of bottoms than they have been at tops."

Granville, Joseph E. "Point 50. . . ." In his *A Strategy of Daily Stock Market Timing for Maximum Profit*, pp. 76–81. 1960.

> According to Granville, odd-lot trading activity truly represents public opinion about the stock market, even though the reliability of odd-lot statistics as a market indicator varies. These six pages provide a very good explanation of how the odd-lot theory is supposed to work, including some of the subtleties ("day orders" versus "open orders," for example).

Hazard, John W. "Odd-Lot Statistics as Forecasters of the Market." In his *Choosing Tomorrow's Growth Stocks Today*, pp. 291–292. 1968.

> "Unfortunately, the statistics can be interpreted in different ways," Hazard notes. Another somewhat skeptical view of the odd-lot theory.

Jacobs, William O. "The Odd-Lot Trading Ratio." In his *Stock Market Profile*, pp. 74–78. 1967.

> Discusses the odd-lot trading ratio, in which odd-lot sales and purchases are expressed as a percentage of total New York Stock Exchange volume. This ratio is used by Jacobs as part of his stock market profile indicator.

Krow, Harvey A. "Odd-Lot Transactions" and "Odd-Lot Balance Index." In his *Stock Market Behavior*, pp. 116–126. 1969.

> Describes an index which reflects whether odd-lot investors are buying or selling on balance. The significance of odd-lot activity is discussed.

Leffler, George L. "Behavior of Odd-Lot Public." In his *The Stock Market*, 3rd ed., p. 579. 1963.

> Leffler does not regard the odd-lot theory favorably. He notes: ". . .The behavior of the odd-lot public may be such as to indicate no trading signals at all."

Lerro, Anthony J., and Swayne, Charles B. "Odd-Lot Theory." In their *Selection of Securities*, pp. 112–115. 1970.

> Various reasons are given why the odd-lot theory may not be as useful as it once was as an advance indicator of stock prices.

Loeb, Gerald M. "Odd-Lot Investors Aren't Always Wrong." In his *The Battle for Investment Survival*, pp. 171–173. 1965.

> A kind word for the little investor who buys stock in odd lots, and a skeptical word for those who believe the theory that odd-lot investors predict the stock market by always being wrong. The author asserts: "Rarely is one able to use successfully the totals of reported odd-lot transactions as a yardstick for market forecasting."

Markstein, David L. "Tracking the Public." In his *How to Chart Your Way to Stock Market Profits*, pp. 201–203. 1966.

> According to Markstein, the small investor in the stock market is likely to be right most of the time, but wrong at critical turning points. Therefore, the odd-lot theory can be of some use.

Widicus, Wilbur W., and Stitzel, Thomas E. "The Odd-Lot Trading Index." In their *Today's Investments for Tomorrow's Security*, pp. 342–345. 1971.

Indicates that odd-lot statistics are sometimes misleading, but are more likely to be useful as a stock market indicator at the bottom of a price trend than at other times.

OPEN-END FUNDS. *See* Mutual Funds

OPTION ACTIVITY RATIO

An index of speculation based on the level of activity in puts and calls (options) compared with volume of trading in the stock market as a whole.

Markstein, David L. "Option Activity Ratio." In his *Investing in the 70s*, pp. 141–143. 1972.

Description of Martin E. Zweig's option activity ratio, which measures speculative activity by keeping track of the percentage of puts and calls in comparison with general trading volume on the New York Stock Exchange. Such a measurement gives clues to when to buy and sell: When a ten-week moving average reaches a certain point, speculation becomes rampant and stocks should be sold.

OVER-THE-COUNTER STOCKS

Unlisted stocks. These securities are not traded on the New York, American, or other stock exchanges. The over-the-counter market is a vast one. There are perhaps ten times as many unlisted stocks as listed ones. Of course, many unlisted corporations are quite small and have stocks that are inactive.

Cobleigh, Ira U. "The Over-the-Counter Market." In *Encyclopedia of Stock Market Techniques*, pp. 98–103. 1970. (cover date: 1971).

A general, positive discussion of investing in over-the-counter securities.

Engel, Louis, "How the 'Over-the-Counter' Market Works." In his *How to Buy Stocks*, 5th rev. ed., pp. 121–134. 1971.

After describing the unlisted-stock market and how it operates, Engel points out that the chief attractiveness of the market is the possibility of finding young, small corporations that will become large corporations in the future.

Fisher, Milton. *How to Make Big Money in the Over-The-Counter Market*. 1970. 237 pp.

> Advice for the adventurous small investor. The author's basic reasoning is that it is much easier for a progressive small corporation to greatly increase its income than it is for a giant blue chip company to do so. Of course, the risk of investing in small firms is generally regarded as high. Fisher covers trading, investing, and speculating in unlisted stocks and especially in new issues. Prospectuses are well explained.

Merritt, Robert D. "The Freewheeling Over-the-Counter Market." In his *Financial Independence through Common Stocks*, pp. 167–173. 1969.

> Unlisted stocks are said to offer great opportunities for price appreciation, but risk factors must be carefully considered.

PENNANTS. *See* Flags and Pennants

PERFORMANCE RATIO. *See* Relative Strength; Trend Following

PERSONAL TRUSTS. *See* Trust Funds

PHILOSOPHY OF THE MARKET. *See* Adages (Wall Street Folklore); Psychology

POINT-AND-FIGURE CHARTS

Stock price graphs that consider price movement only; time periods and volume of trading are ignored. Therefore, an inactive stock with small, infrequent price changes would take up much less space on a point-and-figure chart than an active high flyer. On a conventional bar or line chart, both stocks would require the same amount of horizontal space because of the time element. Point-and-figure charts may be relatively compressed or relatively expanded, depending on what price change the chart maker has decided to make note of. A chart showing one-dollar-per-share (one point) price changes will be more expansive and show more detail than a chart showing only three-dollar-per-share changes.

Cohen, A. W. "Point and Figure Formations Made Easy." In *Encyclopedia of Stock Market Techniques*, pp. 104–116. 1970. (cover date: 1971).

> Thirteen basic chart formations are described and illustrated.

Cohen, Jerome B., and Zinbarg, Edward D. "Point-and-Figure Charting." In their *Investment Analysis and Portfolio Management*, pp. 522–528. 1967.

> An unfavorable view of this system of charting, because the authors believe that forecasting from such charts leads to ambiguities. The point-and-figure method is explained and illustrated.

Dines, James. "How to Point and Figure Stocks Profitably, With Breathtaking Accuracy." In his *How the Average Investor Can Use Technical Analysis for Stock Profits*, pp. 199–396. 1972.

> Dines is perhaps the best-known of point-and-figure interpreters. His colorful, personalized treatment of this kind of charting is quite complete, and covers trends, channels, congestion areas, breakouts, and various kinds of point-and-figure formations. Many charts of actual situations are included.

Krow, Harvey A. "The Point and Figure Method." In his *Stock Market Behavior*, pp. 197–214. 1969.

> Detailed explanation of how to construct and use point-and-figure charts. Two pages of charts show sixteen specific reversal patterns, such as compound fulcrum, inverse head-and-shoulders, inverse compound fulcrum, saucer, and inverse saucer.

Latané, Henry A., and Tuttle, Donald L. "Point-and-Figure Charting." In their *Security Analysis and Portfolio Management*, pp. 364–366. 1970.

> Problems inherent in the interpretation of point-and-figure charts are emphasized.

Lerro, Anthony J., and Swayne, Charles B. "Analysis of Point and Figure Charts." In their *Selection of Securities*, pp. 63–108. 1970.

> Complete explanation of the mechanics of constructing point-and-figure charts of stock price movements. Congestion areas, breakouts, trend lines, formations, and support and resistance areas are discussed. One chapter, "The Projected Target Price," pp. 95–108, is devoted to the setting of objectives.

Markstein, David L. "The 'Ics' Stocks" and "How Charts Tell You When to Buy and Sell." In his *How to Make Your Money Do More*, pp. 143–160. 1971.

> Says that point-and-figure charting has a good record for spotting new trends in stocks. Such arcana as catapults, compound fulcrums, congestion areas, and skillets are discussed, with six pages of illustrations.

Markstein, David L. "Point and Figure Charting." In his *How to Chart Your Way to Stock Market Profits*, pp. 87–123. 1966.

> A complete review of point-and-figure stock charting techniques, including methodology, where to obtain data, congestion area study, trend lines, and counting. Many illustrations are included.

PREFERRED STOCKS (*see also* Convertible Preferred Stocks)

Generally, a class of stock with a fixed dividend rate that has preference over the common stock of the same company in payment of dividends and in distribution of assets if the corporation is liquidated. Straight preferred stocks are usually not preferred by individual investors, because of the lack of opportunity for capital gains.

Allen, Leon B. "What is the Role of Preferred Stocks?" In his *A Method for Stock Profits Without Price Forecasting*, pp. 143–147. 1962.

> Allen says that he does not generally like preferred stocks as investments, because they do not offer protection against inflation. They offer the fixed income of bonds without the safety of bonds. Convertible preferreds are an exception, and should be regarded as offering about the same advantages as convertible bonds.

American Research Council. "Profits in Preferred Stocks: Simple, Cumulative, Participating, and Guaranteed." In *Your Investments*, 18th ed., pp. 113–117. 1970.

> Recommends buying ordinary preferred stocks only when they are overwhelming bargains. Preferred stocks with special features such as participation (extra dividends) and protection (sinking funds) are discussed. Pros and cons of simple preferreds are given, and lists of preferred stocks are included.

Engel, Louis. "What You Should Know About Preferred Stocks." In his *How to Buy Stocks*, 5th rev. ed., pp. 23–28. 1971.

> A simplified explanation of preferred stocks, using the hypothetical Pocket Pole Company as an example.

Graham, Benjamin, and others. "Preferred Stocks." In their *Security Analysis*, 4th ed., pp. 375–383. 1962.

> Discusses the contractual weakness of preferred stocks and argues that bonds are better investments than preferred stocks among fixed-income securities.

Hayes, Douglas A. "Fixed-Income Securities: Preferred Stocks." In his *Investments: Analysis and Management*, 2nd ed., pp. 23–28. 1966.

> General discussion of the advantages and disadvantages of investing in nonconvertible preferred stocks. Emphasis is on the disadvantages.

Merritt, Robert D. "How about Preferred Stocks?" In his *Financial Indepen-dence through Common Stocks*, pp. 255–258. 1969.

> Lists five protective features that should accompany any preferred stock being considered for purchase. Offers a complete method of preferred stock selection.

Widicus, Wilbur W., and Stitzel, Thomas E. "Investing in Preferred Stock . . ." pp. 201–214. In their *Today's Investments for Tomorrow's Security*, pp. 201–204. 1971.

> Presents a rather full discussion of straight preferred stocks but arrives at the conclusion that these securities are best avoided by the average in-vestor. A straight preferred stock generally offers a modest yield com-bined with no chance for capital appreciation.

PREFERRED STOCKS, CONVERTIBLE. *See* Convertible Preferred Stocks

PRICE-EARNINGS RATIO

The figure obtained by dividing the market price of a stock by the stock's annual earnings per share. This ratio is often used as an indicator of whether a par-ticular stock is overpriced or underpriced.

American Research Council. "How to Use Price-Earnings and Price-Dividend Ratios." In *Your Investments*, 18th ed., pp. 175–176. 1970.

> Concise treatment of price-earnings ratios, including the ratio of the Dow-Jones Industrial Average as an indicator of major market highs and major market lows.

Bellemore, Douglas H. "Price-Earnings Ratios—Their Significance and Trend." In his *The Strategic Investor*, pp. 82-91. 1963.

> A general discussion, including historical aspects, of the use of price-earnings ratios to determine if stocks should be bought or sold. Bellemore considers price-earnings ratios for stock groups and for individual stocks.

Dines, James. "Are P/E Ratios the Golden Rule?" In his *How the Average In-vestor Can Use Technical Analysis for Stock Profits*, pp. 600–604. 1972.

> While Dines leans more toward technical analysis (charts) of stocks than study of what are generally referred to as fundamentals, he does think the price-earnings ratio can be valuable if approached in a logical manner. Various studies of this ratio appearing in the *Financial Analysts Journal* are commented upon.

Graham, Benjamin, and others. "Price-Earnings Ratios." In their *Security Analysis*, 4th ed., pp. 229–231, 421–422. 1962.

> Lists eight analytical elements governing the price-earnings ratio, calling five of the factors tangible and three intangible. Elsewhere in the work (pp. 421–422), the authors assert that, in an unusually high price-earnings ratio, a large portion represents expectations and hopes for the future, and this portion is therefore unstable and dependent mainly on psychology.

Molodovsky, Nicholas. "Price/Earnings Ratios: A Critical Reappraisal." In *The Anatomy of Wall Street*, ed. by Charles J. Rolo and George J. Nelson, pp. 216–231. 1968.

> A sophisticated discussion of P-E ratios that is critical of various studies favoring low P-E stocks. The author says that the critical factor is continuing earnings growth, not current P-E ratios.

Rosenberg, Claude N. "What Tools to Use," "Sex Appeal in Stocks," and "My Compounding Growth Guide." In his *Stock Market Primer*, pp. 159–189. 1969.

> A thorough discussion of price-earnings ratios as related to earnings growth rates. Various tables are presented to show reasonable price-earnings ratios for various rates of growth. Both a purely mathematical table and the author's preferred, pragmatic table are shown. In "My Compounding Growth Guide" (pp. 176–189), Rosenberg gives a relatively simple, specific, ten-step method for determining whether or not a particular growth stock should be purchased.

Shade, Philip A. "The Theory of 'Correct' Stock Price Levels" and "The PE Ratio Computation Process—Some Actual Applications." In his *Common Stocks: a Plan for Intelligent Investing*, pp. 178–257. 1971.

> Shade discusses the theoretical interrelationship of risk, returns, and stock prices, and shows how the ideal price-earnings ratio for a hypothetical company can be found. He also demonstrates the computation of ideal P-E ratios for actual companies. Fast-growth companies are discussed, particularly the problem of estimating when fast growth will become slow growth or no growth.

Williamson, J. Peter. "Price/Earnings Ratio Comparisons." In his *Investments*, pp. 160–169. 1971.

> A well-written, intelligent explanation of price-earnings ratios and how they are used to evaluate and compare common stocks. "The price

earnings ratio of a stock is a slightly ambiguous number," the difficulty being in determining what earnings figure to use. Williamson discusses the popularity among security analysts of concentrating on relatively low price-earnings ratios, and then presents several pages devoted to cross-section regression analysis of P-E ratios, with all of its mathematical complexities.

PRICE FILTERS. *See* Filter Technique

PRICE-VOLUME CHARTS
A chart of this type is one on which the price of a particular stock is plotted vertically and the sales volume of the same stock is represented horizontally. That is, the vertical bar chart of the stock's price is expanded horizontally to show volume.

Crocker, Benjamin, and Crocker, Diane W. "Can P/V (Price vs. Volume) Charts Help You Invest?" In *Encyclopedia of Stock Market Techniques*, pp. 150–156. 1970 (cover date: 1971).
> Explains how to make price-volume charts, with a full-page chart of the 1962 crash, the Dow-Jones Industrial Average of prices being plotted vertically, and the New York Stock Exchange volume plotted horizontally. The authors note that price-volume buy or sell signals are most useful with very active stocks, and not so useful with inactive issues.

PROFILE OF THE MARKET. *See* Consensus of Indicators

PROFITS (*see also* Losses)
The fortunate result of buying low and selling high; the opposite of losses.

Jiler, William L. "Profits." In his *How Charts Can Help You in the Stock Market*, pp. 187–193. 1962.
> General discussion of when to take profits and how to arrive at some kind of plan or tactics for investing. Five key questions are listed and discussed.

Loeb, Gerald M. "With Profits Come Problems." In his *The Battle for Stock Market Profits*, pp. 249–251. 1971.
> Loeb states his ideas on a perplexing problem that investors are glad to have: when to take profits.

Rosenberg, Claude N. "On How and When to Drag Down Profits." In his
Psycho-Cybernetics and the Stock Market, pp. 189–195. 1971.

> The author suggests logic and a methodical approach, stressing various
> questions that should be asked about any security. But he adds that there
> is no one solution to the problem of when to sell securities.

Rosenberg, Claude N. "Taking Profits." In his *Stock Market Primer*, pp. 261–
262. 1969.

> A brief consideration of when to take profits from investments to increase
> tax benefits.

PROSPECTUS

A detailed description of a corporation, its activities, and its finances, which is
required to be published when securities are initially issued for public sale.

Fisher, Milton. "How to Read a Prospectus." In his *How to Make Big Money in
the Over-the-Counter Market*, pp. 92–130. 1970.

> A lucid explanation for the small investor of what to look for in reading
> the prospectus of a corporation that is about to "go public" (sell stock
> to the public for the first time). The author, an underwriter of securities,
> advises: "The prospectus must be read with more than care; it must be
> read with imagination and a fund of knowledge . . . ." For additional
> information, Fisher provides a complete reprint of an actual prospectus
> (pp. 107–123) and an analysis of that document (pp. 124–130).

PSYCHOLOGY (*see also* Contrary Opinion)

The emotional and behavioral characteristics of investors and speculators.
Control of the emotions is very important in investing, as the assumption of
risk subjects the psyche to a certain amount of stress.

Bracker, Lewis A., and Wagner, Walter. "Of Love and Hate, Fear and Fantasy,
Rumor and Reason." In their *The Trouble with Wall Street*, pp. 103–124.
1972.

> ". . . Greed and irrationality inevitably lead to disaster," the authors note.
> Loss-producing eccentricities and emotional acts by investors are dis-
> cussed.

Dines, James. "Mass Market Psychology." In his *How the Average Investor Can
Use Technical Analysis for Stock Profits*, pp. 1–133. 1972.

> A rambling consideration of such exotic topics as sex, love, gambling,
> mass psychology, and astrology, all in relation to investing and specula-

tion. Cartoon strips featuring a loser known as "Pigeon" are interspersed throughout the text. Dines' writing is controversial, but certainly not dull.

Haas, Albert, and Don D. Jackson. *Bulls, Bears and Dr. Freud.* 1967. 179 pp.

Rationalization, greed, hope, fear, faith, and even sex are covered in this interesting account of the all-important part that emotions play in investing. In chapter 14, "Market Mental Hygiene," the authors pose a series of questions that will be useful to nervous investors wishing to engage in self-analysis. Jackson is a psychiatrist and Haas is a stockbroker.

Harper, Henry H. *The Psychology of Speculation; The Human Element in Stock Market Transactions.* 1966 (reprint of 1926 edition). 106 pp.

Most of the advice in this book is as appropriate today as it was when first published in 1926. Harper says that successful speculating in the stock market requires "the rare faculty of maintaining a complete mastery over one's impulses, emotions, and ambitions under the most heroic tests of human endurance." Humorous illustrations by Hayden Jones are used throughout the volume.

Kamm, Jacob O. "Not for Everyone." In his *Making Profits in the Stock Market*, pp. 5–8. 1966.

Kamm states that the individual investor is often his own worst enemy. The four personal characteristics that are most required to be a successful investor are individually discussed.

Krow, Harvey A. "Investor Behavior as an Indicator." In his *Stock Market Behavior*, pp. 115–134. 1969.

Concerned mainly with the short interest ratio, the odd-lot balance index, and odd-lot short sales. As a summary, three characteristics of the investing public at market tops and three characteristics at market bottoms are given.

Laurence, Michael. "Conclusion: Success is a State of Mind." In his *Playboy's Investment Guide*, pp. 257–262. 1971.

Emphasizes that the investor or speculator must have emotional control to make money in the stock market. ". . . The speculator's internal make-up determines his reward." This is the final chapter in Laurence's book, and these few pages explain very clearly the speculator's absolute need for psychological self-mastery.

Laurence, Michael. "The Psychology of Successful Stock Speculation." In his *Playboy's Investment Guide*, pp. 66–73. 1971.

> Ten rules are given that the clear-thinking investor should keep in mind at all times. Considerable self-discipline must be exerted to follow these rules, even though most of them are based on ordinary common sense.

Loeb, Gerald M. "Human Foibles Play a Major Role in Shaping Trends" and "Psychology and Style." In his *The Battle for Stock Market Profits*, pp. 273–277, 310–311. 1971.

> Mass or crowd psychology is analyzed in relation to its pervasive effect on the trend of stock prices.

Lurie, S. B. "Market Philosophy." In *Encyclopedia of Stock Market Techniques*, pp. 456–461. 1970 (cover date: 1971).

> Six practical rules of operation are offered, along with four other guidelines that have to do with a philosophy of operation. Lurie emphasizes a common-sense approach to the stock market, similar to the approach used in operating a successful business firm.

Markstein, David L. "Make Psychology Work for You." In his *How to Make Your Money Do More*, pp. 99–173. 1971.

> Thirteen chapters on stock market psychology, including "How 'Crowdism' Affects Your Investments", "Traps You Set for Yourself," and "Traps the Market Lays." Markstein includes charts and a discussion of trend following in this section.

Mittra, Sid. "YIPD: Your Investment Personality Detector." In his *Inside Wall Street*, pp. 1–6. 1971.

> The author presents a twenty-six part quiz (A to Z), so that the reader may determine his or her investment personality. Mittra gives the answers to the quiz on p. 268 of his book—low scores indicate a speculative attitude, those who are cautious will score somewhere in the middle, while high scores show confidence and a sound attitude.

Neal, Charles V. "A Little Self-Analysis Always Helps." In his *How to Keep What You Have, or, What Your Broker Never Told You*, pp. 3–8. 1972.

> "Are you made of stern enough stuff to take a decent chance? Are you naive or reasonably knowledgeable?" Neal suggests these and four other questions for the reader to ask himself before becoming involved in the stock market.

Paris, Alexander P. "Trading Tactics." In his *A Complete Guide to Trading Profits*, pp. 117–196. 1970.

> Discusses the development of a practical trading system and the bridging of the gap between the theory of charting and what might actually happen when the trader enters the market. Paris likens the unsuccessful stock market trader to the horse player who developes a fine system on paper but falls apart when he gets to the track.

Rosenberg, Claude N. *Psycho-Cybernetics and the Stock Market: The Key to Maximum Profits and Peace of Mind*. 1971. 224 pp.

> In this volume, Rosenberg considers the factors of personality and temperament as they relate to success or failure as an investor in the stock market. Some topics covered are risk, losses, luck, gambling, imagination, self-confidence, self-discipline, and profits.

Sauvain, Harry. "Temperament of the Investor." In his *Investment Management*, 3rd ed., pp. 415–416. 1967.

> In just a few paragraphs, Sauvain manages to say nearly all there is to say about investor psychology. "The desire for gain conflicts with the desire for peace of mind . . . . Some people are willing and able to pay the price, and some are not."

Scheinman, William X. "The Market and Its Players." In his *Why Most Investors Are Mostly Wrong Most of the Time*, pp. 1–14. 1970.

> The author believes that the key to stock market success lies in the analysis of the human behavior of investors. His method of predicting the market involves the comparison of the actions of relativley sophisticated investors with relatively unsophisticated investors. See "Divergence Analysis."

Smith, Adam (pseud.) "You: Identity, Anxiety, Money." In his *The Money Game*, pp. 1–123. 1968.

> An interesting discussion of why people win or lose, including crowd psychology ("Is the Market Really a Crowd?"). Smith's sense of humor is much in evidence when he writes about the irrational behavior of speculators. In a serious part of his discourse, he agrees with many other observers of the investment scene in noting that "the strongest emotions in the marketplace are greed and fear."

PUTS AND CALLS (*see also* Option Activity Ratio)

A put is an option to sell (put to the buyer) and a call is an option to buy (call in) one hundred shares of a certain stock at a particular price within a specified period of time, such as ninety days.

Alverson, Lyle T. *How to Write Puts and Calls: A Guide to a Sound Investment Practice.* 1968. 125 pp.

> Alverson is an experienced writer (seller) of options for his own account, and attempts to give the reader the benefit of his experience. Alverson includes comparison formulas to convert premium for one kind of contract to premium for another kind, plus twenty-seven do's and don'ts based on practical experience. (Special note to small investors: Alverson's opinion is that an option writer's total capital would better be at least several hundred thousand dollars.

American Research Council. "Profits in Puts, Calls, Straddles, and Similar Options." In *Your Investments*, 18th ed., pp. 145–151. 1970.

> Informative discussion of puts and calls. Includes tax treatment, uses for speculation, uses to protect paper profits (unrealized gains), uses as a hedge, and other points. A special section covers puts and calls versus warrants for speculation and hedging, with a list of the special advantages of each option form.

Cunnion, John D. *How to Get Maximum Leverage From Puts and Calls.* 1966. 160 pp.

> Emphasizes, in a practical, popularized manner, the various uses of options, whether for conservative purposes (as to protect a profit in a stock) or for speculation. Most aspects of puts and calls are covered, including the esoteric combinations known as straddles, spreads, strips, and straps. The use of options for trading against convertible bonds is explained. Tax aspects of puts and calls are stressed throughout, although this tax information must be checked against latest regulations. The tone of this volume is perhaps a bit too cheerful, as it is just as easy for the speculator to lose with options as it is to win.

Dadekian, Zaven D. *The Strategy of Puts and Calls: Selling Stock Options for Maximum Profit with Minimum Risk.* 1968. 142 pp.

> A somewhat technical, but clearly written, approach to options, emphasizing selling. The author shows how option writing can be done at all levels of risk and return, from very low to very high. The mechanism of stock option transactions is very well covered, as are margin and tax con-

siderations. Various charts, tables, and formulas are included to help the option writer determine potentially profitable situations.

Engel, Louis. "Puts and Calls, Plain and Fancy." In his *How to Buy Stocks*, 5th rev. ed., pp. 189–193. 1971.

An explanation on the elementary level of puts, calls, and straddles. Engel says: ". . . it is probably true that more people who speculate lose money than make money."

Filer, Herbert. "Put and Call Options." In *Encyclopedia of Stock Market Techniques*, pp. 260–267. 1970 (cover date: 1971).

A summary of the characteristics and uses of puts and calls.

Filer, Herbert. *Understanding Put and Call Options: How to Use Them to Reduce Risk in Your Stock Market Operations*. 1959. 123 pp.

The author, one of the leading authorities on puts and calls, says that so far as he could learn, no complete book has ever been written explaining all of the uses and facets of options, before his own. After giving historical information regarding options, Filer covers both the use of options (whether for speculation or to protect profits) and the selling of option contracts. Filer's style of writing is chatty and informal, and he has included a reproduction of an advertising leaflet of ten pages, dated 1875, used by an early option broker.

Fowler, Elizabeth M. *90 Days to Fortune*. 1965. 154 pp.

Fowler is a financial writer for the New York Times. Her book jumps around a bit, but the main subject, more or less, is a man named Jeb Wofford who made a lot of money by buying puts during the market crash of 1962. This is not intended to be a rags to riches story, however, as Wofford had 30 thousand dollars to play around with. The most useful parts of the book are the appendixes, which include Fowler's dozen rules for sensible speculation, plus an excellent summary of practical uses of puts and calls by Paul Sarnoff.

Hazard, John W. "Puts and Calls." In his *Choosing Tomorrow's Growth Stocks Today*, pp. 283–286. 1968.

As the author points out, the small investor usually loses money when he speculates by means of puts or calls. The mechanics of puts and calls are briefly explained.

Loeb, Gerald M. "Puts and Calls." In his *The Battle for Stock Market Profits*, pp. 237–239. 1971.

> A brief discussion of some of the advantages and disadvantages of buying puts and calls.

Malkiel, Burton G., and Richard E. Quandt. *Strategies and Rational Decisions in the Securities Options Market*. 1969. 176 pp.

> A technical, mathematical discussion of the securities options market. Sixteen various strategies, such as "buy put" or "sell straddle," are considered, and the results are charted. The effect of personal income taxes on these strategies also is discussed. From a practical viewpoint, "Suggested Strategies for Certain Investors" (pp. 159–161) will probably be most pertinent. This is a book for serious students of options.

Reinach, Anthony M. *The Nature of Puts and Calls*. 1961. 102 pp.

> Partly devoted to the author's personal economic philosophy, unfortunately, but mainly concerned with the practical considerations of puts and calls. Reinach lists more than twenty specific ways that puts and calls may be used profitably. There is a table showing a dollar range of premiums that options writers and option buyers ought to expect to receive or to pay for thirty-day, sixty-day, ninety-day, six-month, and twelve-month puts and calls. This table covers stock prices from ten dollars to sixty dollars. Premiums are greatly affected by market conditions, stock volatility, and other factors.

Rosenberg, Claude N. "Puts and Calls". In his *Stock Market Primer*, pp. 113–120. 1969.

> The most interesting part of Rosenberg's discussion of puts and calls is his list of conclusions under the heading, "Some Crucial Warnings." His final warning is that puts and calls are so speculative that they should be saved for very rare occasions.

Sarnoff, Paul. *Your Investments Using Puts and Calls*. 1968. 164 pp.

> A clear, popularly written explanation of options, by a former put and call broker. Most of the chapters are in pairs—one chapter from the viewpoint of the writer or seller of options and the other from the viewpoint of the buyer. Pairs of chapters cover such topics as trading strategy, tax tactics, premiums, and margins. A glossary is included, plus tables of typical option prices for sellers and buyers. The guide for buyers is grouped into active issues, inactive issues, and "flyers."

Shulman, Morton. "Puts and Calls." In his *Anyone Can Make a Million*, pp. 75–84. 1966.

> Shulman takes a very pessimistic view of puts and calls, emphasizing that "they are the wildest form of gambling possible in the stock market." He describes the risks in both buying and writing these options, and relates interesting stories about the people who deal in them.

Silverman, Richard. "Protecting Profits with Puts and Calls" and "Big Money from Puts and Calls." In his *$100 Gets You Started*, pp. 112–123. 1965.

> Covers conservative purposes for which stock-option contracts may be purchased, as to protect a profit or to recapture a position, as well as how to try to get rich quick with options. The requirements for selling options are given, including minimum capital usually required.

PYRAMIDING. *See* Margin

RATIO (STOCK-BOND) PLANS. *See* Normal Value Plans; Constant-Ratio Formula

REAL ESTATE INVESTMENT TRUSTS

Associations of one hundred or more shareholders formed to invest in real estate or real estate mortgages. They pay at least 90 percent of income to shareholders, enabling the trusts to qualify for the same tax advantages as other investment companies. Some of the larger real estate investment trusts (REITs) are listed on the major stock exchanges. An equity REIT actually buys real estate, while a mortgage REIT invests in mortgages.

American Research Council. "Real Estate Tax Shelters Available to Investors Through Real Estate Investment Trusts." In *Your Investments*, 18th ed., pp. 163–164. 1970.

> Lists selected larger real estate investment trusts, differentiating the safer mortgage REITs from the riskier equity REITs. Six legal organizational requirements for REITs are briefly commented upon.

Hazard, John W. "Real Estate Investment Companies and Trusts," In his *Choosing Tomorrow's Growth Stocks Today*, pp. 215-217. 1968.

> The publicly-owned real estate investment trust is briefly considered as an investment.

Neal, Charles V. "The Closed-End Funds, an Overlooked Alternative." In his
How to Keep What You Have, or, What Your Broker Never Told You, pp.
221-235. 1972.

> A large part of this chapter on investment companies deals with real
> estate investment companies.

RECESSION RESISTANT INDUSTRIES. *See* Trend Buckers

RECTANGLES
Stock chart formations shaped, as might be expected, like rectangles (some say
they are boxes). A price breakout from a long rectangle or box is thought by
chartists to be highly significant.

Edwards, Robert D., and Magee, John. "The Rectangles . . . ." In their *Technical Analysis of Stock Trends*, 5th ed., pp. 117-128. 1966.

> The writers emphasize that a rectangle is an uncertain indicator in that
> the price of a stock may break out from a rectangle on either the upside or
> the downside.

Markstein, David L. "The Opportunity Patterns: Rectangles" In his *How to
Chart Your Way to Stock Market Profits*, pp. 59-64. 1966.

> Markstein points out that rectangles are congestion areas on stock price
> charts, and can also be known as trading ranges, boxes, flat formations, or
> lines. The price of a stock within a rectangle moves back and forth be-
> tween a resistance level on top and a support level below. A rectangle may
> last for several weeks or several years.

REITs. *See* Real Estate Investment Trusts

RELATIVE STRENGTH (*see also* Trend Following)
The strength of the price movement of an individual stock relative to stock
prices as a whole. A stock that is steadily rising in price as the stock averages are
falling is showing high relative strength. Relative strength may also be measured
for groups of stocks, as for those in a particular industry.

Allen, Leon B. "How I Select Stocks for Investment." In his *A Method for
Stock Profits without Price Forecasting*, pp. 71-89. 1962.

> Describes a method of charting the relative strength of individual stocks.
> Semi-logarithmic graph paper is used to diagram the strength or weakness
> of the price of an individual stock compared with the market average (in
> this case, the Dow-Jones Industrial Average). When to buy and sell is
> discussed, and several charts are used as illustrations.

Cohen, Jerome B., and Zinbarg, Edward D. "Relative Strength." In their
Investment Analysis and Portfolio Management, pp. 516–517. 1967.

> A generally favorable view of relative-strength analysis. Construction of a
> relative-strength graph is explained and illustrated.

Coppock, E. S. C. "Practical Relative Strength Charting." In *Encyclopedia of
Stock Market Techniques*, pp. 117–149. 1970 (cover date: 1971).

> Description of how to construct relative strength charts of individual
> stocks, using weekly relative strength data. Relative strength is charted on
> a current basis, as well as in eight-week and thirty-week moving averages.
> Twelve charts are included, plus a data sheet used by the Trendex Re-
> search Group.

Krow, Harvey A. "Relative Strength." In his *Stock Market Behavior*, pp. 195–
196. 1969.

> Explains how to construct a simple graph of relative strength. A table with
> illustrative data is provided.

Levy, Robert A. *The Relative Strength Concept of Common Stock Price Forecasting*. 1968. 318 pp.

> Somewhat difficult to read, but will be of interest to investors concerned
> with follow-the-leader trend techniques. With the aid of a computer,
> Levy ran various statistical tests on two hundred widely held stocks from
> 1960 to 1965. Most of the tests involved theoretical investing in the ten
> or twenty of these two hundred stocks which had shown the greatest price
> strength in the immediate past (usually six months)—often referred to as
> market leaders. Some of the tests showed surprisingly poor results; others
> were quite profitable, even after commissions. The author claims to have
> disproved the random walk theory of stock price movements.

Loeb, Gerald M. "The Performance Ratio Becomes a New Guideline." In his
The Battle for Stock Market Profits, pp. 174–176. 1971.

> Loeb believes that as more and more investors and speculators are at-
> tracted to stocks that are mathematically out-performing the market, the
> performance or relative-strength method of investing will become more
> and more unreliable.

Markstein, David L. "Measure Your Stock's Strength." In his *How to Make
Your Money Do More*, pp. 161–165. 1971.

> Describes the computation of a cumulative differential line to measure the
> consistent relative strength of a particular stock. Consistent relative
> strength is also known as the momentum of a stock.

Williamson, J. Peter. "Relative Strength in Stock Prices." In his *Investments*, pp. 195–199. 1971.

> Several pages are devoted to a description and discussion of Robert A. Levy's relative-strength technique for making money in the stock market. Williamson asserts that Levy's results "are subject to criticism on a number of grounds."

RESISTANCE LEVELS. *See* Support and Resistance Levels

REVERSAL PATTERNS. *See* Charts or names of specific patterns such as Head-and-Shoulders Formation or Triangles (Coils)

RIGHTS. *See* Stock Rights

ROUNDING TOPS AND BOTTOMS (*see also* Dormant Bottoms)

On stock charts, these are major reversals in price that are so gradual as to be rounded in appearance rather than peaked. The accompanying volume of trading is typically low.

Markstein, David L. "Reversals: Rounding Tops and Bottoms." In his *How to Chart Your Way to Stock Market Profits*, pp. 49–52. 1966.

> Notes that rounding formations are rare and not easy to recognize on charts. This kind of formation is found mainly among stocks that are relatively inactive.

RULES FOR TRADING. *See* Adages (Wall Street Folklore); Formula Plans

SBICs. *See* Small Business Investment Companies

SAUCEPAN

A stock chart price formation shaped roughly like a long-handled cooking utensil.

Lerro, Anthony J., and Swayne, Charles B. "Sauce Pans." In their *Selection of Securities*, pp. 46–47. 1970.

> "The connection between the pan and the handle is significant," the authors point out. That is, the handle of the saucepan represents a breakout or sudden upward movement of the price of a stock as represented on a bar chart.

SAUCERS. *See* Lines and Saucers

SCALE TRADING

Buying a specified number of shares of a particular stock each time the price of the stock moves downward by a certain amount, and selling the same number of shares each time the price of the stock rises by a greater amount. Generally used with stocks that tend to trade regularly within a certain price range. For example, a speculator might buy such a stock each time it drops by a half point and sell each time it rises by a full point. This requires strong nerves, of course, as there is always the danger of a long-term decline in the price of the stock.

American Research Council. "Systematic Short-Term Scale Trading in Low-Priced Stocks." In *Your Investments*, 18th ed., pp. 184–185. 1970.

> Tells what kinds of stocks are most suitable for scale trading, and suggests that profits (or losses) from scale trading may be amplified by a dollar-averaging formula or by a variable-ratio formula. A case study of scale trading with a low-price stock is shown in tabular form.

Leffler, George L. "Modified Scale Trading." In his *The Stock Market*, 3rd ed., pp. 567–568. 1963.

> Description of a conservative scale-trading plan developed by Leffler for the small investor. Buying and selling action is determined by averaging the past four annual highs and lows of a particular stock. Normal value is midway between the average annual high and the average annual low. The plan would have worked very well in leading stocks from 1944 to 1953.

Silverman, Richard. "How to Scale Trade Your Way to Big Profits." In his *$100 Gets You Started*, pp. 75–85. 1965.

> Scale trading is described in detail, including tables of actual trades, based on such schemes as buying on a half-point drop and selling on a one-and-a-half point rise. Needless to say, high commission rates make profitable scale trading difficult to accomplish.

SCARES. *See* Market Scares

SEASONAL (CYCLICAL) VARIATIONS

Fluctuation patterns in stock prices according to hour of the day, day of the week, week of the month, month of the year, season of the year, year within a decade, or some other element of time. Much effort has been expended by statisticians in attempts to learn if stock prices have seasonal or cyclical tendencies.

American Research Council. "Making the Most of Short-Term Price Change—
Seasonal, Monthly, Weekly, Daily—Even Hourly." In *Your Investments*, 18th
ed., pp. 185–186. 1970.

> States that short-term price changes for stocks are likely to be random
> movements (hourly, daily, weekly), but that there is some evidence of
> seasonal movements on a monthly basis. Tables show monthly advances
> and declines in the Dow-Jones Industrial Average since 1897 and monthly
> highs and lows since 1897. Year-end and summer rallies are discussed.

Dewey, Edward R. "The Cycles of Wall Street." In his *Cycles: The Mysterious
Forces That Trigger Events*, pp. 107–128. 1971.

> Dewey believes that periodic cycles exist in the stock market. Some of
> these long-term cycles are discussed and illustrated by menas of charts.
> Dewey's cycles are generally measured in terms of years, rather than weeks
> or months.

Dines, James. "Do Mysterious Cycles Run Wall Street?" In his *How the
Average Investor Can Use Technical Analysis for Stock Profits*, pp. 87–133.
1972.

> A relatively complete discussion of cyclical and seasonal influences on
> stock prices. Dines maintains an objective attitude at all times, even
> toward astrology (not that he is advocating stock market prediction by
> the stars). He approves of the work of Edward Dewey on cycles. A chart
> by Edson Gould, reproduced in Dines' book, is an interesting one showing
> the average ten-year pattern (decade seasonality) of stock prices for the
> seven decades from 1881 to 1950. Many other seasonal patterns are dis-
> cussed.

Foster, Orline D. "Trading by the Clock." In his *Ticker Technique*, pp. 114–
116. 1965.

> Detailed listing of what is likely to happen when trading takes place during
> specific hours (or even half hours) of the day, from 10 A.M. to 3 P.M.

Hirsch, Yale. *The Stock Trader's Almanac*. Annual. 160 pp.

> Hirsch's *Almanac* is a standard source of information about all kinds of
> seasonal variations in stock prices. Each issue contains a stock almanac
> for each month of the year, wherein stock price tendencies during those
> months are explained in detail. Another section, "Directory of Seasonal
> Trading Patterns," is a soup-to-nuts compilation of all types of patterns,
> from thirty-minute variations to ten-year cycles.

Merrill, Arthur A. "Behavior at Certain Times." In his *Behavior of Prices on Wall Street*, pp. 7–38. 1966.

> A consideration of the best times in the year, the month, the week, and the day to buy stocks. Other time patterns are also discussed, such as those occurring around holidays, near income-tax payment dates, after public bad news, and after Federal Reserve Board action. Many illustrative charts are included, and many price-time patterns are rated for significance.

SEAT PRICES. *See* New York Stock Exchange Seat Prices

SECONDARIES

Large blocks of stock that are sold by stockholders, through a group of dealers or investment bankers who underwrite them. Secondaries are not new issues, of course, although they are distributed as new issues are.

Markstein, David L. "Secondaries," pp. 135–136. *Investing in the 70s.* 1972.

> Describes a study made by Robert Koehler of the First National Bank of Chicago's Trust Department. Koehler has shown that an increasing number of secondary stock offerings has a negative effect on stock prices. Koehler recommends a moving monthly average of the number of secondaries issued, as a stock price forecaster.

SELLING STRATEGY (WHEN TO SELL)

A scheme or method devised to let the speculator or investor know when to sell securities. It is more or less a truism in Wall Street that knowing when to sell is much more difficult than knowing when to buy.

Engel, Louis. "When Is the Time to Sell?" In his *How to Buy Stocks*, 5th rev. ed., pp. 302–308. 1971.

> The general theme here is that, if one owns a stock that one would not enthusiastically want to buy more of, one should consider selling. Various danger signals are mentioned, such as a decline in the price-earnings ratio.

Scheinman, William X. "Selling Strategies." In his *Why Most Investors Are Mostly Wrong Most of the Time*, pp. 193–218. 1970.

> ". . . Knowing how and when to sell may be the single most important factor in investment success," Scheinman asserts. In addition to regular selling to take profits or establish losses, hedging and short selling are discussed.

SERVICES, ADVISORY. *See* Investment Advisory Services

SHORT INTEREST (*see also* Odd-Lot Short Sales)

The number of shares that have been sold short of a particular stock issue or of the market as a whole (generally the New York Stock Exchange). The often quoted "short interest ratio" is the ratio of total short interest on the New York Stock Exchange to daily average stock volume. A short interest ratio of more than 1.75 (some say more than 2.00) is regarded as bullish, while less than 0.75 is bearish. This is, of course, a contrary opinion indicator, based on the assumption that short sellers are often wrong.

American Research Council. "'Sophisticated' Short-Selling Indicators." In *Your Investments*, 18th ed., pp. 182–183. 1970.

> Describes the short interest total (New York and American Stock Exchanges) as a stock market indicator, as well as the short interest ratio.

Dines, James. "The Short Interest as a Psychological Indicator." In his *How the Average Investor Can Use Technical Analysis for Stock Profits*, pp. 518–528. 1972.

> In a laudable display of candor, Dines castigates himself for losing faith in the total short interest as a stock market indicator at the beginning of 1969. He states that this "is a good lesson as to how vulnerable everybody is to the contagion of mass psychology." A thorough discussion of how to use the short interest ratio to predict the market is given.

Granville, Joseph E. "The Short Interest Ratio." In his *A strategy of Daily Stock Market Timing for Maximum Profit*, pp. 141–146. 1960.

> Calls a short interest ratio of more than 2.00 very bullish. Tables show changes in short interest, either up or down, at important stock market turning points from 1929 to 1960.

Jacobs, William O. "Short Interest Ratio." In his *Stock Market Profile*, pp. 64–67. 1967.

> While the record of the short interest ratio as a stock market indicator is excellent, according to the author, "it occasionally gives premature or false signals." In any event, this ratio is used by Jacobs as part of his stock market profile system.

Krow, Harvey A. "Short Sales" and "The Short Interest and Ratio." In his *Stock Market Behavior*, pp. 126–131. 1969.

> Says that short interest usually rises to its highest level at exactly the

wrong time—at the bottom of a bear market. Compilation of the short interest ratio is explained.

Latané, Henry A., and Tuttle, Donald L. "Short-Interest-Ratio Theory." In their *Security Analysis and Portfolio Management*, pp. 369–371. 1970.

> The difficulties of interpreting short interest as a stock market indicator are discussed.

Widicus, Wilbur, W., and Stitzel, Thomas E. "Index of Short to Regular Sales." In their *Today's Investments for Tomorrow's Security*, pp. 345–346. 1971.

> The short interest ratio is explained and is said to be a relatively accurate indicator of turning points in stock prices.

SHORT INTEREST TREND

The trend in the number of shares of a particular stock that have been sold short. A falling short interest is often thought to be bearish, while a rising short interest is supposed to be bullish.

Granville, Joseph E. "Applying the Short Interest Trend for Successful Stock Trading." In his *A Strategy of Daily Stock Market Timing for Maximum Profit*, pp. 230–237. 1960.

> Granville considers the observation of a short interest trend to be the most important single technique in the prediction of price movements for individual stocks. He gives some actual examples from 1959–1960, and quotes seven conclusions and rules that should be followed.

SHORT SELLING (*see also* Bear Market)

The selling of borrowed stock, to benefit from an anticipated future price drop. The idea is to replace the borrowed stock with stock bought later at a lower price. (The mechanics of all this are taken care of by the stock broker.) While stocks have been known to drop at a rapid rate, the psychological barrier to short selling is formidable for most people.

American Research Council. "How to Profit by Selling Short." In *Your Investments*, 18th ed., pp. 214–216. 1970.

> The joys and sorrows of short selling are commented upon. Instructions include seven do's and don'ts for short selling and five pros and cons.

Bridwell, Rodger. "Don't Sell America Short." In his *Reality in the Stock Market*, pp. 39–46. 1965.

> A negative view of short selling.

Crane, Burton. "What you Should Know to Go Short." In his *The Sophisti-cated Investor*, pp. 74–82. 1964.

> A generally negative view of short selling, emphasizing the dangers of going against the market.

Edwards, Robert D., and Magee, John. "Short Selling." In their *Technical Analysis of Stock Trends*, 5th ed., pp. 321–325. 1966.

> Psychological barriers to selling stocks short are discussed, although the authors state that traders should seek profits on the short side as well as the long. "There is nothing more reprehensible about selling short than buying long."

Engel, Louis. "What It Means to Sell Short." In his *How to Buy Stocks*, 5th rev. ed., pp. 181–188. 1971.

> A well-written explanation of the mechanism of short selling, although it is difficult to ascertain what the author's attitude is toward short selling by individual investors or speculators.

Foster, Orline D. "Short Selling." In his *Ticker Technique*, pp. 116–118. 1965.

> Short selling is risky, Foster advises, "but in some markets it can prove quite useful." Various rules for short selling are given, such as "Never stay short after the short interest becomes very large."

Granville, Joseph E. "How to Act in a Bear Market." In his *A Strategy of Daily Stock Market Timing for Maximum Profit*, pp. 175–182. 1960.

> Twenty-five rules for successful short selling are explained.

Harper, Henry H. "Retired Business Men in the Stock Market." In his *The Psychology of Speculation*, pp. 19–44. 1966. (reprint of 1926 edition).

> The terrible tale of a man who in 1915 sold Bethlehem Steel short at prices ranging from eighty dollars a share to two hundred dollars a share. Unfortunately, the price then shot up to six hundred dollars a share, causing him to suffer a physical and nervous breakdown, and to exclaim, "In the past year I've suffered every torment known to the demons of hell." Harper compares being short in a bull market to "being chained by the heels to a rising balloon, without any idea of the height to which the gas will carry it."

Leffler, George L. "Short Selling." In his *The Stock Market*, 3rd ed., pp. 219–237. 1963.

> Interesting outline of the history of short selling, plus a good explanation of the technical procedures involved in a short sale.

Loeb, Gerald M. "Selling Short: Bear is Rarely Successful" and "Short Selling Results Have Been Drab Even in a Bear Market." In his *The Battle for Stock Market Profits*, pp. 99-104, 285-288. 1971.

>Loeb takes a dim view of short selling because of the risks and difficulties involved, but gives some suggestions for those who insist on being on the short side at times.

Loeb, Gerald M. "Short Selling." In his *The Battle for Investment Survival*, pp. 308-309. 1965.

>Short selling appears logical in theory, Loeb says, but is very difficult to carry out successfully in real life. Negative information is hard to come by, and most investors or speculators are uncomfortable when holding a short position.

Warren, Ted. "Selling Short." In his *How to Make the Stock Market Make Money for You*, pp. 105-108. 1966.

>Warns that there are plenty of reasons why it is wrong for a novice to sell short. The author discusses several of these reasons, emphasizing the high risk of short selling, as opposed to the probability of profit.

Weaver, Mark. *The Technique of Short Selling; Making Money on Declines in the Stock Market*, rev. ed. 1963. 81 pp.

>One of the headings used in this small volume sums up the author's philosophy very well: "Remaining Long in a Bear Market is Illogical." Weaver discusses the characteristics of stocks suitable for short selling, and also describes stocks that are not suitable. For example, inactive issues with small capitalization are regarded as dangerous to sell short. Twenty-five "Don'ts for the Bear" sum up the rules for careful short selling.

SHORT SELLING ACTIVITY OF NEW YORK STOCK EXCHANGE MEMBERS

Relatively active short selling by members of the New York Stock Exchange is supposed to reflect sophisticated selling and therefore be a negative stock market price indicator. This is in contrast to active short selling by the general public, a positive price indicator in the cynical view of Wall Street.

Heiby, Walter A. "Short Selling Activities of Members of the New York Stock Exchange." In *Encyclopedia of Stock Market Techniques*, pp. 373-381. 1970 (cover date: 1971).

>"Short selling activities of the highly astute members of the New York Stock Exchange may be used to predict the trend of stock prices,"

Heiby says. He describes a stock market indicator which is based on a comparison of member short selling (sophisticated) with non-member short selling (unsophisticated). Members' short selling ratio, non-members' short sales ratio, and the Dow-Jones Industrial Average are shown in chart form for 1957, 1965, and 1966.

SHORT TERM TRADING. *See* Trading, Short Term

SLATTER'S MUTUAL FUND LIQUIDITY INDEX. *See* Mutual Fund Liquidity

SMALL BUSINESS INVESTMENT COMPANIES

Special investment companies, authorized by Congress to put capital into small enterprise by means of loans or purchase of stock. Capital losses by investors in small-business investment companies (SBICs) are fully deductible against ordinary income.

American Research Council. "Small Business Investment Companies Are Tax-Favored—but Speculative." In *Your Investments*, 18th ed., pp. 162–163. 1970.
Lists publicly traded small business investment companies (SBICs).
Risk factors and tax considerations are emphasized.

Hazard, John W. "SBICs." In his *Choosing Tomorrow's Growth Stocks Today*, pp. 209–211. 1968.
Brief discussion of the possibilities of investing in publicly owned small business investment companies. Topics include management, price, leverage, and tax advantages.

SPECIAL SITUATIONS

Securities with unique aspects that promise large capital gains with limited risk but with an uncertain time factor, as the working-out of a situation may take several months or several years. There are many different kinds of special situations. They may result from corporate reorganization or merger, change into a new line of business, large liquid assets relative to stock price, or from other factors. Reasonable price is essential; when a situation has become widely recognized and the stock is overpriced, it can hardly be thought of as special.

American Research Council. "Special-Situation Approaches to Common Stock Selection." In *Your Investments*, 18th ed., pp. 91–101. 1970.
Special situations of various kinds are discussed, including stocks with unusually high volatility, stocks that may be involved in mergers, liquidations,

spin-offs, or asset conversions, stocks that may benefit from litigation or changes in laws, and stocks of corporations with unusually large cash assets. Lists of special-situation stocks are included.

Cohen, Jerome B., and Zinbarg, Edward D. "Special Situations." In their *Investment Analysis and Portfolio Management*, pp. 430–443. 1967.

Special situations that are briefly discussed include: mergers and acquisitions, acquisition-liquidation, merger-hedges, reorganizations, spin-offs, hidden assets, management changes, technological innovation, and changes in regulatory environment.

Ellis, John. "Special Situations." In his *Self-Reliant Investing*, pp. 77–89. 1971.

Ellis considers mergers, reorganizations, tenders and takeovers, spin-offs, company purchase of its own shares, and insider activity.

Graham, Benjamin. "Special Situations or 'Workouts.'" In his *The Intelligent Investor*, 4th rev. ed., pp. 217–219. 1973.

Three more or less typical special situations are described as they existed in early 1971, and again, as they existed in late 1971.

SPECIAL SUBSCRIPTION ACCOUNTS (*see also* Stock Rights)

Special margin accounts set up to enable investors who have received stock rights to purchase that stock at special, low margin requirements, as authorized by the Federal Reserve Board. However, the low margin requirements have a time limit, and the investor must put up additional cash over a period of months.

Lempenau, J. A. "The Special Subscription Account." In *Encyclopedia of Stock Market Techniques*, pp. 436–441. 1970. (cover date: 1971).

Discusses ten advantages and requirements of a special subscription account and its dangers.

Rosenberg, Claude N. "Special Subscription Accounts." In his *Stock Market Primer*, pp. 106–108. 1969.

Good advice on and description of the special form of speculation involving subscription accounts. Both dangers and advantages are covered. Significant changes that have taken place in special subscription account regulations are discussed.

SPECULATION INDEXES

Ratios of activity in lower quality stocks to activity in higher quality stocks. For example, a high level of volume on the American Stock Exchange compared with volume on the New York Stock Exchange would indicate a great interest in speculative issues.

American Research Council. "Speculators' Confidence Index." In *Your Investments*, 18th ed., p. 182. 1970.

> Briefly discusses an index of speculative confidence which compares Standard and Poor's Low-Priced Common Stock Index with Standard and Poor's High-Grade Common Stock Index. Four patterns are listed that are likely to appear at various turning points in the stock market.

Markstein, David L. "Speculative Fever Index." In his *Investing in the 70s*, pp. 138–139. 1972.

> Describes an index which relates volume in stocks of the Dow-Jones Industrial Average (mainly blue chips) to that of an index of low-priced stocks (cats and dogs). A sharp rise in this fever index is a danger signal, so far as stock prices are concerned. The fever index is constructed so that it rises with the volume of low-priced stocks compared with the Dow-Jones Industrials.

"SPIN-ON-A-DIME." *See* Climax Formations

SPLITS. *See* Stock Splits

STOCK-BOND RATIO FORMULAS. *See* Constant-Ratio Formula; Normal-Value Plans

STOCK-BOND YIELD SPREAD

The difference between the average dividend yield on common stocks, such as those in the Dow-Jones Industrial Average, and the average yield from interest on high grade corporate bonds. For example, a stock yield of 4 percent and a bond yield of 6 percent produces a negative spread of 2 percent (negative, because stocks are traditionally supposed to yield more than bonds). The yield spread is often cited as an indicator of stocks being overvalued or undervalued.

American Research Council. "How to Use Stock-Bond Yield Comparisons." In *Your Investments*, 18th ed., p. 176. 1970.

> After a short discussion, a table is presented which shows yield spread between stocks and bonds as a market indicator from 1929 to 1966, illustrating major highs and lows.

Dines, James. "Beginners Seek Value, But Can't Measure It." In his *How the Average Investor Can Use Technical Analysis for Stock Profits*, pp. 618–624. 1972.

> An interesting commentary on stock and bond yields, including an explanation of Edson Gould's Stock Market Altimeter. A chart of the altimeter shows the investment needed to produce one dollar of dividends on the Dow-Jones Industrial Average from 1900 to 1966. A market price of over thirty dollars for one dollar of dividends is generally considered bearish. Dines shows other charts of dividend yields on the Dow-Jones Industrials from 1900 to 1971. Stocks and bonds are compared from 1871 to 1965.

STOCK GROUPS

Lists of stocks classified as to industry. The prices of the stocks in each industry grouping are often used to form stock group price movement indexes.

Dines, James. "Group Analysis." In his *How the Average Investor Can Use Technical Analysis for Stock Profits*, pp. 397–404. 1972.

> Includes the Dines Wolf Pack Theory, which says that "when a few stocks in a group move in a certain direction the rest of the group will tend to follow . . . ." Several pages are devoted to using group analysis to ascertain market direction.

Markstein, David L. "Stock Group Index." In his *Investing in the 70s*, p. 141. 1972.

> Description of a stock market indicator based on the number of stock-group price indexes moving up or down. This indicator gave eight buy or sell signals during the period 1965–1971.

STOCK-OPTION CONTRACTS. *See* Puts and Calls

STOCK-OPTION WARRANTS. *See* Warrants

STOCK RIGHTS (*see also* Special Subscription Accounts)

Certificates issued to stockholders giving them the privilege or right to buy a specified number of additional shares within a certain period of time at a particular price. As this price is usually below the market price, rights generally have monetary value and are traded like other securities.

American Research Council. "Stock Rights." In *Your Investments*, 18th ed., pp. 141–142. 1970.

> Explains three benefits of exercising rights as opposed to selling them.

Four ways to value rights for tax purposes are given and when to buy or
sell rights is considered.

STOCK SPLITS

Increasing the number of shares of corporate stock outstanding by a multiple,
such as two-for-one, three-for-one, or whatever. Stock splits are sometimes
given in the form of stock dividends; a 100 percent stock dividend, for example,
is the same as a two-for-one split.

Markstein, David L. "Do Stock Splits Really Help You?" In his *How to Make
Your Money Do More*, pp. 170–173. 1971.

> A short discussion of the folklore of Wall Street that says that a stock will
> rise in price after being split.

Warren Ted. "Stock Splits." In his *How to Make the Stock Market Make
Money for You*, pp. 128–132. 1966.

> States that the basic motive for corporations to engage in stock splits
> may be that lower-priced stock is easier for corporate insiders to distribute
> at market tops. Therefore, it is dangerous to buy stock on the basis of
> splits.

STOP-LOSS ORDERS

A standing order left with a broker to sell a stock if it drops to a certain price,
to stop the loss. If the price is falling fast, the actual sale may take place well
below the stop-loss point. In the case of a short sale, a stop-loss would go into
effect if the price goes up to a certain point. In recent years, the American
Stock Exchange has not accepted straight stop-loss orders, although it does take
other types of stop orders.

American Research Council. "How to Use Stop Orders." In *Your Investments*,
18th ed., pp. 217–218. 1970.

> Lists five uses of stop orders and discusses risks in using stop-loss orders.

Dines, James. "How 'Stops' Can Help You Never Take a Large Loss." In his
How the Average Investor Can Use Technical Analysis for Stock Profits, pp.
356–368. 1972.

> Dines definitely favors using carefully placed stop orders, and presents an
> unusually complete discussion of stops. The "bottom-guessing buy-stop"
> and when to throw good money after bad are among the topics covered.

Edwards, Robert D., and Magee, John. "Stop Orders." In their *Technical Analysis of Stock Trends*, 5th ed., pp. 328–333. 1966.

> Use of stop orders is recommended. For protective stops, a table of stop distances shows percentages suitable for stocks of various prices and sensitivities. The progressive stop for taking profits is also considered.

Shulman, Morton. "The Stop Loss." In his *Anyone Can Make a Million*, pp. 67–73. 1966.

> Shulman thinks poorly of the stop-loss order as a philosophy of investment, but states that it can be very handy in certain cases. Generally, he discourages the use of this device.

Silverman, Richard. "How to Use Stop-Loss Orders Profitably." In his *$100 Gets You Started*, pp. 237–239. 1965.

> A favorable view of stop orders, emphasizing speculative uses such as stops to automatically establish long positions when a stock breaks out of a trading range on the upside. These are known as "buy-stops."

STRATEGY. *See* Adages (Wall Street Folklore); Psychology; Selling Strategy (When to Sell)

SUPPORT AND RESISTANCE LEVELS (*see also* Charts)

A support level is a price level that a stock has difficulty in breaking through on the downside, and a resistance level is the same on the upside. Buying activity or pressure will increase support levels, and selling pressure will increase at resistance levels. The terms support and resistance are used especially by followers of stock price charts.

American Research Council. "Spotting 'Support' and 'Resistance' Levels." In *Your Investments*, 18th ed., pp. 104–105. 1970.

> Concise commentary on levels of resistance and support including a list of the four ways in which a buying climax can come about.

Bridwell, Rodger. "Supply and Support Levels." In his *Reality in the Stock Market*, pp. 181–184. 1965.

> The manner in which support and resistance (supply) levels are formed is clearly explained. Bridwell describes the actions of investors and traders that contribute to the formation of these levels.

Edwards, Robert D. and Magee, John. "Support and Resistance." In their *Technical Analysis of Stock Trends*, 5th ed., pp. 211–233. 1966.

> Edwards and Magee point out that "some experienced traders have built

their 'systems' almost entirely on . . . support and resistance, paying no attention to . . . specific pictorial patterns of price and volume action . . . ." The authors thoroughly analyze support and resistance phenomena and consider misconceptions by the public.

Jiler, William L. "Support and Resistance." In his *How Charts Can Help You in the Stock Market*, pp. 41–53. 1962.

General discussion of how resistance and support levels are formed within stock price movements. The 50 percent rule is briefly considered, as is unusual volume. Four pages of charts appear in this chapter.

Krow, Harvey A. "Support and Resistance." In his *Stock Market Behavior*, pp. 190–193. 1969.

Describes support and resistance congestion areas found on stock charts.

Lerro, Anthony J., and Swayne, Charles B. "Support and Resistance." In their *Selection of Securities*, pp. 14–19, 89–94. 1970.

General discussion of the dynamics of support and resistance. Two small charts illustrate a congestion area and a prior-resistance area, while two larger illustrations show support areas and resistance areas. The authors explain support and resistance levels for point-and-figure charts on pages 89–94.

Markstein, David L. "How Support and Resistance Levels Time Your Investments for Profit." In his *How to Chart Your Way to Stock Market Profits*, pp. 21–28. 1966.

Describes minor, intermediate, and major resistance levels as well as support levels. Markstein considers support and resistance levels to be extremely important in the technical analysis of stock price movements.

Markstein, David L. "Support and Resistance—Important Keys to Stock Timing." In his *How to Make Your Money Do More*, pp. 137–142. 1971.

An explanation of how to use support and resistance levels in making buy and sell decisions. Lists five points to remember.

Paris, Alexander P. "Support and Resistance." In his *A Complete Guide to Trading Profits*, pp. 37–49. 1970.

Explains the meaning of several phenomena in support and resistance analysis: (1) Trading volume changes within areas of support or resistance. (2) The tendency for stock prices to cluster around whole numbers. (3) The variation in the meaning of support and resistance areas according to how long a particular area has existed. (4) The fact that a support that fails and is penetrated becomes a resistance area for any future rally.

TAPE READING (*see also* Trading, Short-Term)

Very short-term forecasting of stock prices done by observing the flow of transactions as they appear on the stock market ticker tape. Generally attempted only by professional traders.

Foster, Orline D. *Ticker Technique*. Rev. by Robert H. Persons. 1965. 127 pp.

> A section of the book is devoted to each of these aspects of tape reading: (1) The mechanics of the tape; (2) Getting signals off the tape; (3) Three basic approaches to using ticker techniques, including "Transaction-By-Transaction Approach," by Herbert Liesner and "Upticks, Downticks, and True Volume," by Don Worden; and (4) Trading with ticker technique. The final chapter of this book tells how to get started in tape reading, and gives six basic rules that should be followed by the beginner.

Liesner, Herbert. "Transaction-by-Transaction Approach to Tape-Reading." In *Ticker Technique*, by Orline D. Foster, pp. 51–60. 1965.

> A general discussion of how to interpret an actual ticker tape as it comes from the machine. Some pointers on trading are also given.

Loeb, Gerald M. "Detecting 'Good' Buying or 'Good' Selling," "More on Tape Reading," and "What's the Value of Watching 'Tape'"? In his *The Battle for Investment Survival*, pp. 86–88, 281–291. 1965.

> Describes how tape reading can help in spotting the good buys that are high and going higher. By tape reading, the author means "price forecasting based on interpretation of transactions." As always, Loeb favors buying or selling stocks mainly because of price action. His writing is more a philosophical discourse on the value of watching the tape than a practical lecture on actual techniques.

Zieg, Kermit C. *Ticker Tape Trading*. 1970. 127 pp.

> Subtitled "A Study of Tape Trading Principles and Their Profitable Applications." Zieg lists nine principles of tape trading (pp. 42–44), then devotes one chapter of his book to each of these principles. A chapter also elaborates on the fact that the short-term trader is usually his own worst enemy.

TAX-EXEMPT BONDS. *See* Municipal Bonds

TAX TRANSACTIONS

Security sales or purchases in which the tax consequence is the major consideration.

American Research Council. "Basic Tax Factors in Deciding When and What to Sell, Switch, or Rebuy" and "Special Tax-Saving Opportunities in Buying, Selling, and Switching Securities." In *Your Investments*, 18th ed., pp. 198–207. 1970.

> Unusually complete and concise discussion of taxes as related to investments for the individual. Includes "The Case Against Frequent Profit-Taking" and "The Case For Periodic Profit-Taking." Some special tax deductions for investors are listed.

American Research Council. "Tax Shelter and Tax-Savings Approaches to Common Stock Selection." In *Your Investments*, 18th ed., pp. 77–86. 1970.

> Covers stingy dividend payers, tax sheltered dividend payers, regular stock dividend payers and companies with sizable carry-forward tax credits. Lists of stocks having special tax considerations are included.

Cunnion, John D. "Securities Which Offer Tax Protection." In *Encyclopedia of Stock Market Techniques*, pp. 157–174. 1970 (cover date: 1971).

> A general discussion of investments that may be advantageous from a tax viewpoint. Bonds and stocks are both considered.

Graham, Benjamin, and others. "Tax Considerations in Investment Policy." In their *Security Analysis*, 4th ed., pp. 68–70. 1962.

> Includes tax-free as opposed to taxable bonds, the tax position of preferred stocks, and capital gains versus income.

Kreidle, John R., and Stark, Thomas A. "Tax Strategies with Long-Term and Short-Term Capital Gains." In *Encyclopedia of Stock Market Techniques*, pp. 416–421. 1970 (cover date: 1971).

> A detailed examination of the fact that the tax advantage in waiting six months to sell a stock for a long-term capital gain may be completely negated by a relatively small drop in the price of the stock toward the end of the holding period. Break-even values are shown in both chart and tabular form, based on 1970 income tax rates.

Loeb, Gerald M. "Do Tax Losses Mean Savings?" and "Don't Let Tax Questions Cloud Investment Decisions." In his *The Battle for Investment Survival*, pp. 169–170, 198–199. 1965.

> Loeb argues that basic investment timing considerations are usually much more important than income tax considerations.

Loeb, Gerald M. "Tax Transactions are a Market Factor" and "The Trend in Security Taxation." In his *The Battle for Stock Market Profits*, pp. 185–187, 304–308. 1971.

> The author believes that, in most cases, when to sell a stock should be based on investment rather than tax considerations.

Rosenberg, Claude N. "Ugh!!" In his *Stock Market Primer*, pp. 260–266. 1969.

> Most of this chapter is concerned with the tax aspects of stock market losses, although there is also a short discussion of taking profits.

Widicus, Wilbur W., and Stitzel, Thomas E. "Tax Aspects of Investments." In their *Today's Investments for Tomorrow's Security*, pp. 313–336. 1971.

> An interesting, well-written explanation of the general principles involved in keeping taxation on investments as low as possible. Strategy, timing, and tax-free investments are discussed.

TECHNICAL ANALYSIS. *See* specific subjects, such as Charts; Dow Theory; Support and Resistance Levels; Trend Following

TEN PERCENT PLAN

A formula plan for investing which involves selling all stocks held when their monthly average value declines by 10 percent. Stocks are repurchased after their monthly average value goes up by 10 percent.

Leffler, George L. "Ten per Cent Plan." In his *The Stock Market*, 3rd ed., p. 559. 1963.

> The origin, basic features, performance, and merits of the plan are briefly considered. Leffler says performance is poor.

THREE-PEAKS-AND-DOMED-HOUSE FORMATION

A stock price chart formation in which three distinct peaks are followed by the rough outline of a domed house. This complex shape is subject to complex explanations.

Lindsay, George. "The Three Peaks and the Domed House." In *Encyclopedia of Stock Market Techniques*, pp. 442–455. 1970 (cover date: 1971).

> "The majority of all major advances [in the Dow-Jones Industrial Stock Average] ended in a pattern which resembled the Three Peaks and the Domed House," Lindsay observes. "Some came closer to the ideal form than others." Six charts are used to illustrate this formation.

THREE-STEPS-AND-A-STUMBLE THEORY (*see also* Money and Stock Prices)
According to this formulation, a series of three increases in one of the monetary
or interest rates set by the Federal Reserve Board predicts a stumble or drop in
stock prices. The three rates are the discount rate (interest that banks pay), the
margin requirement for securities transactions, and the banks' reserve requirements, which affect how much money banks have to lend.

Dines, James. "Gould's Three-Step-and-Stumble Rule Never Stumbles." In his
How the Average Investor Can Use Technical Analysis for Stock Profits, pp.
547–551. 1972.
> A favorable review of Edson Gould's analysis of the effect of Federal Re-
> serve actions on stock prices. Gould's interesting "Moni-Vane and Stock
> Prices" chart is shown, covering the period 1914–1965. Another chart,
> "Fiscal Policies and Stock Prices," covers 1940–1968.

Latané, Henry A., and Tuttle, Donald L. "Three-Steps-and-a-Stumble Theory."
In their *Security Analysis and Portfolio Management*, pp. 375–376. 1970.
> The authors observe that this theory is an example of the technical treat-
> ment of fundamental factors. The theory is said to have proved fairly re-
> liable in the past.

TICKER TAPE TRADING. *See* Tape Reading

TOMBSTONE FORMATION
A stock chart pattern characterized by a sharp run-up, a period of stability
shown at the flat top, and a rapid decline. Amateur speculators are said to be
especially vulnerable to falling tombstones.

Granville, Joseph E. "The Tombstone Formation." In his *A Strategy of Daily
Stock Market Timing for Maximum Profit*, pp. 229–230. 1960.
> Describes the various tombstones erected over unwary traders by the stock
> of Avco Corporation from 1932 to 1959. The tombstone is said, ap-
> propriately enough, to be a long-range formation.

TOPS AND BOTTOMS. *See* Double Tops and Bottoms; Rounding Tops and
Bottoms; Triple Top

TRADING BY THE CLOCK. *See* Seasonal (Cyclical) Variations

TRADING, SHORT-TERM (*see also* Tape Reading)
Generally thought of as buying and selling a stock in less than a six-month period, thus making the transaction ineligible for long-term capital gains tax treat-

ment. However, to an active trader in stocks, the phrase "short-term" could mean a day or a week.

Bridwell, Rodger. "Trading Away Your Wealth." In his *Reality in the Stock Market*, pp. 30–38. 1965.

> States that the practical odds against consistently realizing profits in short-term trading are 100 to 1, noting, "A rise that took six months can be wiped out in six days."

Hayes, Douglas A. "Common-Stock Strategy: Trading." In his *Investments: Analysis and Management*, 2nd ed., pp. 64–66. 1966.

> Points out the great difficulty of forecasting the short swings of the market. The author recommends that short-term trading be left to professional traders.

Loeb, Gerald M. "How to Invest for Capital Appreciation" and "Advantages of Switching Stocks." In his *The Battle For Investment Survival*, pp. 27–31, 80–82. 1965.

> Loeb believes that the short-term trader often has greater peace of mind than does the long-term holder, because the short-termer does not hold stocks through long and agonizing declines.

Owen, Lewis. "Take Short-Term Gains." In his *How Wall Street Doubles My Money Every Three Years*, pp. 186–188. 1969.

> A recommendation that stocks be sold if they start to drop in price, regardless of capital gains tax considerations. A formula is given to enable the investor to figure how much short-term profit must be taken to equal long-term gain. For example, in the 30-percent income tax bracket, a one thousand-dollar short-term profit will net the investor the same as a long-term gain of 823 dollars.

Rosenberg, Claude N. "The Folly of Gambling in the Stock Market." In his *Psycho-Cybernetics and the Stock Market*, pp. 120–132. 1971.

> A consideration of the emotional problems which may lie in back of the need to engage in excessive stock market activity. Short-term trading is not recommended.

Rosenberg, Claude N. "So You Want to Trade." In his *Stock Market Primer*, pp. 268–272. 1969.

> A critical view of "in and out" or short-term trading. Six specific disadvantages are outlined. Although short-term trading is not recommended at all, the author does include a special set of rules for those who wish to engage in moderate-term trading.

TRADING RULES, MECHANICAL. *See* Formula Plans; Moving Average; Trend Following

TRADING TACTICS. *See* Adages (Wall Street Folklore); Psychology

TRAPS. *See* False Signals

TREASURY BILLS (*see also* Government Bonds)
Short-term U.S. government securities sold on a discount basis. The yield is the difference between purchase price and sale or maturity value. Instead of holding cash, many astute investors or speculators hold Treasury Bills when out of the stock market. Daily prices of bills are quoted in newspapers, not in dollars and cents, but in the form of percentage discounts (bid and asked) from maturity value.

American Research Council. "How to Maximize Income with U.S. Treasury Bills." In *Your Investments*, 18th ed., pp. 126–127. 1970.
> Concise discussion of Treasury Bills as a solution to the problem of what to do with available investment funds. Notes that the attractiveness of bills increases in times of unusually tight money. The methods of purchasing Treasury Bills are briefly considered.

Sullivan, George. "Treasury Bills." In his *The Dollar Squeeze and How to Beat It*, pp. 98–104. 1970.
> Clear explanation of the advantage of Treasury Bills, and how the small investor can acquire them. Shows how to figure the actual cash price of a Treasury Bill. Typical purchase fees of banks and brokers are indicated.

TREND BUCKERS
Corporations or industries that have growing profits during a general economic turndown or recession.

Widicus, Wilbur W., and Stitzel, Thomas E. "Trend Buckers." In their *Today's Investments for Tomorrow's Security*, pp. 300–302. 1971.
> A nicely written summary of the investment possibilities in industries that often do well even during times of widespread recession (assuming the recession is not too acute). Industries that typically resist recession are health, food, and do-it-yourself.

TREND FOLLOWING (*see also* Moving Average; Relative Strength)
Various stock trading methods based on the tendency of stock prices to display inertia and continue in a previously established direction.

American Research Council. "Investment Timing without Forecasting." In *Your Investments*, 18th ed., pp. 197–198. 1970.

> Mainly a consideration of the pros and cons of automatic trend following, as when stocks are bought if the Dow-Jones Industrial Average rises 10 percent and sold if the Dow-Jones Industrials fall 10 percent.

Bridwell, Rodger. "The Trend Followers." In his *Reality in the Stock Market*, pp. 59–62. 1965.

> Bridwell discourages buying stocks only because they are in a rising price trend. Trend following in general is regarded as unwise.

Edwards, Robert D., and Magee, John. "Trendlines and Channels" and "Major Trendlines." In their *Technical Analysis of Stock Trends*, 5th ed., pp. 234–270. 1966.

> The drawing of trend lines for stock prices is considered at some length, and specific techniques are presented, including the recommendation that semilog (ratio) chart paper be used instead of paper with an arithmetic scale. Three tests of authority are given to aid the stock trader in determining if a trend line is valid. Fourteen charts show contrasts in trends, with commentary for each chart.

Jiler, William L. "Trends." In his *How Charts Can Help You in the Stock Market*, pp. 27–40. 1962.

> General discussion of trends and trend following, including various kinds of trend lines (up-curving, down-curving, internal, and others). Four pages of charts are displayed in this chapter.

Krow, Harvey A. "Trend Lines and Trend Channels." In his *Stock Market Behavior*, pp. 166–171. 1969.
How to draw and follow trend lines on charts of stock prices.

Lerro, Anthony J. and Swayne, Charles B. "Trends, Bends, and Angles." In their *Selection of Securities*, pp. 20–29, 74–76. 1970.

> General discussion of trend lines and channels as shown on bar charts of stock prices. The authors examine trend lines and channels that occur on point-and-figure charts on pages 74–76.

Loeb, Gerald M. "Statistical Analysis, Market Trends, and Public Psychology" and "Price Movement and Other Market Action Factors." In his *The Battle for Investment Survival*, pp. 59–67. 1965.

> It is more practical to determine if a stock price is moving up or down, Loeb asserts, than to try to guess about its being overvalued or undervalued.

Markstein, David L. "Profitable Trends Follow Trendlines." In his *How to Chart Your Way to Stock Market Profits*, pp. 29–36. 1966.

> Considers minor, intermediate, and major trend movements. Markstein points out two questions that should be asked about trend lines: (1) How steep is the trend? and (2) How many times has the trend line been tested? Pullbacks, fans, and channels are discussed.

Merrill, Arthur A. "Is the Market Random?" In his *Behavior of Prices on Wall Street*, pp. 90–93. 1966.

> Includes an appendix dealing with market runs. A run is defined as a continuation of price moves in the same direction. Charts illustrate hourly, daily, and weekly runs over a period of years. Hourly and daily runs are more likely to extend themselves than weekly, Merrill notes.

Merrill, Arthur A. "Is Trend Following Profitable?" In his *Behavior of Prices on Wall Street*, pp. 77–78. 1966.

> Outlines the 5 percent penetration method, which is based on the principles of the Dow Theory, but with rigidly defined procedures. Swings of 5 percent are used.

Owen, Lewis. "Buy Only on the Rise." In his *How Wall Street Doubles My Money Every Three Years*, pp. 154–157. 1969.

> Owen is an advocate of buying on strength, defined as purchasing only those stocks that have just had strong price rises.

Paris, Alexander P. "Trendlines." In his *A Complete Guide to Trading Profits*, pp. 50–59. 1970.

> Uptrends are discussed first, then downtrends. Three tests for validity are given, to help determine whether or not a genuine trend exists in the price movements of a particular stock. A short consideration of the psychology of trend line trading is included.

Reid, Jesse B. *Buy High, Sell Higher*! 1966. 208 pp.

> Reid's book is concerned with a trend-following system called UHV (unusually high volume). The idea is to buy a stock only after it has shown a significant price rise accompanied by volume that is unusual for that particular stock. Many examples are given.

Warren, Ted. "Trend Lines: Your Buy and Sell Signals." In his *How to Make the Stock Market Make Money For You*, pp. 88–104. 1966.

> Warns against trying to speculate by means of short trend lines appearing

in daily charts. Twenty monthly charts displaying long-term trend lines of individual stocks are reproduced. Each chart is interpreted.

TREND LINES. *See* Charts; Trend Following

TRIANGLES (COILS)

Progressively smaller or larger price formations resulting in triangular or coil-shaped areas on stock price charts. Stock market technical analysts believe these patterns are significant, although difficult to interpret.

Edwards, Robert D., and Magee, John. "Important Reversal Patterns—the Triangles." In their *Technical Analysis of Stock Trends*, 5th ed., pp. 86–116. 1966.

> Symmetrical triangles (coils), the development of triangles, right-angle triangles, and descending triangles are all considered. The authors say triangles are "an intriguing lot with excellent profit potentialities."

Markstein, David L. "The Opportunity Patterns: Triangles." In his *How to Chart Your Way to Stock Market Profits*, pp. 65–76. 1966.

> Markstein notes that triangles as formations on stock charts are rather difficult to interpret. Symmetrical, ascending, and descending triangles are mentioned, but the important factor, he points out, is the direction of the breakout from the triangle, regardless of type.

Jiler, William L. "The Coil (or Triangle)." In his *How Charts Can Help You in the Stock Market*, pp. 117–123. 1962.

> Discusses symmetrical, ascending, descending, and inverted triangles, with three specific guide-lines as a checklist in following triangle developments. Three pages of charted examples appear in this chapter.

TRIPLE TOP (*see also* Double Tops and Bottoms)

A stock chart formation characterized by three peaks or tops, all reaching about the same price level. Said to be a sign of weakness.

Edwards, Robert D., and Magee, John. "Triple Tops . . ." In their *Technical Analysis of Stock Trends*, 5th ed., pp. 136–139. 1966.

> Triple tops are characterized as few and far between. Methods of recognizing these formations are discussed.

Leffler, George L. "Triple Top." In his *The Stock Market*, 3rd ed., pp. 585–586. 1963.

> A skeptical view of the triple top. As an example, Leffler points out that the Dow-Jones Industrial Average formed an almost perfect triple top between September 1955 and January 1956, and then proceeded to make a new all-time high. The triple top is supposed to forecast weakness but often does not.

TRUST FUNDS

Sums of money (generally large) turned over to banks or other fiduciaries for management and safekeeping. For efficient investment management, smaller amounts of money may be combined to form a common trust fund.

Hazard, John W. "Trust Funds." In his *Choosing Tomorrow's Growth Stocks Today,* pp. 261-269. 1969.

> Lists eight reasons for putting money into a trust fund or common trust fund. Common trust funds are described, and the author warns about confusing these funds with mutual funds.

Sauvain, Harry. "Personal Trusts" and "Common Trust Funds." In his *Investment Management*, 3rd ed., pp. 618–627. 1967.

> General discussion of how banks invest trust funds. Sauvain says there are no published data indicating the banks' investment policies in the management of trust funds. However, he cites a study by the U.S. Office of the Comptroller of the Currency, showing that in 1964 an amount equal to roughly two-thirds of the combined assets of trust departments of commercial banks was invested in common stocks. The amount in common stocks falls to about one-half when assets of common trust funds alone are considered.

Springer, John L. "How Advisers Go Wrong." In his *If They're So Smart, How Come You're Not Rich?*, pp. 167–172. 1971.

> Studies are cited which show that the trust departments of some large banks obtain results that do not even qualify as mediocre.

TURN SIGNALS (*see also* New York Stock Exchange Turn Signal)

Technical indications that the stock market price trend is about to change direction.

Krow, Harvey A. "Putting the Indicators Together." In his *Stock Market Behavior*, pp. 143–156. 1969.

> Describes the various phases of a stock market cycle and tells what technical indicators may be useful along the way. The phases are contraction,

counterwave, resumption of downtrend, bottom, change to uptrend, bull trend, top, and back to contraction.

Markstein, David L. "Bull or Bear Market? The Technical Tests." In his *How to Make Your Money Do More*, pp. 222-238. 1971.

> Various stock market turn signals are described, including The NYSE Turn Signal, The Hi-Lo Index, The Stock Group Index, The Market Fuel Indicator, and Breadth-Momentum. All may be useful, but the infallible indicator does not exist.

TURNAROUND SITUATIONS (*see also* Undervalued Securities)

Corporations which have recently seen hard times for one reason or another, but which because of new management or some other changed factor, appear ready for an upturn in profits.

Widicus, Wilbur W., and Stitzel, Thomas E. "Turnaround Situations." In their *Today's Investments for Tomorrow's Security*, pp. 297-300. 1971.

> Considers the various reasons for turnarounds, emphasizing management, and the risk characteristics of these situations.

UNDERVALUED SECURITIES (*see also* Turnaround Situations)

Stocks or bonds that are priced below what would seem to be a reasonable or normal value, in view of underlying net assets or earning power.

American Research Council. "Value and Financial Approaches to Common Stock Selection." In *Your Investments*, 18th ed. pp. 66-77. 1970.

> Discussion of stocks selling at a low price compared with assets per share or at low price-earnings ratios. Four pros and cons of the value-financial approach are given, and six questions are posed about the earnings statement trends of undervalued companies. Lists of undervalued stocks are included.

Dines, James. "How to Tell 'Underpriced' from 'Overpriced'." In his *How the Average Investor Can Use Technical Analysis for Stock Profits*, pp. 599-607. 1972.

> Generally a discussion of how difficult the fundamental analysis of stocks is, because estimates of future earnings are so unreliable, not to mention the variability of future price-earnings ratios.

Graham, Benjamin, and others. "The Asset-Value Factor in Common-Stock Valuation." In their *Security Analysis*, 4th ed., pp. 551-569. 1962.

> The authors explain how and why asset value is of much less importance today than earning power, for most corporations. They also consider the

special situation of companies with common stock selling for a price per share that is less than net current assets per share, noting that ". . . the purchase of a diversified group of companies on this 'bargain basis' is almost certain to result profitably within a reasonable period of time." Examples are given.

Graham, Benjamin. "Bargain Issues, or Net-Current-Asset Stocks." In his *The Intelligent Investor*, 4th rev. ed., pp. 214–216. 1973.

Benjamin Graham is sometimes referred to as the dean of American security analysts. He also is the leading exponent of undervalued, underpriced securities for the average investor, as opposed to popular growth stocks. When possible, Graham recommends buying into companies having common stock selling at a price per share which is less than net current asset value per share. Such situations generally work out very well, although the time involved may be measured in years rather than months. Also, diversification is essential.

Hayes, Douglas A. "Common-Stock Strategy: Undervalued Issues." *Investments: Analysis and Management*, 2nd ed., pp. 77–82. 1966.

A consideration of both the opportunities and the risks involved in following an undervalued issue strategy. Two specific examples are given for the years 1955 to 1964—one turned out well and the other not so well.

Stillman, Richard N. "Value Will Out." In his *The Strategy of Investment*, pp. 103–118. 1962.

The author discusses what undervalued securities are and how to locate them, concluding: "In summation, then, we commend to the investor a policy of bargain-hunting for undervalued securities."

UPSIDE-DOWNSIDE VOLUME

A comparison of the trading volume of rising stocks with the volume of falling stocks. Usually applies to stocks traded on the New York Stock Exchange.

Dines, James. "Upside-Downside Volume Reveals Internal Market Dynamics." In his *How the Average Investor Can Use Technical Analysis for Stock Profits*, pp. 594–595. 1972.

Two upside-downside volume rules are given to make this indicator more useful.

V FORMATIONS

These are stock price formations in the form of a V at market bottoms or an inverted V at market tops. The important thing about these patterns is that they happen without warning. An excellent example for the market as a whole was the sharp drop and recovery from May 1965 to September 1965.

Jiler, William L. "V Formations." In his *How Charts Can Help You in the Stock Market*, pp. 97–108. 1962.

> General description of V formations, including extended V's. The three components of the true V are given, as well as the four components of the extended V. Five pages of charted examples appear in this chapter.

VALUE APPROACH. *See* Undervalued Securities

VALUE MEDIAN PLANS. *See* Normal-Value Plans

VARIABLE RATIO STOCK-BOND FORMULAS. *See* Normal Value Plans

VASSAR PLAN

A now obsolete investment plan used by Vassar College from 1938 to about 1949. A varying stock-bond ratio was used, depending on the level of the Dow-Jones Industrial Average.

Leffler, George L. "Vassar Plan." In his *The Stock Market*, 3rd ed., pp. 565–566. 1963.

> Brief description of the Vassar Plan. Leffler observes that the plan worked well up to 1946, but was abandoned a couple of years after that.

Persons, Robert H. "The Vassar Plan." In his *Handbook of Formula Plans in the Stock Market*, pp. 69–70. 1967.

> Tells how this variable stock-bond investment formula failed because it was based on stock prices that prevailed during the depression period (1930–1938).

VERTICAL CHARTS. *See* Charts

VOLUME OF TRADING (*see also* Upside-Downside Volume)

The number of shares of stock changing hands during a particular time period, as during an hour, day, or week. May apply to a single stock, a group of stocks, or the market as a whole.

American Research Council. "Focusing on 'Changes in Volume.'" In *Your Investments*, 18th ed., p. 104. 1970.

> Commentary on the technique of buying individual stocks when the price rises on unusually high volume.

American Research Council. "Volume-of-Trading Clues." In *Your Investments*, 18th ed., pp. 180–181. 1970.

> Points out that a reduction in volume of trading almost always shows up before the top of a bull market and before the bottom of a bear market. The 1966 market is singled out as a significant exception.

Dines, James. "Volume Tips Off When 'Big Money' is Getting Out." In his *How the Average Investor Can Use Technical Analysis for Stock Profits*, pp. 580–597. 1972.

> Unusually complete discussion of volume of trading as it affects technical analysis of stock price movements. Volume is considered as it applies to both the stock market as a whole and to individual stocks. Dines says that a stock rise on heavy volume is not necessarily a favorable development. The volume theories of William Gordon, Paul Dysart, Jesse B. Reid, and others are discussed.

Foster, Orline D. "Volume—Why Tape-Readers Think It is Important." In his *Ticker Technique*, pp. 37–42. 1965.

> Reviews characteristics of volume in bull markets, bear markets, dull markets, and irregular markets. Foster discusses volume in relation to these topics: accumulation, distribution, distress selling, short selling, and liquidation. Six general rules for following volume are given.

Jacobs, William O. "Volume Index." In his *Stock Market Profile*, pp. 52–56. 1967.

> Discusses a volume index based on monthly averages of daily trading volume. Jacobs says the index is a good indicator of bull market tops and uses it as part of his stock market profile system.

Kent, William A. "The Volume Gambit." In *Encyclopedia of Stock Market Techniques*, pp. 412–415. 1970 (cover date: 1971).

> A criticism of the traditional view of stock volume. According to the author, a stock may easily make extensive price moves up or down without corresponding increases in volume of sales.

Krow, Harvey A. "Volume of Trading" and "Volume." In his *Stock Market Behavior*, pp. 110–114, 193–194. 1969.

> In "Volume of Trading," Krow gives some basic rules for interpreting the total volume of stock market transactions relative to prices. Day-to-day market volume is sometimes highly significant and sometimes relatively meaningless. In "Volume," Krow discusses how to interpret the volume of individual stocks.

Reid, Jesse B. *Buy High, Sell Higher*! 1966. 208 pp.

> Describes the UHV (unusually high volume) system of investing, wherein a stock is bought only after showing a significant price rise accompanied by volume that is unusual for that particular stock. Many examples are given, with detailed tables of dates, volume, and prices.

Warren, Ted. "Volume: The Important Messages behind the Figures." In his *How to Make the Stock Market Make Money for You*, pp. 119–127. 1966.

> Points out that small or large volume is often a clue to whether price moves in a stock are to be considered of minor or major importance. However, figuring out just what a particular amount of volume means at a particular time is difficult. Warren gives some examples of how he analyzes volume of trading in individual stocks.

Worden, Don. "Upticks, Downticks, and True Volume." In *Ticker Technique*, by Orline D. Foster, pp. 61–94. 1965.

> Worden's concept of true volume emphasizes trading that takes place in a particular stock in large quantities or blocks and gives a lesser place to volume in small, one hundred-share amounts. It is also restricted to trading on upticks (price moving up) or downticks (price moving down), as opposed to transactions in which there is no change in price.

VOLUME-PRICE TREND METHOD

A statistical index of the volume of trading that is required to lift the price of a stock by a certain percentage or to drop the price by a certain percentage. The interaction of buying pressure and selling pressure is measured.

Markstein, David L. "Volume-Price Trend Charting," In his *How to Chart Your Way to Stock Market Profits*, pp. 125–161. 1966.

> Includes how to construct a volume-price trend chart, how to read the chart, trading tactics or strategy, and six case histories with charts and explanations. Five trading rules for using these charts are also included.

WALL STREET FOLKLORE. *See* Adages (Wall Street Folklore)

WARRANT HEDGING

Buying the common stock of a corporation and selling the corresponding warrants short, or buying the warrants of a corporation and selling the corresponding stock short. Various proportions of stock and warrants are used, based on some fairly involved considerations.

Silverman, Richard. "How to Hedge Risky Warrants for Small but Safe Profits." In his *$100 Gets You Started*, pp. 104–111. 1965.

> A simple method of hedging is described, in which common stock is sold short and the corresponding warrants (same corporation) are bought. Tables show results of various mixes of stock and warrants.

Thorp, Edward O., and Kassouf, Sheen T. *Beat the Market; A Scientific Stock Market System*. 1967. 221 pp.

> The Thorp-Kassouf system involves selling overvalued warrants short as the warrants approach their expiration date and worthlessness, while at the same time buying the corresponding common stock to complete the hedge. Often easier said than done, because of restrictions that stock exchanges place on short selling of warrants that are ready to expire. Thorp and Kassouf also describe reverse hedging, where warrants are bought and the common stock sold short. An appendix gives the mathematical theory of warrant hedging.

WARRANTS

Certificates giving the holder the privilege of buying a specified amount of a particular common stock at a certain price. A warrant usually has an expiration date but may be perpetual. Warrants are similar to rights except that they are valid longer.

American Research Council. "Stock Warrants." In *Your Investments*, 18th ed., pp. 142–144. 1970.

> Explains the five main considerations in picking a warrant for capital gains. A formula is included for figuring the value of a warrant, as are comments on hedging with warrants and selling warrants short.

Cobleigh, Ira U. "The Wonderful World of Warrants." In his *All About Stocks*, pp. 28–36. 1970.

> Mr. Cobleigh calls warrants "the most exciting and volatile of all marketable securities." He lists five specific suggestions for the aid of those who wish to speculate in warrants.

Fried, Sidney. *Speculating with Warrants*. 1971. 57 pp.

> Fried is a well-known authority on warrant speculation and publisher of a special service dealing with warrants. His booklet covers the arithmetic of warrant leverage, selling warrants short, and hedging with warrants. Many actual examples are given. While the riskiness of warrants is mentioned, Fried emphasizes that dealing in this type of certificate can be lucrative.

Graham, Benjamin. "Stock-Option Warrants." In his *The Intelligent Investor*, 4th rev. ed., pp. 228–232. 1973.

> Graham is not fond of stock-option warrants. He calls their recent emergence and relative prominence "near fraud, an existing menace, and a potential disaster," and compares them to French *assignats* of 1789–1796, another kind of "magic paper."

Loeb, Gerald M. "Warrants and Convertibles: Volatile and Dazzling Performers." In his *The Battle for Stock Market Profits*, pp. 331–335. 1971.

> Not all convertibles are volatile and dazzling, of course; the author is concerned mainly with the risk-reward aspects of warrants.

Rosenberg, Claude N. "Warrants." In his *Stock Market Primer*, pp. 109–112. 1969.

> Basic explanation, including how to evaluate warrants. Rosenberg advises that an investor should not buy warrants unless he is really enchanted with the corresponding common stock's future, and stresses that the warrant market is highly speculative.

Shulman, Morton. "Warrants." In his *Anyone Can Make a Million*, pp. 101–120. 1966.

> Shulman says warrents are an excellent speculative vehicle. He discusses them only as a straight purchase (no short selling and hedging). To round out the chapter, four basic points to seek in buying warrants are given.

Silverman, Richard. "How Warrants Can Make You Rich." In his *$100 Gets You Started*, pp. 124–131. 1965.

> Warrants can also make you poor, but the author stresses the speculative possibilities that have existed in the past, as when a particular warrant rose in price from five cents to twenty-five dollars in two years. The basic principles of warrants are nicely explained.

YALE PLAN

A modified constant-ratio investment plan (see "Constant-Ratio Formula") that was used by Yale University from the late 1930s to the early 1950s. The key to the plan was fluctuation in portfolio value rather than an external central value of some kind.

Leffler, George L. "Yale Plan." In his *The Stock Market*, 3rd ed., p. 566. 1963.

> Brief description of the Yale Plan. Leffler says that the plan, which was abandoned around 1954, was a very conservative one.

Persons, Robert H. "The Constant-Ratio Formula." In his *Handbook of Formula Plans in the Stock Market*, pp. 58–63. 1967.

> The Yale University formula investing plan is briefly described in this discussion of constant-ratio plans.

YIELD SPREAD. *See* Stock-Bond Yield Spread

YIELD VALUE APPROACH. *See* Dividend Value Approach

ZONE PLAN. *See* Keystone Plan

BIBLIOGRAPHY

Allen, Leon B. *A Method for Stock Profits without Price Forecasting*. Garden City, N.Y.: Doubleday, 1962. 216 pp.

Alverson, Lyle T. *How to Write Puts and Calls; a Guide to a Sound Investment Practice*. New York: Exposition Press, 1968. 125 pp. $6.00

American Research Council. *Your Investments*, 18th ed. New York: McGraw-Hill, 1970. 226 pp. $7.95

"Anonymous Investor." *Wiped Out; How I Lost a Fortune in the Stock Market while the Averages Were Making New Highs*. New York: Simon & Schuster, 1966. 125 pp. $3.50

Barnes, Leo, ed. *Current Issues on the Frontiers of Financial Analysis*. (Hofstra University Yearbook of Business, series 7, vol. 4.) Hempstead, N.Y.: Hofstra University, 1970. 300 pp. $6.00

Bellemore, Douglas H. *The Strategic Investor*. New York: Simmons-Boardman, 1963. 394 pp.

Bracker, Lewis A., and Wagner, Walter. *The Trouble with Wall Street*. Englewood Cliffs, N.J.: Prentice-Hall, 1972. 235 pp. $6.95

Bridwell, Rodger. *Reality in the Stock Market*. Vancouver, Canada: Winfield Press, 1965. 210 pp.

Chase, Richard H., and others. *Computer Applications in Investment Analysis*. (Tuck Bulletin No. 30.) Hanover, N.H.: Dartmouth College, Amos Tuck School of Business Adminstration, 1966. 54 pp. $2.00

Cobleigh, Ira U. *All about Stocks; a Guide to Profitable Investing in the '70s*. New York: Weybright & Talley, 1970. 243 pp. $6.95

Cohen, Jerome B., and Zinbarg, Edward D. *Investment Analysis and Portfolio Management*. Homewood, Ill.: Dow Jones-Irwin, 1967. 778 pp. $13.25

Crane, Burton. *The Sophisticated Investor; a Guide to Stock Market Profits.* Rev. by Sylvia Crane Eisenlohr. New York: Simon & Schuster, 1964. 249 pp. $5.95

Cunnion, John D. *How to Get Maximum Leverage from Puts and Calls.* Larchmont, N.Y.: Business Reports, Inc., 1966. 160 pp. $3.00

Dacey, Norman F. *Dacey on Mutual Funds.* New York: Crown, 1970. 272 pp. $6.95

Dadekian, Zaven D. *The Strategy of Puts and Calls; Selling Stock Options for Maximum Profit with Minimum Risk.* New York: Corinthian Editions (Scribners), 1968. 142 pp. $5.95

Dewey, Edward R. *Cycles; the Mysterious Forces that Trigger Events.* New York: Hawthorn, 1971. 211 pp. $6.95

Dines, James. *How the Average Investor Can Use Technical Analysis for Stock Profits; an In-Depth Work on Stock Market Technical Analysis, Mob Psychology, and Fundamentals.* New York: Dines Chart Corp., 1972. 685 pp. $19.95

Drew, Garfield A. *New Methods for Profit in the Stock Market, with a Critical Analysis of Established Systems.* Burlington, Vt: Fraser Publishing Co., 1966 (reprint of 1955 edition). 384 pp. $7.50

Edwards, Robert D., and Magee, John. *Technical Analysis of Stock Trends*, 5th ed. Springfield, Mass.: John Magee, 1966. 486 pp. $16.00

Ellis, Charles D. *Institutional Investing.* Homewood, Il!.: Dow Jones-Irwin, 1971. 253 pp. $9.95

Ellis, John. *Self-Reliant Investing.* Chicago: Regnery, 1971. 219 pp. $5.95

Encyclopedia of Stock Market Techniques. Larchmont, N.Y.: Investors Intelligence, 1970 (cover date: 1971). 733 pp. $24.95

Engel, Louis. *How to Buy Stocks*, 5th rev. ed. Boston: Little, Brown, 1971. 340 pp. $7.95

Filer, Herbert. *Understanding Put and Call Options; How to Use Them to Reduce Risk in Your Stock Market Operations.* New York: Crown, 1959. 123 pp.

Fisher, Milton. *How to Make Big Money in the Over-the-Counter Market.* New York: William Morrow, 1970. 237 pp. $5.95

Foster, Orline D. *Ticker Technique; the Art of Tape Reading.* Rev. by Robert H. Persons, with additional material by Don Worden and Herbert Liesner. Palisades Park, N.J.: Investors' Press, 1965. 127 pp. $5.95

Fowler, Elizabeth M. *90 Days to Fortune*. New York: Ivan Obolensky (Astor-Honor), 1965. 154 pp. $4.95

Fried, Sidney. *Speculating with Warrants*. New York: R. H. M. Associates, 1971. 57 pp. $3.95

Graham, Benjamin. *The Intelligent Investor; a Book of Practical Counsel*, 4th rev. ed. New York: Harper & Row, 1973. 318 pp. $7.95

Graham, Benjamin, and others. *Security Analysis: Principles and Technique*, 4th ed. New York: McGraw-Hill, 1962. 778 pp. $12.95

Granville, Joseph E. *A Strategy of Daily Stock Market Timing for Maximum Profit*. Englewood Cliffs, N.J.: Prentice-Hall, 1960. 289 pp. $17.95

Haas, Albert, and Jackson, Don D. *Bulls, Bears and Dr. Freud*. New York: World, 1967. 179 pp.

Hamilton, William P. *The Stock Market Barometer; a Study of Its Forecast Value Based on Charles H. Dow's Theory of the Price Movement, with an Analysis of the Market and Its History Since 1897*. New York: Richard Russell Associates, 1960 (reprint of 1922 edition). 278 pp. $4.95

Harper, Henry H. *The Psychology of Speculation; the Human Element in Stock Market Transactions*. Burlington, Vt.: Fraser Publishing Co., 1966 (reprint of 1926 edition). 106 pp. $3.00

Hayes, Douglas A. *Investments: Analysis and Management*, 2nd ed. New York: Macmillan, 1966. 501 pp. $10.95

Hazard, John W. *Choosing Tomorrow's Growth Stocks Today*. Garden City, N.Y.: Doubleday, 1968. 305 pp.

Hirsch, Yale. *The Stock Trader's Almanac*. Old Tappan, N.J.: The Hirsch Organization. Annual. 160 pp. $6.95

Jacobs, William O. *Stock Market Profile: How to Invest with the Primary Trend*. West Nyack, N.Y.: Parker Publishing Co., 1967. 184 pp.

Jiler, William L. *How Charts Can Help You in the Stock Market*. New York: Trendline (Standard & Poor's Corp.), 1962. 202 pp. $10.00

Kamm, Jacob O. *Making Profits in the Stock Market*, 3rd rev. ed. Cleveland: World, 1966. 180 pp.

Knowlton, Winthrop, and Furth, John L. *Shaking the Money Tree; How to Find New Growth Opportunities in Common Stocks*. New York: Harper & Row, 1972. 190 pp. $7.50

Krefetz, Gerald and Marosi, Ruth. *Money Makes Money and the Money Money Makes Makes More Money; the Men Who are Wall Street*. New York: World, 1970. 271 pp. $7.50

Krow, Harvey A. *Stock Market Behavior; the Technical Approach to Understanding Wall Street*. New York: Random House, 1969. 241 pp. $10.00

Latané, Henry A., and Tuttle, Donald L. *Security Analysis and Portfolio Management*. New York: Ronald Press, 1970. 752 pp. $13.50

Laurence, Michael. *Playboy's Investment Guide*. Chicago: Playboy Press, 1971. 276 pp. $7.95

Lawrence, John F., and Steiger, Paul E. *The 70s Crash and How to Survive It*. New York: World, 1970. 215 pp. $6.95

Leffler, George L. *The Stock Market*, 3rd ed. Rev. by Loring C. Farwell. New York: Ronald Press, 1963. 654 pp. $9.50

Lerro, Anthony J., and Swayne, Charles B. *Selection of Securities: Technical Analysis of Stock Market Prices*. Braintree, Mass.: D. H. Mark, 1970. 131 pp. $5.95

Levy, Robert A. *The Relative Strength Concept of Common Stock Price Forecasting; an Evaluation of Selected Applications of Stock Market Timing Techniques, Trading Tactics, and Trend Analysis.* Larchmont, N.Y.: Investors Intelligence, 1968. 318 pp. $15.00

Loeb, Gerald M. *The Battle for Investment Survival*, rev. ed. New York: Simon & Schuster, 1965. 320 pp. $5.95

Loeb, Gerald M. *The Battle for Stock Market Profits (Not the Way It's Taught at Harvard Business School)*. New York: Simon & Schuster, 1971. 352 pp. $6.95

Malkiel, Burton G., and Quandt, Richard E. *Strategies and Rational Decisions in the Securities Options Market*. Cambridge, Mass.: MIT Press, 1969. 176 pp. $7.95

Markowitz, Harry M. *Portfolio Selection: Efficient Diversification of Investments*. (Cowles Foundation for Research in Economics at Yale University, Monograph 16.) New York: Wiley, 1959. 344 pp. (Now published by Yale University Press, $12.50.)

Markstein, David L. *How to Chart Your Way to Stock Market Profits*. West Nyack, N.Y.: Parker Publishing Co., 1966. 259 pp. (Now published by Arc Books, Inc., $5.95.)

Markstein, David L. *How to Make Your Money Do More; the Complete Stock Market Adviser*. New York: Trident, 1971. 285 pp. $6.95

Markstein, David L. *Investing in the 70s; Profitable Approaches for Middle-Income Investors*. New York: Crowell, 1972. 182 pp. $5.95

Mead, Stuart B. *Mutual Funds; a Guide for the Lay Investor*. Braintree, Mass.: D. H. Mark, 1971. 161 pp. $5.95

Merrill, Arthur A. *Behavior of Prices on Wall Street; Market Inclinations Help Prediction, Produce Profits*. Chappaqua, N.Y.: Analysis Press, 1966. 171 pp. $10.00

Merritt, Robert D. *Financial Independence through Common Stocks*, rev. ed. New York: Simon & Schuster, 1969. 416 pp. $6.50

Mittra, Sid. *Inside Wall Street*. Homewood, Ill.: Dow Jones-Irwin, 1971. 287 pp. $8.50

Neal, Charles V. *How to Keep What You Have, Or, What Your Broker Never Told You*. Garden City, N.Y.: Doubleday, 1972. 314 pp. $7.95

Owen, Lewis. *How Wall Street Doubles My Money Every Three Years; the No-Nonsense Guide to Steady Stock Market Profits*. New York: Bernard Geis, 1969. 289 pp. $6.95

Paris, Alexander P. *A Complete Guide to Trading Profits*. Philadelphia: Whitmore, 1970. 196 pp. $4.95

Peisner, Robert N. *How to Select Rapid Growth Stocks; Six Practical Investment Tools for Finding Stocks with a Potential for Rapid Growth*. New York: Dutton, 1966. 160 pp. $4.95

Person, Carl E. *The Save-By-Borrowing Technique; Building Your Fortune— From Loan to Profit*. Garden City, N.Y.: Doubleday, 1966. 289 pp. $5.95

Persons, Robert H. *Handbook of Formula Plans in the Stock Market*. Rye, N.Y.: American Research Council, 1967. 92 pp. $3.95

Reid, Jesse B. *Buy High, Sell Higher!* New York: Hawthorn, 1966. 208 pp.

Reinach, Anthony M. *The Nature of Puts and Calls*. New York: The Bookmailer, 1961. 102 pp.

Ritter, Lawrence S., and Silber, William L. *Money*. New York: Basic Books, 1970. 221 pp. $5.95

Rolo, Charles J., and Nelson, George J., eds. *The Anatomy of Wall Street; a Guide for the Serious Investor*. Philadelphia: Lippincott, 1968. 307 pp. $7.50

Rosenberg, Claude N. *Psycho-Cybernetics and the Stock Market; the Key to Maximum Investment Profits and Peace of Mind*. Chicago: Playboy Press, 1971. 224 pp. $6.95

Rosenberg, Claude N. *Stock Market Primer*, rev. ed. New York: World, 1969. 351 pp. $6.95

Sarnoff, Paul. *Your Investments Using Puts and Calls*. Rye, N.Y.: American Research Council, 1968. 164 pp.

Sauvain, Harry. *Investment Management*, 3rd ed. Englewood Cliffs, N.J.: Prentice-Hall, 1967. 666 pp. $12.50

Scheinman, William X. *Why Most Investors Are Mostly Wrong Most of the Time*. New York: Weybright & Talley, 1970. 268 pp. $10.00

Sederberg, Arelo. *The Stock Market Investment Club Handbook; How to Organize, Maintain and Profit from an Investment Club*. Los Angeles: Sherbourne, 1971. 277 pp. $7.50

Shade, Philip A. *Common Stocks: a Plan for Intelligent Investing*. Homewood, Ill.: Irwin, 1971. 326 pp. $5.05

Shulman, Morton. *Anyone Can Make a Million*. New York: McGraw-Hill, 1966. 276 pp. $4.95

Silverman, Richard. *$100 Gets You Started*. New York: Macmillan, 1965. 264 pp. $5.95

Smith, Adam (pseud.) [George W. Goodman]. *The Money Game*. New York: Random House, 1968. 302 pp. $6.95

Smith, Ralph L. *The Grim Truth about Mutual Funds*. New York: G. P. Putnam's Sons, 1963. 122 pp.

Sobel, Robert. *The Great Bull Market; Wall Street in the 1920s*. New York: Norton, 1968. 175 pp. $1.65

Springer, John L. *If They're So Smart, How Come You're Not Rich?* Chicago: Regnery, 1971. 235 pp. $5.95

Sprinkel, Beryl W. *Money and Markets; a Monetarist View*. Homewood, Ill.: Irwin, 1971. 305 pp. $5.05

Stillman, Richard N. *The Strategy of Investment*. New York: Holt, Rinehart & Winston, 1962. 180 pp.

Sullivan, George. *The Dollar Squeeze and How to Beat It*. New York: Macmillan, 1970. 204 pp. $5.95

Thorp, Edward O., and Kassouf, Sheen T. *Beat the Market; a Scientific Stock Market System*. New York: Random House, 1967. 221 pp. $8.95

Warren, Ted. *How to Make the Stock Market Make Money for You*. Los Angeles: Sherbourne, 1966. 319 pp. $5.95

Weaver, Mark. *The Technique of Short Selling; Making Money on Declines in the Stock Market*, rev. ed. Palisades Park, N.J.: Investors' Press, 1963. 81 pp. $4.95

Widicus, Wilbur W., and Stitzel, Thomas E. *Today's Investments for Tomorrow's Security*. Homewood, Ill.: Dow Jones-Irwin, 1971. 415 pp. $9.95

Williamson, J. Peter. *Investments; New Analytic Techniques*. New York: Praeger, 1971. 325 pp. $12.50

Wysong, Perry. *How You Can Use the Wall Street Insiders*. Fort Lauderdale, Fla.: Wilton House, 1971. 188 pp. $4.95

Zerden, Sheldon. *Best Books on the Stock Market; an Analytical Bibliography*. New York: Bowker, 1972. 195 pp. $12.95

Zerden, Sheldon. *Margin: Key to a Stock Market Fortune*. New York: Pilot Books, 1969. 53 pp. $2.00

Zieg, Kermit C. *Ticker Tape Trading*. Larchmont, N.Y.: Investors Intelligence, 1970. 127 pp. $7.95

SELECTED
PERIODICAL ARTICLES

ADAGES (WALL STREET FOLKLORE)

Hoffland, D. L. "The Folklore of Wall Street." *Financial Analysts Journal*, vol. 23, May–June, 1967, pp. 85–88.

Criticism of popular trading methods.

ADVANCE-DECLINE LINE

Dysart, P. L. "Bear Market Signal? A Sensitive Breadth Index Has Just Flashed One." *Barron's*, vol. 47, September 4, 1967, p. 9.

How to use advance-decline lines.

Zakon, A. J., and Pennypacker, J. C. "An Analysis of the Advance-Decline Line as Stock Market Indicator." *Journal of Financial and Quantitative Analysis*, vol. 3, September 1968, pp. 299–314.

Advance-decline line is poor leading indicator of stock prices.

ADVISORY SERVICES. *See* Investment Advisory Services

BARRON'S CONFIDENCE INDEX. *See* Confidence Index

BEAR MARKET

"Anatomy of a Bear." *Financial World*, vol. 132, December 24, 1969, pp. 3–4.

Bauman, W. S. "How Do Investors Preserve Capital in a Bear Market?" *Commercial and Financial Chronicle*, vol. 205, February 2, 1967, p. 512.

"Bear Markets—Past and Present." *Financial World*, vol. 132, August 13, 1969, pp. 3-4.

Biggs, B. M. "This Too Shall Pass; A Timely Look at the Aftermath of Other Speculative Bubbles." *Barron's*, vol. 50, June 22, 1970, p. 5.

"Charts That Show What Went Wrong on Wall Street." *Changing Times*, vol. 24, October 1970, pp. 24-27.
    Nine charts of various averages and indexes.

Russell, R. "Leg Upward? Bear Market Rallies, Says a Dow Theorist, Can Be Tricky." *Barron's*, vol. 46, September 5, 1966, p. 5.

Russell, R. "Track of the Bear; a Dow Theorist Traces the Pattern of Market Declines." *Barron's*, vol. 45, July 26, 1965, pp. 9-10.

BLUE CHIPS

"Blue Chips vs. Glamours." *Financial World*, vol. 132, October 8, 1969, pp. 3-4.

Christy, G. A. "Blue Chips in an Inflationary Climate—A Negative View." *Trusts & Estates*, vol. 108, November 1969, pp. 1073-1077.

"Disappointing Blue Chips." *Financial World*, vol. 127, April 5, 1967, p. 10.

Fee, C. R., and Broady, G. K. "Selecting Next Decade's Blue Chips Means Shunning Short Term Trading," *Commercial and Financial Chronicle*, vol. 207, May 30, 1968, p. 2137.

Layne, A. A. "Are You Stuck With a Blue Chip Loser? . . . Here are the Expert's Recommendations." *Medical Economics*, vol. 49, May 22, 1972, pp. 119-127.

"Today's Blue Chip May Be Tomorrow's Dog; Record of the Past 20 Years Proves It." *Forbes*, vol. 96, November 1, 1965, pp. 14-16.

BONDS

Ascher, L. W. "Selecting Bonds for Capital Gains." *Financial Analysts Journal*, vol. 27, March-April, 1971, pp. 74-79.

Atkinson, T. R. "Why Bond Investors Should Find a Favorable Climate in Next Decade." *Commerical and Financial Chronicle*, vol. 207, June 13, 1968, p. 2333.

"Can You Get 8% on Good-Grade Bonds?" *Changing Times*, vol. 27, February 1973, p. 33.

Ellis, C. D. "Bonds for Long Term Investors." *Financial Analysts Journal*, vol. 26, March–April, 1970. pp. 81–85.

Grady, F. C. "Managing Bond Portfolios on a Profitable Basis." *Commercial and Financial Chronicle*, vol. 209, June 12, 1969, pp. 2578–2579.

Homer, S. "Utilizing Bonds Fully for Portfolio Performance." *Commercial and Financial Chronicle*, vol. 209, March 27, 1969, pp. 1344–1345.

"Invest in Bonds the Mutual Fund Way." *Changing Times*, vol. 26, July 1972, p. 16.
    Mutual bond funds.

"Investors Discover Bond Pitfalls." *Financial World*, vol. 134, July 22, 1970, p. 6.

Layne, A. A. "To Calm a Jittery Portfolio, Buy Bond Funds; By Following These Guidelines, You Can Add the Stability, Income, and Safety that Your Present Investments May Lack." *Medical Economics*, vol. 49, October 9, 1972, pp. 88–93.

Levinson, W. A. "What You've Always Wanted to Know about Bonds, But Were Too Growth-Stock Minded to Ask." *Medical Economics*, vol. 49, June 5, 1972, pp. 94–119.

McDiarmid, F. J. "Will There Always Be a Bond Market?" *Public Utilities Fortnightly*, vol. 78, September 29, 1966, pp. 40–48.

Madrick, J. G. "The Bond Funds; When the Hare Slows Down, Put Your Money on the Tortoise." *Money*, vol. 1, October 1972, pp. 99–100.
    Mutual bond funds.

"More and More People Are Buying Bonds, because Yields have Hit Record Highs. It's a Good Time to Make Sure You Understand the Ins and Outs of Bonds and the Bond Market." *Changing Times*, vol. 23, July 1969, pp. 25–29.

Price, T. R. "New Era in Bonds." *Commercial and Financial Chronicle*, vol. 216, August 17, 1972, p. 457.

Price tells how bond investors can fare better than common stock buyers.

Price, T. R. "Unorthodox Path to Profits: New Era in Bonds." *Commercial and Financial Chronicle*, vol. 216, August 17, 1972, p. 457.

Shapiro, H. D. "Who Are All Those New Bond Managers and What Are They Up To." *Institutional Investor*, vol. 7, January 1973, pp. 49–53.

Performance-oriented bond investing.

Wright, J. W. "Aggressive Approach to Bond Investment." *Trusts & Estates*, vol. 109, May 1970, pp. 409–411.

Wright, J. W. "Bonds are Imprudent Investments." *Trusts & Estates*, vol. 108, January 1969, pp. 82–84.

BONDS, CONVERTIBLE. *See* Convertible Bonds

BONDS, GOVERNMENT. *See* Government Bonds

BONDS, MUNICIPAL. *See* Municipal Bonds

BOOKS (LITERATURE)

"Best Bets for an Investor's Bookshelf; the Deluge of How-to-Get-Rich Books. Only a Handful Are Good." *Business Week*, December 23, 1972, pp. 118–119.

Markstein, D. L. "Twenty Ways to Increase Your Investment Knowledge; Guides to the Various Techniques and Philosophies, from Ultra-Conservative to Speculative, Are Briefly Reviewed." *Burroughs Clearing House*, vol. 53, February 1969, pp. 28–29.

BORROWING TO INVEST. *See* Leverage; Margin

BREADTH OF MARKET. *See* Advance-Decline Line

BUY-AND-HOLD

Erpf, A. G. "Investing for Long-Term Is Wisest Policy." *Commercial and Financial Chronicle*, vol. 208, October 3, 1968, p. 1313.

Greene, N. R. "The Miracle of Long-Term Investing in Common Stocks." *Commercial and Financial Chronicles*, vol. 205, January 19, 1967, p. 242.

"It's Easier to Win than Lose." *Business Week*, May 29, 1965, p. 118.
    Return on stocks from 1926 to 1960.

Loeb, G. M. "Investors Should Buy and Sell Instead of Buying and Sitting." *Commercial and Financial Chronicle*, vol. 214, December 2, 1971, p. 1643.
    Negative view of buy-and-hold policy.

"Stocks that Survived From 1907, and Those that Didn't." *Magazine of Wall Street*, vol. 121, November 11, 1967, pp. 9–12.

CASH

Snelling, D. E. "Short-Term Investment of Excess Cash." *Management Accounting*, vol. 50, January, 1969, pp. 31–35.

CHARTS

"Charts that Show What Went Wrong on Wall Street." *Changing Times*, vol. 24, October 1970, pp. 24–27.
    Nine charts of various averages and indexes.

Markstein, D. L. "Can Stock Charts Really Help?" *Burroughs Clearing House*, vol. 54, November 1969, p. 15.

Markstein, D. L. "Charting—a Quick Review." *Banking*, vol. 59, December 1966, p. 8.

Markstein, D. L. "Undeniable Contribution Stock Chartists Make." *Commercial and Financial Chronicle*, vol. 206, November 23, 1967, pp. 1946–1947.

"Reading the Future in the Past; Techniques of Chartist, Whose Approach is Gaining in Popularity." *Business Week*, August 14, 1965, pp. 107–108.

"Stock Chartist Tries to Pierce the Foggy Trend." *Business Week*, July 5, 1969, pp. 66–67.

CHARTS, POINT-AND-FIGURE. *See* Point-and-Figure Charts

CLIMAX FORMATIONS

Markstein, David L. "Spin-on-a-Dime or Bottom Climaxes." *Burroughs Clearing House*, vol. 54, July 1970, pp. 15–16.

CLOSED-END FUNDS. *See* Investment Companies

COMMON TRUST FUNDS. *See* Trust Funds

COMPUTER ANALYSIS

Bean, A. M. "Portfolio Analysis and Stock Selection by Computer." *Financial Executive*, vol. 35, February 1967, pp. 26–27.

Blake, C. W., and Riegle, D. W. "Data Processing Key to Investment Success." *Financial Analysts Journal*, vol. 24, January–February, 1968, pp. 134–146.

Clay, L. T. "Computers in Investment Analysis." *Financial Analysts Journal*, vol. 22, January–February, 1966, pp. 70–71.

"The Computer as a Research Tool: A Tabulation of Services Available to Institutions." *Institutional Investor*, vol. 5, October 1971, pp. 37–48.
  Lists 106 services: name, type, year started, description, and cost.

"Computers in Investment; Strictly for Professionals." *Economist*, vol. 217, December 11, 1965, pp. 1251–1252.

Eiteman, D. K. "Computer Program for Common Stock Valuation." *Financial Analysts Journal*, vol. 24, July–August, 1968, pp. 107–111.

Feuerstein, A. E., and Maggi, P. G. "Computer Investment Research." *Financial Analysts Journal*, vol. 24, January–February, 1968, pp. 154–158.

Feuerstein, A. E. "Investment Decision by Computers." *Bankers Monthly*, vol. 84, September 1967, p. 48.

Gal, J. J. "Man-Machine Interactive Systems and Their Application to Financial Analysis." *Financial Analysts Journal*, vol. 22, May–June, 1966, pp. 126–136.

Grunewald, A. E. "Computer Assisted Investment Analysis." *Michigan State University Business Topics*, vol. 15, Spring 1967, pp. 11–18.

Gumperz, J. "Computer as a Financial Tool; Some of Its Advantages and Limitations." *Financial Analysts Journal*, vol. 22, May–June, 1966, pp. 118–119.

Hardy, C. "Computer Investment Systems: What They Are, How They Work." *Banking*, vol. 64, October 1971, p. 50.

Howard, G. C. "Use of Computers in Investment Analysis." *Commercial and Financial Chronicle*, vol. 204, December 8, 1966, pp. 2038-2039.

Kopecky, C. L. "Using Computers to Outguess People." *Banking*, vol. 64, January 1972, pp. 20–24.
    Use of computer for investment analysis.

Lerner, E. M. "Use of Computers in Secirity Analysis." *Trusts and Estates*, vol. 106, August 1967, pp. 751–753.

Savage, J. P. "Computerized Investment Management—and Stricter Standards for Performance Measurement." *Trusts & Estates*, vol. 106, May 1967, pp. 471–473.

Stone, D. E. "Caveats in Computer-Aided Financial Analysis." *Financial Analysts Journal*, vol. 24, January–February, 1968, pp. 149–153.

Thomas, D. L. "Calculation Risks; Computers and Winning Friends and Influencing Decisions on Wall Street." *Barron's*, vol. 45, June 28, 1965, p. 3.

Thomas D. L. "Computerized Gunslingers; Electronic Brains Increasingly Are Calling the Shots in Wall Street." *Barron's*, vol. 49, March 24, 1969, p. 3.

Thomas D. L. "Electronic Investing." *Barron's*, vol. 47, August 14, 1967, p. 3.

Thomas D. L. "Smart Money, Giant Brains; Despite Limitations, Computers Can Be a Useful Investment Tool." *Barron's*, vol. 51, August 30, 1971, p. 3.

Thomas, D. L. "Where the Action Is: Computers Have Increased Volatility—and Risk—in the Stock Market." *Barron's*, vol. 47, August 28, 1967, p. 3.

"Wall Street's Newest Drudge and Genius." *Business Week*, July 9, 1966, pp. 117–118.

CONFIDENCE INDEX

Dell'Aria, P. S., and Granville, J. E. "Bull vs. Bear: Two Conflicting Views of the Barron's Confidence Index." *Barron's*, vol. 46, September 12, 1966, p. 3.

Gaumnitz, J. E., and Salabar, C. A. "The Barron's Confidence Index—An Examination of Its Value as a Market Indicator." *Financial Analysts Journal*, vol. 25, September–October, 1969, pp. 16–17.

Regan, P. J. "False Alarm; Barron's Confidence Index Is More Bullish than It Looks." *Barron's*, vol. 51, February 8, 1971, p. 9.

CONTRARY OPINION

Caubis, A. "Timing, Economic Guides for the Contrary Investor." *Commercial and Financial Chronicle*, vol. 208, October 24, 1968, p. 1621.

CONVERTIBLE BONDS

Brigham, E. F. "Analysis of Convertible Debentures: Theory and Some Empirical Evidence." *Journal of Finance*, vol. 21, March 1966, pp. 35–54.

"The Case for Convertibles." *Dun's Review and Modern Industry*, vol. 87, April 1966, pp. 43–44.

"Convertible Securities—The Parachute that Failed to Open." *Forbes*, vol. 104, September 15, 1969, pp. 30–31.

Cretien, P. D. "Convertible Bond Premiums as Predictors of Common Stock Price Changes." *Financial Analysts Journal*, vol. 25, November–December, 1969, pp. 90–95.

Hubbard, C. L., and Johnson, T. "Profits from Writing Calls with Convertible Bonds." *Financial Analysts Journal*, vol. 25, November–December, 1969, pp. 78–89.

"The Ins and Outs of Convertible Securities . . . The Advantages and the Problems." *Changing Times*, vol. 21, March 1967, pp. 43–45.

Kogan, D. P. "Convertible Hedge: It's a Useful Way to Limit Risk in a Declining Market." *Barron's*, vol. 46, June 27, 1966, p. 9.

McKenzie, R. R. "Convertible Debentures, 1956-65." *Quarterly Review of Economics & Business*, vol. 6, Winter 1966, pp. 41-51.

Shanahan, B. "Convertible Bonds—Best of Two Worlds?" *Magazine of Wall Street*, vol. 124, May 10, 1969, pp. 25-26.

Soldofsky, R. M. "Yield-Risk Performance of Convertible Securities." *Financial Analysts Journal*, vol. 27, March-April, 1971, pp. 61-65.

Turov, D. "Lien and Hungry; Speculative Appetite is Growing for Convertible Bonds." *Barron's*, vol. 51, April 26, 1971, p. 9.

Turov, D. "Riskless Reward? Skillful Traders May Reap One by Hedging in Convertible Bonds." *Barron's*, vol. 51, March 22, 1971, p. 9.

Vinson, C. E. "Rates of Return on Convertibles: Recent Investor Experience." *Financial Analysts Journal*, vol. 26, July-August, 1970, pp. 110-114.

Wilson, R. S. "Special Advantages of Convertible Bonds in a Rising Market." *Magazine of Wall Street*, vol. 117, October 16, 1965, pp. 120-123.

CONVERTIBLE PREFERRED STOCKS

Giddings, P. M. "Happiness: Stocks that Double While You Pocket 5%. How Can You Get That Kind of Return on a Growth Investment? By Buying a Convertible Preferred or Bond instead of the Company's Common Stock." *Medical Economics*, vol. 50, March 19, 1973, pp. 115-126.

"Relic of the 1920s Returns." *Business Week*, August 13, 1966, p. 80.

Rosenberg, J. "Convertible Preferreds." *Barron's*, vol. 46, October 24, 1966, p. 9.

DIVERSIFICATION

Aranyl, J. "Portfolio Diversification." *Financial Analysts Journal*, vol. 23, September-October, 1967, pp. 133-139.

Dulan, H. A. "Shifting from Diversification to Yield Emphasis in Common Stock Portfolios." *Financial Analysts Journal*, vol. 21, July-August, 1965, pp. 98-108.
    Seeking relatively high dividend income is advantageous.

Evans, J. L., and Archer, S. H. "Diversification and the Reduction of Dispersion: an Empirical Analysis." *Journal of Finance*, vol. 23, December 1968, pp. 761–767.

Jennings, E. H. "An Empirical Analysis of Some Aspects of Common Stock Diversification." *Journal of Financial and Quantitative Analysis*, vol. 6, March 1971, pp. 797–812.

Lintner, J. "Security Prices, Risk, and Maximum Gains from Diversification." *Journal of Finance*, vol. 20, December 1965, pp. 587–615.

Mao, J. C. T. "Essentials of Portfolio Diversification Strategy." *Journal of Finance*, vol. 25, December 1970, pp. 1109–1121.

Smith, K. V., and Schreiner, J. C. "Direct vs. Indirect Diversification." *Financial Analysts Journal*, vol. 26, September–October, 1970, pp. 33–38.
    Direct diversification through individual stocks vs. indirect diversification through mutual funds.

Wagner, W. H., and Lau, S. C. "The Effect of Diversification on Risk." *Financial Analysts Journal*, vol. 27, November–December, 1971, pp. 48–53.

DIVIDEND VALUE APPROACH

Molodovsky, N. "Common Stock Valuation." *Financial Analysts Journal*, vol. 21, March–April, 1965, pp. 104–123.

Pike, J. R., and Haugen, R. "Prospective Market Price as an Element in Stock Analysis—a Rationale and Method." *Trusts and Estates*, vol. 106, February 1967, pp. 131–136.
    Prospective market price as determined by expected dividends.

Seligman, D. "Why the Stock Market Acts That Way; Some New Theories about the Intrinsic Worth of Common Stocks. . . ." *Fortune*, vol. 74, November 1966, pp. 154–157.

DIVIDENDS. *See* Income Stocks

DOLLAR AVERAGING

"Averaging Out the Ups and Downs in Stock Prices." *Changing Times*, vol. 26, April 1972, p. 22.

"Dollar Averaging; Investment Tool." *Financial World*, vol. 126, August 31, 1966, p. 11.

"Dollar-Averaging Method Eliminates Timing Risk." *Magazine of Wall Street*, vol. 122, May 25, 1968, pp. 16–18.

"How Dollar Cost Averaging Pays." *Industry Week*, vol. 167, September 21, 1970, p. 34.

"How to Out-Perform the Market." *Financial World*, vol. 132, October 22, 1969, p. 50.

"New Look at Dollar-Cost-Averaging." *Financial World*, vol. 134, September 9, 1970, p. 18.

Rhodabarger, T. D. "How to Time Your Way to Bigger Mutual Fund Profits. Investment-Timing Plans Make Market Fluctuations Work to Your Advantage. Here are Three of Them to Choose From." *Medical Economics*, vol. 49, June 19, 1972, pp. 91–109.
    Dollar averaging, 10 percent filter, and seven-step bond-stock plan.

Sargent, D. R. "How to Profit from Market Swings. Even if Your Crystal Ball is Clouded, You Can Turn Stock Price Dips and Surges to Your Advantage by Following a Systematic Plan of Dollar Averaging. . . ." *Medical Economics*, vol. 45, April 1, 1968, pp. 84–89.

DOUBLE TOPS AND BOTTOMS

Markstein, D. L. "Opportunity in Double." *Burroughs Clearing House*, vol. 54, May 1970, p. 16.

DOW THEORY

Markstein, D. L. "Dow Theory—Does It Really Work?" *Burroughs Clearing House*, vol. 53, June 1969, p. 16.

Russell, R. "Leg Upward? Bear Market Rallies, Says a Dow Theorist, Can Be Tricky." *Barron's*, vol. 46, September 5, 1966, p. 5.

Russell, R. "Track of the Bear; a Dow Theorist Traces the Pattern of Market Declines." *Barron's*, vol. 45, July 26, 1965, pp. 9–10.

DUAL FUNDS

"Enthusiastic Reception Indicated for New Dual-Purpose Funds." *Trusts and Estates*, vol. 106, February 1967, pp. 144–145.

Gentry, J. A., and Pike, J. R. "Dual Funds Revisited." *Financial Analysts Journal*, vol. 24, March–April, 1968, pp. 149–157.

Glenn, A. "Two Mints in One? Dual Funds Promise to Double Both Risk and Reward." *Barron's*, vol. 47, January 23, 1967, p. 5.

Johnston, G. S. "Are Dual-Purpose Funds Contradictory in Nature?" *Commercial and Financial Chronicle*, vol. 207, January 4, 1968, p. 51.

Johnston, G. S., Curley, M. L., and McIndoe, R. A. "Are Shares of Dual-Purpose Funds Undervalued?" *Financial Analysts Journal*, November–December, 1968, pp. 157–163.

Lieberman, M. D. "Assured Pay-Off; It Leads Attraction to Deep-Discount Dual Funds." *Barron's*, vol. 52, November 6, 1972, p. 9.

Loomis, C. J. "Two for the Price of One." *Fortune*, vol. 75, February, 1967, pp. 201–202.

Shelton, J. P., Brigham, E. F., and Hofflander, A. E. "An Evaluation and Appraisal of Dual Funds." *Financial Analysts Journal*, vol. 23, May–June, 1967, pp. 131–139.

Stevenson, R. A. "Dual Funds Discounts—a New Technical Indicator?" *Commercial and Financial Chronicle*, vol. 210, September 18, 1969, pp. 898–899.

ELLIOT WAVE PRINCIPLE

Collins, C. J. "Market Ebb Tide: Elliott's Wave Theory Suggests That the Lows are Still to Come." *Barron's*, vol. 50, April 27, 1970, p. 5.

EMOTIONS OF INVESTORS. *See* Psychology

FEDERAL RESERVE BOARD ACTIONS. *See* Money Supply and Stock Prices; Three-Steps-and-a-Stumble Theory

FILTER TECHNIQUE

Fama, E. F. "The Behavior of Stock Market Prices." *Journal of Business*, vol. 38, January, 1965, pp. 34–105.

   Regards filter technique as unprofitable.

Fama, E. F., and Blume, M. E. "Filter Rules and Stock Market Trading." *Journal of Business*, vol. 39, January 1966, pt. 2, pp. 226–241.

Gould, A., and Buchsbaum, M. "Filter Approach Using Earnings Relatives." *Financial Analysts Journal*, vol. 25, November–December, 1969, p. 61.

Kisor, M., and Messner, V. A. "Filter Approach and Earnings Forecasts." *Financial Analysts Journal*, vol. 25, January–February, 1969, pp. 109–115.

Peck, L. G. "Critique of the Filter Technique." *Financial Analysts Journal*, vol. 22, May–June, 1966, p. 156.

Trent, E. "The Trent Formula; How to Maximize Profits, Minimize Losses, in the Stock Market." *Barron's*, vol. 52, November 20, 1972, p. 9.

   Use of the 12½ percent price filter with Dow-Jones averages.

FLAGS AND PENNANTS

Markstein, David L. "Flags and Pennants." *Burroughs Clearing House*, vol. 55, January 1971, pp. 16–17.

FOREIGN INVESTMENTS

"Easy Way to Buy Stocks in Foreign Firms. (American Depository Receipts.)" *Changing Times*, vol. 23, March 1969, p. 46.

Fountain, J. "American Depository Receipts and Their Uses." *Financial Analysts Journal*, vol. 25, January–February, 1969, pp. 15–20.

FORMULA PLANS

Grunewald, A. E., and R. C. Klemkosky. "If You Believe Growth is Dead, Try the Formula Timing Plan." *Michigan State University Business Topics*, vol. 20, Summer 1972, pp. 59–65.

Rhodabarger, T. D. "How to Time Your Way to Bigger Mutual Fund Profits. Investment-Timing Plans Make Market Fluctuations Work to Your Advantage. Here are Three of Them to Choose from." *Medical Economics*, vol. 49, June 19, 1972, pp. 91–109.

> Dollar averaging, 10 percent filter, and seven-step bond-stock plan.

FUNDAMENTAL ANALYSIS. *See* specific subjects, such as Growth Stocks; Price-Earnings Ratio; Undervalued Securities; and so forth.

GENERAL MOTORS INDICATOR

Stovall, R. H. "Directional Signal; What's Good for General Motors is Good for the Market." *Barron's*, vol. 49, October 27, 1969, p. 9.

Stovall, R. H. "GM Bellwether." *Magazine of Wall Street*, vol. 121, December 9, 1967, p. 32.

GLAMOUR STOCKS. *See* Growth Stocks; High Velocity Stocks

GOVERNMENT BONDS

Connell, C. A. "Time for Government Bonds?" *Dun's Review*, vol. 94, July 1969, pp. 41–42.

Edwards, M. B. "Payment of Estate Tax with U.S. Bonds: Still a Useful Device with a Potential Trap." *Journal of Taxation*, vol. 37, September 1972, pp. 141–143.

Gaines, T. C. "Maximizing Profits in Treasuries and Municipals." *Commercial and Financial Chronicle*, vol. 209, March 13, 1969, pp. 1144–1145.

Kudish, D. J. "Bond Primer for the Equity-Oriented Fiduciary." *Trusts & Estates*, vol. 110, March 1971, pp. 200–203.

Reierson, R. L. "The Bond Market and the Investor." *Trusts & Estates*, vol. 108, March 1969, pp. 290–294.

Spencer, M. M. "How Tax Considerations Enhance Investment Opportunities in Government Bonds." *Journal of Taxation*, vol. 27, September 1967, pp. 150–154.

GROWTH STOCKS

Andrews, J. R. "The Fundamental Case for Investing in Growth." *Financial Analysts Journal*, vol. 26, November–December, 1970, pp. 55–64.
Hypothetical projections are given to 1980.

Babcock, G. C. "Concept of Sustainable Growth." *Financial Analysts Journal*, vol. 26, May–June, 1970, pp. 108–114.

Babson, D. L. "Select Growth Stocks for Higher Total Return." *Commercial and Financial Chronicle*, vol. 215, May 4, 1972, p. 1417.
Growth stocks as opposed to income stocks.

Brigham, E. F., and Pappas, J. L. "Duration of Growth, Changes in Growth Rates, and Corporate Share Prices." *Financial Analysts Journal*, vol. 22, May–June, 1966, pp. 157–162.

Cragg, J. G., and Malkiel, B. G. "Consensus and Accuracy of Some Predictions of the Growth of Corporate Earnings." *Journal of Finance*, vol. 23, March 1968, pp. 67–84.

Graber, D. E. "Real and Illusory Earnings Growth." *Financial Analysts Journal*, vol. 25, March–April, 1969, pp. 52–54.

Harvey, C. W., and Bond, C. C. "How to Catch a Fast-Growth Stock Ascending. Two Officers of a Successful Growth Fund Reveal the Criteria that Help Its Management Spot Emerging High Fliers. . . ." *Medical Economics*, vol. 48, February 1, 1971, pp. 81–86.
Authors are officers of T. Rowe Price New Horizons Fund.

Huang, S. S. C. "Study of the Performance of Rapid Growth Stocks; Investment Analysis." *Financial Analysts Journal*, vol. 21, January–February, 1965, pp. 58–59.

Jones, C. H. "Growth Rate Appraiser—a Tool for Portfolio Managers." *Financial Analysts Journal*, vol. 24, September–October, 1968, pp. 109–111.

Levin, J. "Growth Rates: the Bigger They Come the Harder They Fall." *Financial Analysts Journal*, vol. 28, November–December, 1972, pp. 71–77.

Levin, J. "Growth Stock Projections; How Accurate Are They." *Commercial and Financial Chronicle*, vol. 204, December 29, 1966, pp. 2314–2315.

Mao, J. C. T. "Valuation of Growth Stocks; the Investment Opportunities Approach." *Journal of Finance*, vol. 21, March 1966, pp. 95–102.

Miller, E. K. "The Case for Growth Stocks." *Commercial and Financial Chronicle*, vol. 215, February 17, 1972, p. 571.

Milne, R. D. "Mathematics of Growth." *Financial Analysts Journal*, vol. 25, January–February, 1969, pp. 11–14; March–April, 1969, pp. 13–15; May–June, 1969, pp. 13–16; July-August, 1969, pp. 13–15; September–October, 1969, pp. 13–15; November–December, 1969, pp. 12–14.

>   Simplified presentation of least-squares techniques for measuring earnings growth trends.

Molodovsky, N. "Selecting Growth Stocks." *Financial Analysts Journal*, vol. 24, September–October, 1968, pp. 103–106.

O'Neill, C. R. "Investing in Growth Stocks: There Are Only Two Things Which Can Change the Price of a Stock—Either a Change in Earnings or a Change in Price-Earnings Ratio." *Trusts & Estates*, vol. 112, January 1973, pp. 34–35.

Shapiro, M. "Great Crash in Growth Stocks." *Dun's*, vol. 97, January 1971, pp. 30–32.

Shapiro, M. "Trading in Tulips? An Old Street Hand Appraises the Mania for Growth Stocks." *Barron's*, vol. 48, August 26, 1968, p. 1.

Smilen, K. B., and Safian, K. "Growth Stocks vs. Cyclicals; Their Separate Trends Are the Basis of a New Analytical Tool." *Barron's*, vol. 46, July 25, 1966, p. 9.

Wendt, P. F. "Current Growth Stock Valuation Methods." *Financial Analysts Journal*, vol. 21, March–April, 1965, pp. 91–103.

HEAD-AND-SHOULDERS FORMATION

Markstein, D. L. "Head and Shoulders: Foreteller of Change." *Burroughs Clearing House*, vol. 54, April 1970, pp. 19–20.

HEDGE FUNDS

"Funds that Use Short Sale Tactics; Smart Wall Street Investors Are Cutting Their Risk by Going into Hedge Funds." *Business Week*, April 2, 1966, p. 108.

"Hedge-Fund Miseries." *Fortune*, vol. 83, May 1971, pp. 269–270.

"Hedge Funds—New Investment Force." *Financial World*, vol. 131, June 18, 1969, pp. 10–11.

"Heyday of the Hedge Funds." *Dun's Review*, vol. 19, January 1968, pp. 23–25.

Lenzner, R. "Where Have All the Hedge Funds Gone?" *Institutional Investor*, vol. 6, February 1972, pp. 34–37.

Loomis, C. J. "Hard Times Come to the Hedge Funds." *Fortune*, vol. 81, January 1970, pp. 100–103.

Sosnoff, M. T. "Hedge Fund Management: New Respectability for Short Selling." *Financial Analysts Journal*, vol. 22, July–August, 1966, pp. 105–108.

HEDGING

Edwards, R. G. "Hedging Technique to Make the Closed-Ends More Attractive." *Commercial and Financial Chronicle*, vol. 205, June 1, 1967, p. 2141.

Kogan, D. P. "Convertible Hedge: It's a Useful Way to Limit Risk in a Declining Market." *Barron's*, vol. 46, June 27, 1966, p. 9.

Turov, D. "Riskless Reward? Skillful Traders May Reap One by Hedging in Convertible Bonds." *Barron's*, vol. 51, March 22, 1971, p. 9.

HIGH VELOCITY STOCKS

"Blue Chips vs. Glamours." *Financial World*, vol. 132, October 8, 1969, pp. 3–4.

Mathews, C. "What Makes a Glamour Stock?" *Dun's Review*, vol. 90, October 1967, pp. 36–37.

INCOME STOCKS

Dulan, H. A. "Shifting from Diversification to Yield Emphasis in Common Stock Portfolios." *Financial Analysts Journal*, vol. 21, July–August, 1965, pp. 98–108.

   Seeking relatively high dividend income is advantageous.

Levin, J. "Achieve Growth Goal with Quality Income Stocks." *Commercial and Financial Chronicle*, vol. 215, May 4, 1972, p. 1417.

Income stocks, as opposed to growth stocks.

Levin, J. "For Long Term, Growth, Buy Income Stocks." *Commercial and Financial Chronicle*, vol. 207, January 18, 1968, pp. 254–255.

Levin, J. "Many Happy Returns; in Recent Years, a Study Shows, Income Stocks Have Outperformed Growth Issues." *Barron's*, vol. 45, August 16, 1965, p. 5.

Whitmore, F. "Capital Gains Mania vs. Power of the Dividend." *Commercial and Financial Chronicle*, vol. 208, November 21, 1968, section 2, pp. 34–36.

Whitmore, F. "Yield-Dividend Income Approach for Maximizing Investment Return." *Commercial and Financial Chronicle*, vol. 207, February 29, 1968, p. 873.

INCOME TAX. *See* Tax Transactions

INSIDER TRANSACTIONS

Carniol, N. M. "Can Insider Transactions Be Used as a Guide to Market Performance?". *Magazine of Wall Street*, vol. 124, August 30, 1969, pp. 19–20.

"Inside the Insiders Report." *Forbes*, vol. 101, March 1, 1968, pp. 41–42.

Shaw, R. B. "A Timely and Revealing Study of Insider Buying and Selling." *Magazine of Wall Street*, vol. 116, March 20, 1965, pp. 16–19.

INSTITUTIONAL INVESTING

Biel, H. H. "Why Institutional Investors Control the Stock Market's Future Course. *Commercial and Financial Chronicle*, vol. 206, July 27, 1967, p. 337.

Cohen, M. F. "Growing Institutionalization of the Securities Market." *Commercial and Financial Chronicle*, vol. 205, section 2, January 12, 1967, pp. 16–17.

Cohen, M. F. "Institutional Investing and the Securities Market." *Commercial and Financial Chronicle*, vol. 204, December 29, 1966, p. 2306.

"The Computer as a Research Tool: a Tabulation of Services Available to Institutions." *Institutional Investor*, vol. 5, October 1971, pp. 37–48.

Lists 106 services: name, type, year started, description, and cost.

Gentry, J. A. "Do Institutional Investors Buy and Sell Common Stock with Similar Characteristics?" *Quarterly Review of Economics & Business*, vol. 8, Winter 1968, pp. 21–29.

Geyer, C. T. "A Primer on Institutional Trading." *Financial Analysts Journal*, vol. 25, March–April, 1969, pp. 16–25.

Kirk, J. "A Critical Look at the Institutional Investor." *Banking*, vol. 60, March 1968, p. 8.

Mennis, E. A. "New Trends in Institutional Investing." *Financial Analysts Journal*, vol. 24, July–August, 1968, pp. 133–138.

"Power of Institutional Investors." *Fortune*, vol. 72, December 1965, p. 233.

Welles, C. "The Public: Who Needs 'Em?" *Institutional Investor*, vol. 6, March 1972, pp. 33–51. ("The Little Man Returns, or So It Seems," pp. 34–36; "How the Street Is Putting the Little Man out of the Market," pp. 37–41; "What Happens When the Little Man Is Gone from the Stock Market for Good?" pp. 42–51.)

West, R. R. "Institutional Trading and the Changing Stock Market." *Financial Analysts Journal*, vol. 27, May–June, 1971, pp. 17–24.

West, S. "Weep Not for the Little Man." *Institutional Investor*, vol. 6, June 1972, pp. 76–77.

Reply to C. Welles, above.

INTRINSIC VALUE. *See* Dividend Value Approach

INVESTMENT ADVISORY SERVICES

Cheney, H. L. "How Good Are Subscription Investment Advisory Services?" *Financial Executive*, vol. 37, November 1969, pp. 30–35.

Hardy, C. C. "For Market Forecasters, It Was a Pretty Good Year; Most High Priced Stock Letters Foresaw 1972's Big Upswing, but Those Relying on Economic Fundamentals Read the Future Best." *Money*, vol. 2, February 1973, pp. 75–78.

> Includes general discussion of advisory services.

Pascoe, J. "Investment Advisory Services: Which Ones Were Right?" *Medical Economics*, vol. 48, January 18, 1971, pp. 94–100.

> Ten popular, published services are named and individually analyzed about advice given in 1968 and 1970.

Schutzer, A. I. "Mutual Fund Advisory Services: Can They Make You a Winner? A New Study Shows that They Can Indeed Pick the Big Performers. . . ." *Medical Economics*, vol. 49, October 23, 1972, pp. 183–192.

> Eight published services are named and individually analyzed.

Thomas D. L. "Thundering Bull; the Market for Investment Advisory Services Is Booming." *Barron's*, vol. 52, September 4, 1972, p. 3.

> Various services are described.

Zweig, M. E. "Darts, Anyone? As Stock Pickers, Market Seers, the Pros Fall Short." *Barron's*, vol. 52, February 19, 1973, p. 22

INVESTMENT CLUBS

"Investment Clubs: Way to Buy Stocks for $10 a Month." *Changing Times*, vol. 22, October 1968, pp. 25–28.

Nicholson, G. A., and O'Hara, T. E. "Investment Clubs." *Financial Analysts Journal*, vol. 24, May–June, 1968, pp. 141–146.

INVESTMENT COMPANIES

Brignoli, R. J. "Irrationality: the Case of the Closed-End Fund Discount." *Commercial and Financial Chronicle*, vol. 216, November 30, 1972, p. 1765.

Edwards, R. G. "Hedging Technique to Make the Closed-Ends More Attractive." *Commercial and Financial Chronicle*, vol. 205, June 1, 1967, p. 2141.

Leuthold, S. "Reward vs. Risk; Both Must Be Weighed in Choosing Professional Money Management." *Barron's*, vol. 51, February 15, 1971, p. 9.

Madrick, J. G. "The Negative-Load Funds; Priced Well Below the Value of Their Assets, Many Closed-End Funds Combine a Good Growth Record with Healthy Current Yields." *Money*, vol. 2, March 1973, pp. 43–48.

Pratt, E. J. "Myths Associated with Closed-End Investment Company Discounts." *Financial Analysts Journal*, vol. 22, July–August, 1966, pp. 79–82.

Treynor, J. L. "How to Rate Management of Investment Funds." *Harvard Business Review*, vol. 43, January–February, 1965, pp. 63–75.

LEVERAGE

"Maximizing Investment Potentials through High-Leverage Situations." *Magazine of Wall Street*, vol. 127, November 21, 1970, pp. 12–15.

Murphy, J. E. "Effect of Leverage on Profitability, Growth, and Market Valuation of Common Stock." *Financial Analysts Journal*, vol. 24, July–August, 1968, pp. 121–123.

Nelson, P. G. "I Mortgaged My Home to Speculate." *Medical Economics*, vol. 45, October 28, 1968, pp. 179–187.
　　Physician used new mortgage on home as source of funds for speculation.

Stovall, R. H. "Science, Leverage, and the Aggressive Investor." *Magazine of Wall Street*, vol. 121, February 3, 1968, p. 34.

LITERATURE OF INVESTING. *See* Books (Literature)

LONG-TERM INVESTING. *See* Buy-and-Hold

LOSSES

Brussel, J. A. "Speculating in Mutual Funds Murdered Me . . . Wound Up Taking More than a Plunge . . . Took a Bath." *Medical Economics*, vol. 47, March 30, 1970, p. 122.

Jen, F. C., and Shick, R. A. "Optimal Tax Loss Strategy for a Portfolio." *Trusts and Estates*, vol. 108, September 1969, pp. 905–910.

Reid, R. A. "How I Ran $35,000. into a Shoestring . . . Read This—and Open a Savings Account." *Medical Economics*, vol. 49, March 13, 1972, pp. 81–85.

White, F. P. "I'm a Two-Time Loser on SBICs." *Medical Economics*, vol. 45, May 27, 1968, p. 135.
> A doctor's disaster in publicly-traded SBICs.

LOW-PRICED STOCKS

"High Value in Low-Priced Stocks Target of the Small Investor." *Magazine of Wall Street*, vol. 120, June 10, 1967, pp. 12–15.

Merjos, A. "Strictly for Swingers; Low-Priced Stocks Rise and Fall Faster than Most." *Barron's*, vol. 47, February 27, 1967, p. 5.

Merjos, A. "Swinging Index; *Barron's* 20 Low-Priced Stocks Tend to Go to Extremes." *Barron's*, vol. 50, November 23, 1970, p. 9.

"Why Low-Priced Stocks Need Not Be Dangerous Duds." *Magazine of Wall Street*, vol. 123, March 1, 1969, pp. 13–15.

MARGIN

Goldberg, W. "Stock Market's Reaction to Margin Changes." *Trusts & Estates*, vol. 106, November 1967, pp. 1067–1068.

"How Traders Beat the 70 per cent Margin; Unregulated Loan Companies Are Reappearing." *Business Week*, April 8, 1967, pp. 51–52.

Moore, T. G. "On Margin; a Scholar Explodes Some Persistent Myths." *Barron's*, vol. 46, May 16, 1966, p. 1.
> Favors the elimination of legal margin requirements.

"Personal Business." *Business Week*, April 30, 1966, pp. 141–142.
> Use of margin by individual investor.

"Trading on Margin." *Financial World*, vol. 138, December 6, 1972, pp. 3–4.

MECHANICAL INVESTMENT FORMULAS. *See* Filter Technique; Formula Plans; Moving Average; Trend Following

MONEY SUPPLY AND STOCK PRICES

Barone, R. "The Use of Money in Stock Price Models." *Business Economics*, vol. 7, September 1972, pp. 23-26.

Biggs, B. M. "Money Supply Analysis is a Useful Market Tool." *Barron's*, vol. 51, October 11, 1971, pp. 14-15.

Chadwick, N. S. "A Little Known Way to Help Predict Stock Market Trends." *Banking*, vol. 75, October 1967, pp. 8-10.
    Use of total loans and investments of commercial banks as a stock market indicator.

"An Econometric Stab at Stock Forecasting; Experts Disagree about the Basic Concepts, and Their Predictions Diverge." *Business Week*, May 29, 1971, pp. 36-38.
    Models constructed by M. W. Keran and A. G. Shilling disagree somewhat.

Fanning, J. E. "A System for Forecasting the Market." *Financial Analysts Journal*, vol. 27, September-October, 1971, pp. 23-26.

Homa, K. E., and Jaffee, D. M. "Supply of Money and Common Stock Prices." *Journal of Finance*, vol. 26, December 1971, pp. 1045-1066.

Keran, M. W. "Expectations, Money, and the Stock Market." *Federal Reserve Bank of St. Louis Review*, vol. 53, January 1971, pp. 16-31.

Keran, M. W. "A Structural Model of the Stock Market." *Business Economics*, vol. 6, September 1971, pp. 23-28.

LeRoy, S. F. "Explaining Stock Prices." *Federal Reserve Bank of Kansas City Monthly Review*, March 1972, pp. 10-19.

Leveson, S. M. "Money and Stock Prices." *Business Economics*, vol. 3, Summer 1968, p. 40.
    Changes in money supply not reliable as predictor of stock prices.

Malkiel, B. G., and Quandt, R. E. "The Supply of Money and Common Stock Prices: Comment." *Journal of Finance*, vol. 27, September 1972, pp. 921-926.
    Comment on article by K. E. Homa and D. M. Jaffee, above. Malkiel and Quandt state that real life investing that made exclusive use of econometric models would be extremely hazardous.

Mascia, J. S. "Monetary Change and Equity Values: Do Changes in the Supply of Money Contribute to More Accurate Stock Market Forecasting?" *The Bankers Magazine*, vol. 152, Summer 1969, pp. 51–60.

Palmer, M. "Money Supply, Portfolio Adjustments, and Stock Prices." *Financial Analysts Journal*, vol. 26, July–August, 1970, pp. 19–22.

Poole, A. C. "Relationship of Money Market to Stock Market and the Economy." *Commercial and Financial Chronicle*, vol. 204, September 8, 1966, p. 865.

Rudolph, J. A. "The Money Supply and Common Stock Prices." *Financial Analysts Journal*, vol. 28, March–April, 1972, pp. 19–25.
> States that there are short-term correlations between changes in money supply and stock prices.

Seligman, B. "Money Supply/Stock Prices." *Magazine of Wall Street*, vol. 123, November 9, 1968, p. 38.

Seligman, B. "Tight Money and Its Effect on Common Stock Prices." *Magazine of Wall Street*, vol. 122, May 25, 1968, p. 37.

Wright, J. W. "Money Supply—a Key to Stock Market Predictions." *Banking*, vol. 63, January 1971, pp. 51–52.

MONTHLY INVESTMENT PLAN

Slatter, J. "No Get-Rich-Quick Scheme; Monthly Investment Plan Has Fared about as Well as the Averages." *Barron's*, vol. 46, August 29, 1966, p. 5.

MOST ACTIVE STOCKS

West, F. R. "Negative Indicator; the 20 Most Active Stocks Point to Further Market Declines." *Barron's*, vol. 50, April 6, 1970, p. 5.

West, F. R. "New Market Tool? Strength or Weakness in the Most Active List is Often Meaningful." *Barron's*, vol. 49, April 28, 1969, p. 5.

MOVING AVERAGE

James, F. E. "Monthly Moving Averages—an Effective Investment Tool?" *Journal of Financial and Quantitative Analysis*, vol. 3, September 1968, pp. 315–326.

    Monthly moving averages not effective.

Van Horne, J. C., and Parker, G. G. C. "The Random Walk Theory: an Empirical Test." *Financial Analysts Journal*, vol. 23, November–December, 1967, pp. 87–92.

    Moving average trading rules not profitable.

Van Horne, J. C., and Parker, G. G. C. "Technical Trading Rules: a Comment." *Financial Analysts Journal*, vol. 24, July–August, 1968, pp. 128–131.

    Weighted moving average trading rules not profitable.

MUNICIPAL BONDS

Bratter, H. "Tax-Exempt Municipals." *Banking*, vol. 61, September 1968, pp. 53–54.

Gaines, T. C. "Maximizing Profits in Treasuries and Municipals." *Commercial and Financial Chronicle*, vol. 209, March 13, 1969, pp. 1144–1145.

Harries, B. W. "Standard & Poor's Corporation New Policy on Rating Municipal Bonds." *Financial Analysts Journal*, vol. 24, May–June, 1968, pp. 68–71.

Hastie, K. L. "Determinants of Municipal Bond Yields." *Journal of Financial and Quantitative Analysis*, vol. 7, June 1972, pp. 1729–1748.

Horton, J. J. "Statistical Rating Index for Municipal Bonds." *Financial Analysts Journal*, vol. 25, March–April, 1969, pp. 72–75.

Kirk, J. "What's What in the World of Municipal Bond Ratings." *Banking*, vol. 60, August 1967, p. 8.

Madrick, J. G. "The Munificent Municipals: Robust Returns, Tax Free, Make Them Worthy Rivals to Other Bonds and Stocks. Even for Middle-Bracket Investors." *Money*, vol. 1, December 1972, pp. 65–70.

Packer, S. B. "Municipal Bond Ratings." *Financial Analysts Journal*, vol. 24, July–August, 1968, pp. 93–97.

Reilly, J. F. "Outlook for Municipal Bonds." *Financial Analysts Journal*, vol. 23, September–October, 1967, pp. 93–95.

Riehle, R. C. "Moody's Municipal Ratings." *Financial Analysts Journal*, vol. 24, May–June, 1968, pp. 71–73.

Walsh, W. F. "Municipal Bonds; Some Portfolio Strategems." *Burroughs Clearing House*, vol. 53, May 1969, pp. 26–27.

MUTUAL FUND LIQUIDITY

Slatter, J. "Erratic Market Guide; Mutual Fund Liquidity Ratio Sometimes Gets Its Signals Crossed." *Barron's*, vol. 50, December 14, 1970, p. 5.

Slatter, J. "New Market Guide? Mutual Fund Liquidity, the Record Suggests, Often Calls the Turn." *Barron's*, vol. 47, February 6, 1967, p. 5.

MUTUAL FUNDS

Bogle, J. C. "Mutual Fund Performance Evaluation." *Financial Analysts Journal*, vol. 26, November–December, 1970, pp. 25–33.

Brussel, J. A. "Speculating in Mutual Funds Murdered Me . . . Wound Up Taking More than a Plunge . . . Took a Bath." *Medical Economics*, vol. 47, March 30, 1970, p. 122.

Cohen, K. J., and Pogue, J. A. "Some Comments Concerning Mutual Fund versus Random Portfolio Performance." *Journal of Business*, vol. 41, April 1968, pp. 180–190.

Day, J. "Mutual Funds—Comments of a Seasoned Observer." *Magazine of Wall Street*, vol. 124, April 26, 1969, p. 22.

Day, J. "Shaken Faith in Mutual Funds." *Business Management*, vol. 40, April 1971, p. 24.

Ellis, Charles D. "The Route to the Right Mutual Fund; This Bumpy Year for Funds Hasn't Dented Their Virtues. Here's How to Pick Wisely—and Sidestep Some Traps." *Money*, vol. 1, November 1972, pp. 65–68.

Friend, I., and Vickers, D. "Portfolio Selection and Investment Performance." *Journal of Finance*, vol. 20, September 1965, pp. 391–415.
    Performance of mutual funds.

Glenn, A. "Bought, Not Sold; No-Load Funds Have Become Increasingly Popular with Investors." *Barron's*, vol. 51, May 24, 1971, p. 3.

"Invest in Bonds the Mutual Fund Way." *Changing Times*, vol. 26, July 1972, p. 16.
    Mutual bond funds.

Jensen, M. C. "Performance of Mutual Funds in the Period 1945–1964." *Journal of Finance*, vol. 23, May 1968, pp. 389–416.

Layne, A. A. "To Calm a Jittery Portfolio, Buy Bond Funds; by Following These Guidelines, You Can Add the Stability, Income, and Safety that Your Present Investments May Lack." *Medical Economics*, vol. 49, October 9, 1972, pp. 88–93.

Leuthold, S. "Reward vs. Risk; Both Must Be Weighed in Choosing Professional Money Management." *Barron's*, vol. 51, February 15, 1971, p. 9.
    Volatility as related to the performance of mutual funds.

Leuthold S. "What's the Score? You Can't Always Tell from Mutual Fund Performance Records." *Barron's*, vol. 51, February 1, 1971, p. 3.

Levy, H., and Sarnat, M. "Investment Performance in an Imperfect Securities Market and the Case for Mutual Funds." *Financial Analysts Journal*, vol. 28, March 1972, pp. 77–81.
    Mutual funds reduce risk for the small investor.

Levy, R. A. "What Price Performance? Most Mutual Funds, a Study Shows, Take Excessive Risks." *Barron's*, vol. 51, July 5, 1971, pp. 11–14.
    Rates 140 leading funds according to volatility-adjusted performance.

Madrick, J. G. "The Bond Funds: When the Hare Slows Down, Put Your Money on the Tortoise." *Money*, vol. 1, October 1972, pp. 99–100.
    Mutual bond funds.

Mills, H. D. "On the Measurement of Fund Performance." *Journal of Finance*, vol. 25, December 1970, pp. 1125–1131.

"Mutual Funds Pay Off for the Patient." *Magazine of Wall Street*, vol. 125, January 31, 1970, pp. 9–12.

Rhodabarger, T. D. "How to Time Your Way to Bigger Mutual Fund Profits. Investment-Timing Plans Make Market Fluctuations Work to Your Advantage. Here are Three of Them to Choose From." *Medical Economics*, vol. 49, June 19, 1972, pp. 91–109.
    Dollar averaging, 10 percent filter, and seven-step bond-stock plan.

Robinson, P. "Some Pointers on Evaluating Mutual Funds." *Burroughs Clearing House*, vol. 53, December 1968, pp. 30–31.

Schutzer, A. I. "How to Pick the Best-Performing Mutual Funds; You Can Replace Yesterday's Winners with Tomorrow's by Using the Guidelines Developed by Arthur Lipper III . . ." *Medical Economics*, vol. 46, December 22, 1969, pp. 83–91.

Schutzer, A. I. "Mutual Fund Advisory Services: Can They Make You a Winner? A New Study Shows That They Can Indeed Pick the Big Performers. . . ." *Medical Economics*, vol. 49, October 23, 1972, pp. 183–192.
    Eight published services are named and individually analyzed.

Sharpe, W. F. "Mutual Fund Performance." *Journal of Business*, vol. 39, January 1966, pt. 2, pp. 119–138.
    On the measurement of performance.

Stauffer, C. H., and Vogel, R. C. "Parameters of Mutual Fund Performance." *Business Economics*, vol. 6, September 1971, pp. 58–63.

Treynor, J. L., and Mazuy, K. K. "Can Mutual Funds Outguess the Market." *Harvard Business Review*, vol. 44, July–August, 1966, pp. 131–136.

Treynor, J. L. "How to Rate Management of Investment Funds." *Harvard Business Review*, vol. 43, January–February, 1965, pp. 63–75.

"What Ails the Mutual Fund Industry: a Safe Place for Small Investors Became a Playground for Speculators." *Business Week*, March 3, 1973, pp. 48–52.

"What You Should Know about the Mutual Funds." *Magazine of Wall Street,* vol. 121, March 16, 1968, pp. 9–12.

Williamson, J. P. "Measurement and Forecasting of Mutual Fund Performance: Choosing an Investment Strategy." *Financial Analysts Journal,* vol. 28, November–December, 1972, pp. 78–80.

NEW ISSUES

Harsham, P. "What it Takes to Speculate Profitably in New Stocks: New Issues are Riskier than Ever, but the Tips of a Doctor Who's Made $10,000 a Month on Them can Save You Some Lumps." *Medical Economics,* vol. 50, February 19, 1973, pp. 215–224.

McDonald, J. G., and Fisher, A. K. "New Issue Stock Price Behavior." *Journal of Finance,* vol. 27, March 1972, pp. 97–102.
> Initial, short-term behavior is of no predictive significance.

Reilly, F. K. "Further Evidence on Short-Run Results for New Issue Investors." *Journal of Financial and Quantitative Analysis,* vol. 8, January 1973, pp. 83–90.
> New issues show short-run price appreciation but are difficult to acquire at offering prices.

Reilly, F. K., and Hatfield, K. "Investor Experience with New Stock Issues." *Financial Analysts Journal,* vol. 25, September–October, 1969, pp. 73–80.
> New issues are generally undervalued at offering prices.

"Should You Invest in New Stock Issues? Is This a Road to Quick Profit? How Do You Tell Winners from Dogs?" *Changing Times,* vol. 26, September 1972, pp. 24–27.

Stoll, H. R., and Curley, A. J. "Small Business and the New Issues Market for Equities." *Journal of Financial and Quantitative Analysis,* vol. 5, September 1970, pp. 309–322.
> New issues show short-run price appreciation.

ODD-LOT SHORT SALES

Kisor, M., and Niederhoffer, V. "Odd-Lot Short Sales Ratio: It Signals a Market Rise." *Barron's,* vol. 49, September 1, 1969, p. 8.

Ludovici, A. "Odd-Lot Short Sales Presages Market Rally." *Commercial and Financial Chronicle*, vol. 204, October 20, 1966, p. 1388.

ODD-LOT THEORY

Drew, G. A. "Clarification of the Odd-Lot Theory." *Financial Analysts Journal*, vol. 23, September–October, 1967, pp. 107–108.
>   Reply to T. J. Kewley and R. A. Stevenson, and a defense of odd-lot theory.

Drew. G. A. "Little Men, What Now? Odd-Lot Figures Point to a Further Rise in Stocks." *Barron's*, vol. 51, February 22, 1971, p. 5.

"Is the Odd-Lotter Always Wrong?" *Business Week*, May 6, 1967, p. 147.

Kaish, S. "Odd Lot Profit and Loss Performance." *Financial Analysts Journal*, vol. 25, September–October, 1969, pp. 83–89.

Kewley, T. J., and Stevenson, R. A. "Odd-Lot Theory as Revealed by Purchase and Sale Statistics for Individual Stocks." *Financial Analysts Journal*, vol. 23, September–October, 1967, pp. 103–106.
>   Odd-lot theory of little value.

Kewley, T. J., and Stevenson, R. A. "The Odd-Lot Theory for Individual Stocks: a Reply." *Financial Analysts Journal*, vol. 25, January–February, 1969, pp. 99–104.
>   Reply to G. A. Drew.

Markstein, D. L. "Is the Public Ever Right about Stocks?" *Burroughs Clearing House*, vol. 53, August 1969, pp. 20–21.

Slatter, J. "Lambs in the Street; Odd-Lotters Are No Better at Picking Stocks than at Calling Turns." *Barron's*, vol. 46, January 31, 1966, p. 5.

Slatter, J. "True to Form: Odd-Lotters Are No Better at Selection than at Timing." *Barron's*, vol. 47, February 20, 1967, p. 5.

"Strange Case of the Odd-Lotters." *Financial World*, vol. 135, March 3, 1971, pp. 3–4.

Wu, H. K. "Odd-Lot Trading in the Stock Market and Its Market Impact." *Journal of Financial and Quantitative Analysis*, vol. 7, January 1972, pp. 1321–1341.

>Odd-lotters are often correct in timing of net purchases.

OPTION ACTIVITY RATIO

Zweig, M. E. "New Technical Tool; The Option Activity Ratio Has Flashed a Bull Signal." *Barron's*, vol. 50, November 30, 1970, p. 5.

Zweig, M. E. "Option to Sell; New Puts/Calls Ratio Is Signaling an Intermediate Market Decline." *Barron's*, vol. 51, May 10, 1971, p. 9.

OPTIONS. *See* Puts and Calls

OVER-THE-COUNTER STOCKS

Cobleigh, I. U. "OTC—Everybody's Stock Market." *Commercial and Financial Chronicle*, vol. 209, April 24, 1969, p. 1765.

Cobleigh, I. U. "O-T-C Market; Birthplace of the Blue Chips." *Commercial and Financial Chronicle*, vol. 208, October 31, 1968, p. 1725.

Hershman, A. "Over-the-Counter: Frantic, Frenetic, Frazzled." *Dun's Review*, vol. 92, August 1968, pp. 32–37.

Jessup, P. F., and Upson, R. B. "Opportunities in Regional Markets." *Financial Analysts Journal*, vol. 26, March–April 1970, pp. 75–79.

Maynard, H. M. "Now's the Time to Consider Over-the-Counter Stocks; Possibilities for Rapid Growth in the O.T.C. Market Are Flourishing . . ." *Medical Economics*, vol. 49, September 11, 1972, pp. 236–249.

"Special Situations: Over-the-Counter, Says Ralph Coleman, Is Where You Find Them." *Barron's*, vol. 47, December 25, 1967, p. 5.

PERSONAL TRUSTS. *See* Trust Funds

POINT-AND-FIGURE CHARTS

"Point-and-Figure Method." *Magazine of Wall Street*, vol. 125, October 25, 1969, pp. 17–19.

PREFERRED STOCKS

Cobleigh, I. U. "Unique Virtues of Preferred Stock." *Commercial and Financial Chronicle*, vol. 207, January 25, 1968, p. 325.

"Preferred Stocks Interest Private and Large Corporate Investors." *Magazine of Wall Street*, vol. 126, August 29, 1970, pp. 9–11.

PREFERRED STOCKS, CONVERTIBLE. *See* Convertible Preferred Stocks

PRICE-EARNINGS RATIO

Beidleman, C. R. "Limitations of Price-Earnings Ratios." *Financial Analysts Journal*, vol. 27, September–October, 1971, pp. 86–91.
    Criticism of the concept of "normal" price-earnings ratios for individual stocks.

Fluegel, F. K. "Rate of Return on High and Low P/E Ratio Stocks." *Financial Analysts Journal*, vol. 24, November–December, 1968, pp. 130–133.

Foster, E. M. "Price-Earnings Ratio and Corporate Growth." *Financial Analysts Journal*, vol. 26, January–February, 1970, pp. 96–99; July 1970, pp. 115–118.

Hammel, J. E., and Hodes, D. A. "Factors Influencing Price-Earnings Multiples." *Financial Analysts Journal*, vol. 23, January–February, 1967, pp. 90–92.

Joy, O. M., and Jones C. P. "Another Look at the Value of P/E Ratios." *Financial Analysts Journal*, vol. 26, September–October, 1970, pp. 61–64.

Leuthold, S. "Spotting Tops and Bottoms; Multiples of Normalized Earnings, Book Values are Useful Guides." *Barron's*, vol. 52, June 1972, p. 5.

Levy, R. A., and Kripotos, S. L. "Earnings Growth, P/E's, and Relative Price Strength." *Financial Analysts Journal*, vol. 25, November–December, 1969, p. 60.

> States that price-earnings ratios are of relatively little use in the profitable selection of stocks.

Levy, R. A. "On the Safety of Low P/E Stocks." *Financial Analysts Journal*, vol. 29, January–February, 1973, pp. 57–59.

> Stocks with low price-earnings ratios presented no particular advantage during long market declines.

McWilliams, J. D. "Prices, Earnings, and P-E Ratios." *Financial Analysts Journal*, vol. 22, May–June, 1966, pp. 137–142.

Miller, P. F., and Widmann, E. R. "Price Performance Outlook for High and Low P-E Stocks." *Commercial and Financial Chronicle*, vol. 204, September 29, 1966, section 2, pp. 26–28.

Miller, P. F., and Beach, T. E. "Recent Studies of P/E Ratios—a Reply." *Financial Analysts Journal*, May–June, 1967, pp. 109–110.

> Reply to N. Molodovsky and defense of low price-earnings ratio approach.

Molodovsky, N. "Recent Studies of P/E Ratios." *Financial Analysts Journal*, vol. 23, May–June, 1967, pp. 101–108.

> Neither high nor low price-earnings ratios are advantageous in themselves.

Molodovsky, N. "Stock Values and Stock Prices." *Financial Analysts Journal*, vol. 24, November–December, 1968, pp. 134–148.

Murphy, J. E., and Stevenson, H. W. "Price-Earnings Ratios and Future Growth of Earnings and Dividends." *Financial Analysts Journal*, vol. 23, November–December, 1967, pp. 111–114.

Nicholson, S. F. "Price Ratios in Relation to Investment Results." *Financial Analysts Journal*, vol. 24, January–February 1968, pp. 105–109.

O'Neill, C. R. "Investing in Growth Stocks: There are Only Two Things Which Can Change the Price of a Stock—Either a Change in Earnings or a Change in Price-Earnings Ratio." *Trusts & Estates*, vol. 112, January 1973, pp. 34–35.

"P/E—Clue to Good Buys in Stocks." *Changing Times*, vol. 26, March 1972, pp. 21–22.

"P/E Ratios—Market Clue?" *Financial World*, vol. 136, November 24, 1971, pp. 3–4.

Perham, J. C. "The Riddle of the P/E Ratio; Some of Wall Street's Top Analysts Explain a Tricky Business." *Dun's*, vol. 100, September 1972, pp. 38–42.

Robichek, A. A., and Bogue, M. C. "A Note on the Behavior of Expected Price/ Earnings Ratios over Time." *Journal of Finance*, vol. 26, June 1971, pp. 731–735.

Vanderpoel, W. R. "Brief for Price-Earnings Ratio as an Effective Forecasting Tool." *Commercial and Financial Chronicle*, vol. 207, May 9, 1968, p. 1861.

Vanderpoel, W. R. "High versus Low Multiple Stocks: Their Performance Indications." *Commercial and Financial Chronicle*, vol. 206, November 30, 1967, p. 2029.

PSYCHOLOGY

Harsham, P. "Profiting from Stock Market Psychology; Investors' Emotions Can Sway Stock Prices far More than Economic Factors Do. . . ." *Medical Economics*, vol. 45, March 18, 1968, pp. 79–83.

Kent, W. A., and Lewison, J. "Why You Lost—Wall Street's Cultural Hangup." *Financial Analysts Journal*, March–April, 1971, pp. 33–35.

Meyerholz, J. C. "Must Investor's Personality Impede Successful Investing?" *Trusts & Estates*, vol. 108, August 1969, p. 817

Slovic, P. "Psychological Study of Human Judgment: Implications for Investment Decision-Making." *Journal of Finance*, vol. 27, September 1972, pp. 779–799.

Stone, W. E. "Stock Market Forecasting: Using Technical Analysis to Measure Investor Psychology." *Trusts & Estates*, vol. 111, January 1972, pp. 47–53.

PUTS AND CALLS

Bierman, H. "The Valuation of Stock Options." *Journal of Financial and Quantitative Analysis*, vol. 2, September 1967, pp. 327–334.

Crane, N. E. "Taking the Mystery Out of Options; A Wall Street Professional Describes the Basic Features of These Investments Which Are Steadily Growing in Use." *Financial World*, vol. 138, October 25, 1972, p. 25.

Day, J. W. "Puts and Calls, a Perfect Way to Make Money?" *Business Management*, vol. 39, January 1971, p. 13.

Gross, L. "Put Option—the Short Sale Substitute." *Commercial and Financial Chronicle*, vol. 216, August 31, 1972, p. 621.

Hubbard, C. L., and Johnson, T. "Profits from Writing Calls with Convertible Bonds." *Financial Analysts Journal*, vol. 25, November–December, 1969, pp. 78–89.

Pacey, M. D. "Option Pick-Up; Fresh Capital, New Ideas Spur the Put-and Call Trade." *Barron's*, vol. 49, September 22, 1969, p. 11.

"Puts and Calls: Dream or Delusion? The Option Business Is Starting to Boom. Is This a Game for Sophisticates? Or for Suckers? Who Is Raking in the Chips?" *Forbes*, vol. 109, June 1, 1972, p. 44.

Smith, K. V. "Option Writing." *Financial Analysts Journal*, vol. 24, May–June, 1968, pp. 135–138.

Stoll, H. R. "Relationship Between Put and Call Option Prices." *Journal of Finance*, vol. 24, December, 1969, pp. 801–924.

Taylor, H. M. "Evaluating a Call Option and Optimal Timing Strategy in the Stock Market." *Management Science*, vol. 14, September 1967, pp. 111–120.

Zweig, M. E. "New Technical Tool; the Option Activity Ratio Has Flashed a Bull Signal." *Barron's*, vol. 50, November 30, 1970, p. 5.

Zweig, M. E. "Option to Sell; New Puts/Calls Ratio Is Signaling an Intermediate Market Decline." *Barron's*, vol. 51, May 10, 1971, p. 9.

REAL ESTATE INVESTMENT TRUSTS

Armstrong, T. F. "The Past, Present and Future of the Mortgage Trust." *Trusts and Estates*, vol. 109, November 1970, pp. 942–944.

Bailey, E. N. "Real Estate Investment Trusts: an Appraisal." *Financial Analysts Journal*, vol. 22, May–June, 1966, pp. 107–114.

Bowler, W. R. "What's Right with the REITs? They've Held Up Well in a Sloppy Stock Market—and the Yields Are High." *Dun's*, vol. 101, March 1973, pp. 137–138.

Donohue, J. "REITs: Are They Substitutes for Fixed Income Securities?" *Institutional Investor*, vol. 5, December 1971, pp. 66–69.

"Mortgage Investment Trusts." *Financial World*, vol. 125, March 30, 1966, p. 13.

"Real Estate Investment Trusts; Way to Hedge against Inflation." *Changing Times*, vol. 23, November 1969, pp. 6–9.

Schulkin, P. A. "Real Estate Investment Trusts." *Financial Analysts Journal*, vol. 27, May–June, 1971, pp. 33–40.

"Sorting out the Real Estate Investment Trusts." *Fortune*, vol. 82, August 1970, pp. 173–175.

Thomas, D. L. "Fresh Appraisal; Real Estate Investment Trusts Regain Favor on Wall Street." *Barron's*, vol. 48, October 28, 1968, p. 3.

RECTANGLES

Markstein, D. L. "Opportunity Pattern." *Burroughs Clearing House*, vol. 54, August 1970, pp. 20–22.

RELATIVE STRENGTH

"Case against the Random Walk." *Fortune*, vol. 74, July 1, 1966, pp. 159–160.
    Ideas of R. A. Levy.

Hurwitz, L. D. "Stock Selection Method Based on per cent Performance." *Commercial and Financial Chronicle*, vol. 204, August 4, 1966, pp. 418–419.

Jensen, M. C. "Random Walks: Reality or Myth: Comment." *Financial Analysts Journal*, vol. 23, November–December, 1967, pp. 77–85.
    Criticism of conclusions of R. A. Levy.

Levy, R. A. "Conceptual Foundations of Technical Analysis." *Financial Analysts Journal*, vol. 22, July–August, 1966, pp. 83–89.

A defense of trend following and relative strength.

Levy, R. A., and Kripotos, S. L. "Earnings Growth, P/Es, and Relative Price Strength." *Financial Analysts Journal*, vol. 25, November–December, 1969, p. 60.

States that price-earnings ratios are of relatively little use in the profitable selection of stocks.

Levy, R. A. "The Principle of Portfolio Upgrading." *Industrial Management Review*, vol. 9, Fall 1967, pp. 82–96.

Levy, R. A. "Random Walks; Reality or Myth." *Financial Analysts Journal*, vol. 23, November–December, 1967, pp. 69–77.

States that recent, relative price strength is predictive.

Levy, R. A. "Random Walks: Reality or Myth—Reply." *Financial Analysts Journal*, vol. 25, January–February, 1966, pp. 129–132.

Reply to M. C. Jensen.

Levy, R. A. "Relative Strength as a Criterion for Investment Selection." *Journal of Finance*, vol. 22, December 1967, pp. 595–610.

Levy, R. A. "Technical, Fundamental and Random Walk Selection." *Commercial and Financial Chronicle*, vol. 207, April 4, 1968, p. 1372.

Favorable view of trend following and relative strength.

RESISTANCE LEVELS. *See* Support and Resistance Levels

RIGHTS. *See* Stock Rights

ROUNDING TOPS AND BOTTOMS

Markstein, David L. "Stock Market Signal—the Rounding Turn." *Burroughs Clearing House*, vol. 54, June 1970, pp. 21–22.

SEASONAL (CYCLICAL) VARIATIONS

Griffith, R. "Concept of Seasonal Market Rallies Fallacious." *Commercial and Financial Chronicle*, vol. 206, November 16, 1967, p. 1849.

"The January Indicator." *Business Week*, February 3, 1973, p. 53.
> Stock prices in January predict the rest of the year.

Kaisch, S. "Are There Seasonal Patterns in Stock Prices?" *Michigan Business Review*, vol. 21, January 1969, pp. 8–11.

SECONDARIES

Fredman, A. J., and Wert, J. E. "Analysis of Secondary Distributions." *Financial Analysts Journal*, vol. 24, November–December, 1968, pp. 165–168.

Koehler, R. "Surge of Secondaries." *Barron's*, vol. 51, November 29, 1971, p. 9.
> Three-month moving average of number of secondary offerings as a stock market indicator.

Rhodabarger, T. D. "A New Tool for Calling Stock Turns." *Medical Economics*, vol. 49, August 28, 1972, p. 65.

SELLING STRATEGY (WHEN TO SELL)

Lempenau, J. J. "When to Sell a Good Stock: Five Warning Signals. The Next Time Your Stocks Rise, Consider the Wisdom of Taking Profits. . . ." *Medical Economics*, vol. 47, June 8, 1970, pp. 94–99.

SHORT INTEREST

Biggs, B. M. "Dubious Guide; the Short Interest, Says a Skeptic, Means Less than Many Think." *Barron's*, vol. 50, May 18, 1970, p. 9.

Biggs, B. M. "Short Interest: a False Proverb." *Financial Analysts Journal*, vol. 22, July–August, 1966, pp. 111–116.

Hanna, M. "Short Interest: Bullish or Bearish?—Comment." *Journal of Finance*, vol. 23, June 1968, pp. 520–523.
> Criticism of article by J. J. Seneca.

Mayor, T. H. "Short Trading Activities and the Price of Equities. . . ." *Journal of Financial and Quantitative Analysis*, vol. 3, September 1968, pp. 283–298.
> Short interest not predictive of stock prices.

Seneca, J. J. "Short Interest—Bearish or Bullish?" *Journal of Finance*, vol. 22, March 1967, pp. 67–70.

Seneca, J. J. "Short Interest: Bullish or Bearish? Reply." *Journal of Finance*, vol. 23, June 1968, pp. 524–527.

> Reply to M. Hanna.

Smith, R. D. "Short Interest and Stock Market Prices." *Financial Analysts Journal*, vol. 24, November–December, 1968, pp. 151–154.

SHORT SELLING

"Dangerous Game; Selling Short Is One Way to Make Money in Wall Street That's Best Left to Professionals. For the Average Investor, the Risks Are Too Great." *Financial World*, vol. 138, November 22, 1972, pp. 9–10.

"Funds that Use Short-Sale Tactics; Smart Wall Street Investors Are Cutting Their Risk by Going into Hedge Funds." *Business Week*, April 2, 1966, p. 108.

Harrison, M. "Tactics for a Bear." *Magazine of Wall Street*, vol. 119, December 24, 1966, pp. 359–361.

> Strategy for the short seller.

"Is Short Selling Bullish or Bearish?" *Business Week*, December 3, 1966, pp. 129–130.

McEnally, R. W., and Dyl, E. A. "The Risk of Selling Short." *Financial Analysts Journal*, vol. 25, November–December, 1969, pp. 73–76.

> Short selling may not be as risky as is commonly thought.

"Short Sales; Path to Profits?" *Financial World*, vol. 125, February 9, 1966, p. 6.

Sosnoff, M. T. "Hedge Fund Management: New Respectability for Short Selling." *Financial Analysts Journal*, vol. 22, July–August, 1966, pp. 105–108.

Thomas, C. W. "Primer for Shorts; How to Survive and Even Prosper in a Bear Market." *Barron's*, vol. 50, November 2, 1970, p. 9.

SHORT TERM TRADING. *See* Trading, Short Term

SMALL BUSINESS INVESTMENT COMPANIES

Donnelly, R. A. "Success at a Discount; Small Business Investment Companies Sell Way below Book Value." *Barron's*, vol. 51, March 22, 1971, p. 3.

"The Dream That Failed." *Forbes*, vol. 100, July 15, 1967, pp. 20–21.

"SBICs: Venturing into New Fields." *Financial World*, vol. 132, November 19, 1969, p. 8.

White, F. P. "I'm a Two-Time Loser on SBICs." *Medical Economics*, vol. 45, May 27, 1968, p. 135.
    A doctor's disaster in publicly traded SBICs.

SPECIAL SITUATIONS

"Special Situations; Over-the-Counter, Says Ralph Coleman, Is Where You Find Them." *Barron's*, vol. 47, December 25, 1967, p. 5.

SPLITS. *See* Stock Splits

STOCK-BOND YIELD SPREAD

Christy, G. A. "Rationalization of the Stock-Bond Yield Spread." *Quarterly Review of Economics & Business*, vol. 7, Spring 1967, pp. 63–70.

Seligman, B. "Inverse Bond-Stock Yield." *Business Economics*, vol. 3, Fall 1967, pp. 95–97.
    Inverse yield spread is said to be normal now.

"Yield Spread—Stock Signal?" Financial World, vol. 130, October 23, 1968, pp. 21–22.

STOCK RIGHTS

Soldofsky, R. M., and Johnson, C. R. "Rights Timing." *Financial Analysts Journal*, vol. 23, July–August, 1967, pp. 101–104.

STOCK SPLITS

Fama, E. F., and others. "The Adjustment of Stock Prices to New Information." *International Economic Review*, vol. 10, February 1969, pp. 1–21.

> Buying stocks merely because splits have taken place is not a profitable practice.

Hausman, W. H., West, R. R., and Largay, J. A. "Stock Splits, Price Changes, and Trading Profits: a Synthesis." *Journal of Business*, vol. 44, January 1971, pp. 69–77.

"If Your Stock Splits, Are You Better Off?" *Changing Times*, vol. 26, December 1972, pp. 37–38.

Johnson, K. B. "Stock Splits and Price Change." *Journal of Finance*, vol. 21, December 1966, pp. 675–686.

"A New Look at Stock Splits." *Magazine of Wall Street*, vol. 124, July 5, 1969, pp. 13–15.

STOP-LOSS ORDERS

Barnes, R. M. "Statistical Method for Setting Stops in Stock Trading." *Operations Research*, vol. 18, July 1970, pp. 665–688.

SUPPORT AND RESISTANCE LEVELS

Markstein, D. L. "Support and Resistance—Keys to Stock Timing." *Burroughs Clearing House*, February 1970, p. 16.

TAX-EXEMPT BONDS. *See* Municipal Bonds

TAX TRANSACTIONS

Edwards, M. B. "Payment of Estate Tax with U.S. Bonds: Still a Useful Device with a Potential Trap." *Journal of Taxation*, vol. 37, September 1972, pp. 141–143.

Gelband, J. F. "Controlling Your Tax Liability." *Magazine of Wall Street*, vol. 121, November 11, 1967, pp. 32–34.

Grinaker, R. L. "How to Evaluate the Effect of Taxes in Deciding Whether to Hold or Sell Securities." *Journal of Taxation*, vol. 27, November 1967, pp. 262–265.

Holbrook, M. E. "Year-End Tax Moves." *Barron's*, vol. 52, November 27, 1972, p. 9.

Jen, F. C., and Shick, R. A. "Optimal Tax Loss Strategy for a Portfolio." *Trusts and Estates*, vol. 108, September 1969, pp. 905–910.

Kreidle, J. R., and Stark, T. A. "The Long Term Capital Gain Fallacy." *Commercial and Financial Chronicle*, vol. 209, May 1, 1969, p. 1914.

Morrison, W. L. "Tax Planning for the Unusual Securities Transaction." *Journal of Taxation*, vol. 29, October 1968, pp. 240–244.

Spencer, M. M. "How Tax Considerations Enhance Investment Opportunities in Government Bonds." *Journal of Taxation*, vol. 27, September 1967, pp. 150–154.

TECHNICAL ANALYSIS. *See* specific subjects, such as Charts; Dow Theory; Support and Resistance Levels; Trend Following.

THREE-STEPS-AND-A-STUMBLE THEORY

Gould, E. "Market Pitfalls? Three-Step-and-Stumble Rule is Flashing Red." *Barron's*, vol. 48, May 6, 1968, p. 9.

Gould, E. "Three Steps and Stumble? An Analyst Appraises the Outlook for the Stock Market." *Barron's*, vol. 45, December 27, 1965, p. 3.

TRADING RULES, MECHANICAL. *See* Formula Plans; Moving Average; Trend Following

TRADING, SHORT-TERM

Arms, R. W. "Jack Be Nimble; an Analyst Has Developed a New Index for Traders." *Barron's* vol. 47, August 7, 1967, p. 5.
> Very short-term trading indicator.

Babson, D. L. "Portfolio-Churning Consequences in Today's Investment Mania Fad." *Commercial and Financial Chronicle*, vol. 205, May 4, 1967, p. 1745.

Fee, C. R., and Broady, G. K. "Selecting Next Decade's Blue Chips Means Shunning Short Term Trading." *Commercial and Financial Chronicle*, vol. 207, May 30, 1968, p. 2137.

Harvey, S. A. "Short-Term Trading for Stock Market Profits." *Commercial and Financial Chronicle*, vol. 214, August 26, 1971, p. 605.

Loeb, G. M. "Investors Should Buy and Sell Instead of Buying and Sitting." *Commercial and Financial Chronicle*, vol. 214, December 2, 1971, p. 1643.

TREND BUCKERS

"Market Mavericks." *Financial World*, vol. 126, August 31, 1966, p. 14.

TREND FOLLOWING

Cretien, P. D. "Long-Term Trend Analysis: Risk and Potential in Stock Market Prices." *Commercial and Financial Chronicle*, vol. 216, July 6, 1972, p. 3.
> Projection and analysis of trend in Standard & Poor's Composite 500 Stock Index, year by year, to 1980.

Levy, R. A. "Conceptual Foundations of Technical Analysis." *Financial Analysts Journal*, vol. 22, July–August, 1966, pp. 83–89.
> A defense of trend following and relative strength.

Levy, R. A. "Technical, Fundamental and Random Walk Selection." *Commercial and Financial Chronicle*, vol. 207, April 4, 1968, p. 1372.
> Favorable view of trend following and relative strength.

Markstein, D. L. "Analyst Use of Trendlines and Fanlines." *Burroughs Clearing House*, vol. 54, March 1970, p. 18.

Pinches, George E. "The Random Walk Hypothesis and Technical Analysis." *Financial Analysts Journal*, vol. 26, March–April, 1970, pp. 104–110.

Profitable mechanical trading rulse are extremely difficult to devise.

Trent, E. "The Trent Formula; How to Maximize Profits, Minimize Losses, in the Stock Market." *Barron's*, vol. 52, November 20, 1972, p. 9.

Use of 12½ percent price filter with Dow-Jones averages.

TRIANGLES (COILS)

Markstein, David L. "Triangulate for Profit." *Burroughs Clearing House*, vol. 55, November 1970, p. 16.

TRUST FUNDS

Aarons, E. F. "Let a Bank Manage Your Investments? Many Banks Now Offer Investment Counsel for Accounts Too Small to Be of Interest to Most Money Managers . . ." *Medical Economics*, vol. 45, May 27, 1968, pp. 106–111.

Twenty-seven banks are named that manage portfolios under $100,000. Annual fees are quoted.

Ehrlich, E. E. "Functions and Investment Policies of Personal Trust Departments." *Federal Reserve Bank of New York Monthly Review*, vol. 54, October 1972, pp. 255–270.

Hardy, C. "Shopping for the Right Trust Officers." *Medical Economics*, vol. 49, May 22, 1972, pp. 90–98.

How to judge bank trust departments.

Schutzer, A. I. "Which Bank Can Make a Modest Trust Fund Grow? Some Banks Get First-Rate Investment Performance out of Their Common Trust Funds, Others Do Poorly. Now a New *Medical Economics* Survey Shows You How to Pick a Winner." *Medical Economics*, vol. 48, July 5, 1971, pp. 98–103.

The top ten bank common trust funds—best performing—are named for 1970, 1969–1970, and 1966–1970.

Stern, W. P. "Performance and the Trust Officer." *Trusts and Estates*, vol. 107, November 1968, pp. 1035–1039.

Stern, W. P. "Performance, Trust Funds, and the Investment Scene." *Commercial and Financial Chronicle*, vol. 209, April 24, 1969, pp. 1768–1769.

TURN SIGNALS

Markstein, D. L. "Three Ways to Discern a Stock Market Turn." *Burroughs Clearing House*, vol. 53, July 1969, p. 16.

UNDERVALUED SECURITIES

Hayes, D. A. "Undervalued Issue Strategy." *Financial Analysts Journal*, vol. 23, May–June, 1967, pp. 121–127.

"High Value in Low-Priced Stocks Target of the Small Investor." *Magazine of Wall Street*, vol. 120, June 10, 1967, pp. 12–15.

Hoddeson, D., and Lipper, A. "Buy Low, Sell High; Studies of Relative Value Suggest That's Still Good Advice." *Barron's*, vol. 47, June 19, 1967, p. 3.

"Trust in Value; That's How, Says Mike Danko, It Pays to Handle Your Funds." *Barron's*, vol. 48, March 18, 1968, p. 3.

UPSIDE-DOWNSIDE VOLUME

Tompkins, E. H. "Upside-Downside Volume—a New Market Indicator?" *Barron's*, vol. 45, August 23, 1965, p. 10.

VOLUME OF TRADING

Crouch, R. L. "Volume of Transactions and Price Changes on the New York Stock Exchange." *Financial Analysts Journal*, vol. 26, July–August, 1970, pp. 104–109.

"Heavy Volume; Market Signal?" *Financial World*, vol. 124, December 22, 1965, pp. 3–4.

WALL STREET FOLKLORE. *See* Adages (Wall Street Folklore)

WARRANTS

Anreder, S. S. "Not Just for Swingers; Warrants Lately Have Become Almost Respectable." *Barron's*, vol. 50, December 7, 1970, p. 5.

Kassouf, S. T. "Warrant Price Behavior—1945 to 1964." *Financial Analysts Journal*, vol. 24, January–February, 1968, pp. 123-126.

Miller, J. D. "Effects of Longevity on Values of Stock Purchase Warrants." *Financial Analysts Journal*, vol. 27, November–December, 1971, pp. 78-85.

"New Day for Warrants." *Dun's*, vol. 95, May, 1970, pp. 29-31.

Parkinson, M. "Empirical Warrant-Stock Relationships." *Journal of Business*, vol. 45, October 1972, pp. 563-569.

"Rebirth of the Warrant." *Forbes*, vol. 103, February 15, 1969, pp. 26-27.

"Rediscovery of Warrants." *Dun's*, vol. 99, March 1972, p. 91.

Schnitzler, G. "Warrants: Which Way? Which Ones?" *Commercial and Financial Chronicle*, vol. 216, July 27, 1972, p. 233.
    Stock warrants are diluted by high dividend yield on related common.

Schwartz, W. "The Importance of Using Warrants." *Institutional Investor*, vol. 5, December 1971, pp. 54-55.
    Warrants are recommended for their leverage possibilities.

Shelton, J. P. "Relation of the Price of a Warrant to the Price of Its Associated Stock." *Financial Analysts Journal*, vol. 23, May–June 1967, pp. 143-151; July–August, 1967, pp. 88-99.

Siegel, H. "Warrants: Which Way? Which Ones?" *Commercial and Financial Chronicle*, vol. 216, July 27, 1972, p. 233.
    A reply to G. Schnitzler, above, stating that stock warrants are not diluted by high dividend yield on related common.

"Trading in Warrants—Pitfalls and Potentials." *Magazine of Wall Street*, vol. 124, July 5, 1969, pp. 26-28.

Turov, D. "Stock or Warrant? Figuring Out Which One to Buy Can Be Important." *Barron's*, vol. 50, March 9, 1970, p. 9.

"Warrants." *Magazine of Wall Street*, vol. 129, February 18, 1972, pp. 12–16.

"Warrants—Risks Outweigh Rewards." *Financial World*, vol. 129, May 8, 1968, p. 8.

YIELD SPREAD. *See* Stock-Bond Yield Spread

DIRECTORY
OF PERIODICALS

The Bankers Magazine. Warren, Gorham & Lamont, Inc., 89 Beach St., Boston, Mass. 02111. Quarterly. $34 a year.

Bankers Monthly. Bankers Monthly, Inc., 1500 Skokie Blvd., Northbrook, Ill., 60062. Monthly. $9 a year.

Banking (American Bankers Association). Simmons-Boardman Publishing Corp., P. O. Box 530, Bristol, Conn.06010 (editorial offices: 350 Broadway, New York, N.Y. 10013). Monthly. $8 a year.

Barron's. Dow Jones & Co., Inc., 200 Burnett Road, Chicopee, Mass. 01021 (editorial offices: 22 Cortlandt St., New York, N.Y. 10007). Weekly. $21 a year.

Burroughs Clearing House. Burroughs Corp., Box 418, Detroit, Mich. 48232. Monthly. Controlled circulation.

Business Economics. National Association of Business Economists, 888 17 St. N.W., Washington, D.C. 20006. Quarterly. $15 a year; $10 a year to libraries open to the public.

Business Management. Ceased publication, October 1971.

Business Week. McGraw-Hill, Inc., 1221 Avenue of the Americas, New York, N.Y. 10020. Weekly. $12.95 a year.

Changing Times. Kiplinger Washington Editors, Inc., Editors Park, Md. 20782. Monthly. $7 a year.

The Commercial and Financial Chronicle. William B. Dana Co., 25 Park Place, New York, N.Y. 10007. Semiweekly. $95 a year.

Dun's (formerly *Dun's Review*). Dun & Bradstreet Publications Corp., 666 Fifth Ave., New York, N.Y. Monthly. $7 a year.

Dun's Review. See *Dun's.*

The Economist. The Economist Newspaper, Ltd., 54 St. James St., London
  SW1, England. Weekly. $41 a year (air mail, $56 a year).

Federal Reserve Bank of Kansas City Monthly Review. Federal Reserve Bank of
  Kansas City, Kansas City, Mo. 64198. Monthly. Free.

Federal Reserve Bank of St. Louis Review. Federal Reserve Bank of St. Louis,
  St. Louis, Mo. 63166. Monthly. Free.

Financial Analysts Journal. Financial Analysts Federation, 219 E. 42 St., New
  York, N.Y. 10017. Bimonthly. $12 a year.

Financial Executive. Financial Executives Institute, Inc., 50 W. 44 St., New
  York, N.Y. 10036. Monthly. $12.50 a year.

Financial World. Macro Publishing Corp., 17 Battery Place, New York, N.Y.
  10004. Weekly. $28 a year.

Forbes. Forbes, Inc., 60 Fifth Ave., New York, N.Y. 10011. Semimonthly.
  $9.50 a year.

Fortune. Time, Inc., 541 North Fairbanks Court, Chicago, Ill. 60611. Monthly.
  $12 a year.

Harvard Business Review. Graduate School of Business Administration, Harvard
  University, Boston, Mass. 02163. Bimonthly. $15 a year.

Industrial Management Review. See *Sloan Management Review.*

Industry Week. Penton Publishing Co., Penton Plaza, 1111 Chester Ave., Cleveland, Ohio 44114. Weekly. $25 a year.

Institutional Investor. Institutional Investor Systems, Inc., Circulation Depart-
  ment, 2160 Patterson Street, Cincinnati, Ohio 45214 (editorial offices:
  140 Cedar St., New York, N.Y. 10006). Monthly. $40 a year.

International Economic Review. Wharton School of Finance and Commerce,
  University of Pennsylvania, Philadelphia, Pa. 19104. Three times a year.
  $15 a year.

The Journal of Business (Graduate School of Business, University of Chicago).
  University of Chicago Press, 5801 Ellis Ave., Chicago, Ill. 60637. Quarterly.
  $8 a year.

The Journal of Finance. Graduate School of Business, New York University,
  100 Trinity Place, New York, N.Y. 10006. Five times a year. $12.50 a year.

Journal of Financial and Quantitative Analysis. Graduate School of Business Administration, University of Washington, Seattle, Washington 98195. Five times a year. $10 a year to individuals; $15 a year to institutions.

The Journal of Taxation. Journal of Taxation, Inc., 512 N. Florida Ave., Tampa, Fla. 33602. Monthly. $36 a year.

The Magazine of Wall Street. See *Wall Street Business Analyst.*

Management Accounting. National Association of Accountants, 919 Third Ave., New York, N.Y. 10022. Monthly. $10 a year.

Management Science. Institute of Management Sciences, 146 Westminster St., Providence, R.I. 02903. Monthly. $32 a year.

Medical Economics. Medical Economics Co., Oradell, N.J. 07649. Biweekly. $25 a year (controlled free circulation to physicians).

Michigan Business Review. Graduate School of Business Administration, University of Michigan, Ann Arbor, Mich. 48104. Five times a year. Apply.

Michigan State University Business Topics. Graduate School of Business Administration, Michigan State University, East Lansing, Mich. 48823. Quarterly. Apply.

Money. Time, Inc., 541 N. Fairbanks Court, Chicago, III. 60611. Monthly. $15 a year.

Operations Research. Operations Research Society of America, 428 E. Preston St., Baltimore, Md. 21202. Six times a year. $20 a year.

Public Utilities Fortnightly. Public Utilities Reports, Inc., Suite 502, 1823 L St. N.W., Washington, D.C. 20036. Biweekly. $26 a year.

Quarterly Review of Economics & Business. Bureau of Economics and Business Research, College of Commerce and Business Administration, University of Illinois, Urbana, III. 61801. Quarterly. $6 a year.

Sloan Management Review (formerly *Industrial Management Review*). Alfred P. Sloan School of Management, Massachusetts Institute of Technology, Cambridge, Mass. 02139. Three times a year. $10 a year.

Trusts & Estates. Communication Channels, Inc., 461 Eighth Ave., New York, N.Y. 10001. Monthly. $24 a year.

Wall Street Business Analyst (formerly *The Magazine of Wall Street*). Colonial Communications Corp., 465 Endo Blvd., Garden City, N.Y. 11530. Monthly. $20 a year.

AUTHOR INDEX

TITLE INDEX

SUBJECT INDEX